Russia's Carnival

Russia's Carnival

The Smells, Sights, and Sounds of Transition

Christoph Neidhart

ROWMAN & LITTLEFIELD PUBLISHERS, INC.
Lanham • Boulder • New York • Oxford

ROWMAN & LITTLEFIELD PUBLISHERS, INC.

Published in the United States of America
by Rowman & Littlefield Publishers, Inc.
A Member of the Rowman & Littlefield Publishing Group
4720 Boston Way, Lanham, Maryland 20706
www.rowmanlittlefield.com

P.O. Box 317, Oxford OX2 9RU, United Kingdom

British Library Cataloguing in Publication Information Available

Library of Congress Cataloging-in-Publication Data

Neidhart, Christoph, 1954–
  Russia's carnival : the smells, sights, and sounds of transition /
Christoph Neidhart.
      p. cm.
Includes bibliographical references and index.
  ISBN 0-7425-2041-2 (cloth : perm. paper)—ISBN 0-7425-2042-0 (paper
: perm. paper)
  1. Russia (Federation)—Social conditions—1991– I. Title.
  HN530 .2 .A8 N44 2002
  306'.0947—dc21

                                                     2002012108

Printed in the United States of America

♾™ The paper used in this publication meets the minimum requirements of
American National Standard for Information Sciences—Permanence of Paper
for Printed Library Materials, ANSI/NISO Z39.48–1992.

Contents

Acknowledgments

Many people have contributed to the completion of this book. First and foremost, hundreds of the former Soviet Union's citizens shared their experiences and insights with me, some in brief encounters, others over a long period. They helped me to understand what was going on in their society, beyond the news and politics. They made my years in Russia and the former Soviet republics exciting, compelling, and mostly agreeable. I feel a deep obligation to them. While at times my book may sound critical of some leftover Soviet habits, I have great admiration for the way the Russian people and their neighbors in the republics have coped with the tremendous transition their societies are undergoing. Special thanks go to my friends in the former Soviet Union, in particular Ira Kipriyanova, Leonid Gozman, Mati Sirkel, Marina Sleptsova, Andreas Schwander, Boris Shumatsky, Katya Gvozdeva, and our home help Ludmilla; to Zygmunt Dzięciołowski in Warsaw, who was the first to teach me how to navigate through a Soviet-style, connected society; and especially to my best friend Klaus-Helge Donath in Moscow, with whom I shared house, office, library, and experiences.

This project would never have been started without my editors at the Swiss weekly *Die Weltwoche*, Hanspeter Born and Elsbeth Tzermias, who supported my journalistic projects in every possible way. Harvard University's Davis Center of Russian Studies, its scholars and staff, provided an environment, detached from everyday journalism, in which I found the time, space, and intellectual stimulation to engage in writing this book. Professors Richard Pipes and Marshall Goldman made it possible for me to join the Davis Center, while its director, Timothy Colton, reviewed an early version and generously supported the project in moments when it nearly stalled. I owe my debt of gratitude to them, as I do to Harvard University. Ana Siljak, Svetlana Boym, Virginie Coulloudon, and Barbara Keys read drafts and gave invaluable advice, critical assessments, and patient assistance. This book has been greatly improved by their suggestions. I also thank my friends and office mates, Robert Krikorian in particular, Sean Pollock, and David Brandenberger; again and again, they helped me to overcome my deficiencies in English, a second language to me. June Masuda coached me through my first attempts to write publishable English and helped me by editing a draft.

Other people who with friendship, ideas, advice, and criticism have contributed to this book are Larry Wolff, Mark Kramer, Julie Bucker, Jeffrey Collins, John LeDonne, Katya Antonyuk, Gregory Feifer, Margret Mellert, Nina Toepfer, Gulnora Aminova, and many more. Finally, I would like to express my awe, and my thanks, to the people who turned a manuscript into a book, the editors at Rowman & Littlefield, in particular Susan McEachern, Matt Hammon, Alden Perkins, Dave Compton, and Kimberly Ball. And, of course, I thank my wife and parents for their help, encouragement, and love.

Christoph Neidhart, Tokyo, July 4, 2002

1

Introduction

Is Democracy Visible?

Today's Russia *smells* different from the Soviet Union, and different from Russia of any previous time. Russia *looks* different—as do the other post-Communist societies compared to before the fall of Communism. Russia *sounds* different, her *touch* is different, the food *tastes* as never before. People dress differently from the way they used to. Life has become better, I'm tempted to add, recalling the scents, tastes, appearances, sounds, and textures of the Soviet Union.

Speaking of a country's smell might be problematic—all the more so if the country in question spans eleven time zones and includes climates as diverse as Russia's, from arctic to semitropical, from maritime to extremely continental. Nevertheless, few people who have traveled the Soviet Union would deny a scent of "socialism" common to the whole of Soviet Russia and even to the republics, despite their historic and ethnic otherness.

The Soviet Union's smell was hard to describe but easy to recognize, as was socialism's color: gray. Socialism had its particular stench and a characteristic dust. The houses smelled of cabbage, of wet socks and sweat; the backyards reeked of diesel and trash, and sometimes of coal. Even the vastness of Siberia's far north, the tundra, smelled of oil. And no one seemed to care.

Russia and the former Soviet republics have changed radically in some places—even beyond recognition—although they have changed only superficially in others. Everyday life has been transformed, especially in the cities. People dress differently and behave differently; they own goods they would never have dreamed of owning a decade ago. They organize their lives in ways no one could have imagined doing in the Soviet era. Nor

1

could anyone have predicted what ideals, goals, and role models many former Soviet citizens now worship.

What can one read into these transformations? How should one in hindsight interpret the Soviet society? Was the Soviet Union the modern industrialized society it claimed to be or was it merely mimicking one, as I believe? Are the changes of the last decade only superficial, as some critics maintain?[1] Or do they reflect a massive upheaval in Russian society? Can one detect a degree of democratization by observing the increasing plurality in appearances?

What is democracy for today's Russia? Freedom or plurality? This book explores these and related issues, based on my observations over almost a decade of covering Russia and the newly emerging states as a journalist. I traveled the former Soviet Union extensively. From 1990 to 1997, I was stationed in Moscow and St. Petersburg as the correspondent for *Die Weltwoche,* a weekly Swiss newspaper. In this job, my editors often allowed me to focus on more than narrowly political or economic stories—particularly on people's everyday lives and on my personal experiences.

Working in the Soviet Union was full of surprises, confusion, and nuisances that made my daily life different—often difficult—from what I had known and expected. Many of my interactions with Russians revealed their significance long after the fact; it took me years to grasp certain patterns, the economic *raison d'être* of many friendships, for example, and the networks they keep together. Looking at my own experiences through the prism of eminent works of scholars and writers, in particular Bakhtin, Brodsky, Likhachev, Lotman, Sinyavsky, and Zinoviev, has helped me to understand the (post-)Soviet condition—and I had plenty of time to read during the long Moscow winter nights. In addition, scholars who do not deal directly with Russia, but who analyze Western societies, their paths to modernity, and their self-fashioning, such as Elias, Giddens, Hall, Harvey, Kern, Sennett, Barthes, and Eco, have strongly influenced my views. Their ideas prompted me to search for parallels between Russia's current development and the West. Indeed, at times, the historian Stephen Kern's account of the Western world between 1890 and 1914 reads like a distant echo of what can be observed in Russia and the former Soviet republics these days.[2]

Instead of hiding behind the authority of "established facts," I collected what I personally encountered as a journalist, a friend, a guest, and a customer. In my writing, I rely on my perceptions and on what I have learned from friends—whose identities are not revealed—and casual acquaintances as much as on official interviews. Being an outsider who lived on the inside, I consider myself especially suited for this task. As Sayuri stresses in *Memoirs of a Geisha*, one does not ask a rabbit to describe itself as it hops through the grass, for how would it know? If we want to hear about the field, however, no one is better suited to tell us than the hare, though one has to take into account that it will be but one rabbit's perspective.[3] In this book, I assume the role of the rabbit. My grassy field is the (post-)Soviet cities rather than the rural areas. Politics is made in the cities and so are fashions. Transitions happen here first, and they happen faster and more palpably. Some readers may find my findings arbitrary, accidental, or atypical. With a few exceptions, I use neither statistics nor polls as authoritative evidence (and one poll I do quote has been widely disputed), but I am convinced that most of my examples represent the Soviet and post-Soviet realities very well.

To evaluate the transformation of Russian society, we must first revisit the Soviet system. The Soviet people used to live in two realities: in the harsh, repressive, state-imposed system and in a parallel existence with their friends and relatives. To a certain extent, this was a dream world, or as the Soviet intelligentsia preferred to call it, their "spiritual world." The privileged, well-read Soviet artists, academics, doctors, teachers, and engineers viewed with condescension the lowly spheres of everyday life. However, with the collapse of the oppressive regime, their *virtual* reality has all but vanished, too.

The USSR looked like an industrialized (Western) society; its facilities mirrored those of any European country. It had railroads, radio, television, air travel, and private cars. Many of its institutions (for example trade unions) bore the same names as their genuine Western counterparts. But they functioned in a fundamentally different way. Thus, to assess the magnitude of the shake-up since the Soviet Union collapsed, one must understand how Soviet life really worked. This might, at times, make my findings appear retrospective. But how can one appreciate the distance post-Soviet societies have come in only a decade, if not by reassessing the poor conditions from whence they started? How can one judge the "market" or "bazaar economy" if one forgets its actors' mindset at the beginning of the transition and Russia's lack of the most basic element of a modern economy: a currency?

Russia and the former republics have gone through an enormous change, the dimensions of which can hardly be overestimated. To compare today's society with its predecessor diachronically, I use as frames of reference the five human senses: sight, sound, scent, taste, and touch. Additionally, assuming that there are senses for proximity and temporality, I investigate the transitions that can be perceived by these senses. I read meaning into my findings to identify hints of radical change and evidence for my assumption that the grassroots of Russian society is readying itself for democracy, or pluralism. True, my views may be called subjective, since I generalize and skim over many concerns. And often I state the obvious.

Societies structure time with markers, such as holidays or public festivals, with feast and dance. In Europe, winter solstice has been celebrated since pre-Christian times. It then indicated death and renewal of the annual cycle. Carnival, as it still (or again) exists in some parts of Europe, has its roots in the festive realization of end and beginning (of the agricultural year).[4] It is the perfect example of a calendrical marker: for a limited period of time, the world is turned upside down, or inside out, as the late Russian scholar Mikhail Bakhtin so aptly described. His work on Rabelais, together with the Fasnacht, the carnival in Basel, Switzerland, I grew up with, have greatly influenced this book. There has been little scholarly research done on the Fasnacht or on the Swabian-Alemannic carnival in general. However, Bakhtin's ideas accord with the Basel people's views of their Fasnacht. His assessment of carnival as a played revolution of "preclass and prepolitical social order" lost to history[5] may be overly positive—utopian, as his critics have it. Umberto Eco believes him wrong; Eco sees carnival as a safety valve and thus a "paramount example of law enforcement."[6] Indeed, in the fifteenth century, carnival lost its antiauthoritarian character and subversive power; it became more and more organized.[7] But it persisted as a calendrical festival, though gradually losing relevance. Many cities eventually prohibited the fools' feast, particularly the wearing of masks. In the nineteenth century, it was revived as a carnival of the bourgeois elite, a masquerade of the affluent; that carnival tolerated the poor and the margins of the society only as onlookers. However, the Swabian-Alemannic region, particularly the city of Basel, as an act of historicism, eventually reverted to a form of carnival closer to its medieval origins. Strictly within its temporal limits, the Basel Fasnacht is more archaic, anarchic, and antiauthoritarian than others. It knows no stage, "is not a spectacle seen by the people; they live it, and everyone participates because its very idea embraces all the people," as Bakhtin characterized the medieval carnival. It makes "a man renounce his official state."[8] I thus grew up with a carnival that, within its given limits, playfully suspended law and order, including the time regime. Its "free and familiar contact between people," who are usually separated hierarchically, readies a society to "mass action," as Bakhtin put it.[9]

Thence, to me, carnival suggests itself to be juxtaposed with the huge popular rallies I witnessed in Eastern Europe and the Soviet Union, first in the Baltic capitals in 1988, later in Yerivan (Armenia) and Baku (Azerbaijan), in Prague in the fall of 1989, and subsequently in Russia. These mass actions turned society upside down; they accelerated time. Were they revolutions? Velvet revolutions, since they claimed hardly any casualties? Or just spontaneous carnivals reinforcing the established order?

In medieval Europe, according to Bakhtin, carnivals were enacted, but phony, revolutions. If we follow Eco, they perpetuated the status quo. In any case, at the conclusion, society returned to its established order.

Yet, even revolutions occur gradually. As a temporal landmark, the revolutionary events—the moment the people take to the streets, for example—indicate a protracted transition, not in cyclical time like carnival but in history, in which there is no established order to return to. The upheaval as such is the catharsis of a more gradual transformation.

Russia's failed coup of August 1991 was neither a carnival (society did not revert to its status quo ante) nor a revolution (only a few figureheads of the ruling elite were toppled—and some subsequently made a comeback). The coup was either an unfinished revolution or a carnival turned serious. As with carnivals, appearances mattered more than reality. August "played out" on the nation's television screens and its images were heavily manipulated. But was the coup the catharsis in Russia's transition toward democracy, as the Russian reformers would have it?

What is democracy for today's Russians, then? Today, the country is more genuinely industrialized, modern, and westernized than ever and has experienced a noticeable increase in diversity. Does this indicate an increasing political plurality? Would the emerging plurality in appearances I observe in this book indicate democracy? What does democracy mean to Russians and citizens of the former Soviet republics? A parliament, free elections, or the existence of competing political parties? Freedom of speech, a free and pluralistic press, or a press free to publish lies and slander, to insult people? Freedom to conduct business, to travel, to settle freely? For some people in the former Soviet Union, democracy means dignity, to be treated as human beings, to be respected as individuals. A woman once told me that it was "democratic" that her doctor told her what he was doing to treat her; for other women, democracy meant not being harassed by their gynecologists. According to polls, many Russians understand democracy as human rights, including a free press and, more importantly, the freedom to do business. Only 5 percent of the people monitored by the All-Union Center for the Research of Public Opinion in a 1994 poll named free elections as the core of democracy.[10]

For some, democracy seems synonymous with "anything goes" or is a justification of social Darwinism. Certain media see the availability of pornography as a sign of democracy. Moscow journalist Nadezhda Azhgikhina writes: "The democratic press has made soft porn a kind of trademark of democracy, according to the principle that everything that was prohibited must be good. And nobody cares or feels ashamed, pornography is considered as a pleasant reminder of the Western lifestyle."[11]

For a substantial portion of post-Soviet society, democracy means chaos, corruption, criminality, injustice, and poverty. Many Russians blame democracy for the widespread fraud and deception. To them, the arbitrary dictatorship of the Communist Party, responsible for mass terror and millions of murders, now stands for stability, justice, and order.

An acquaintance, a forty-year-old unemployed accountant, a typical, middle-aged ex-Soviet man, once blamed democracy for his difficulty in finding a girlfriend. When the Communists were in power, women were easy to get, this chubby, unpleasant man complained. Prostitution did not exist; he got sex for free. Now all the women wanted money, he said, blaming the political changes for his bad luck. But, I replied, had not he grown a bit older? And was he not in worse shape than once upon a time? My questions made him angry. No, he countered, it was the democrats' fault. Many such as he have made democracy responsible for their passing youth.

In a Potemkin-like sense, the Soviet Union was democratic: on the surface, it appeared to be democratic, just as Count Potemkin's villages appeared to be villages, but were in fact only facades. Despite the CPSU's (Communist Party of the Soviet Union's) monopoly, which was guaranteed by the constitution, the population seemed involved in the shaping of policy; it was represented by "elected" officials. Political participation, however, was but an exercise in indoctrination and a way to keep current with "democratic" etiquette. Views were dictated, not exchanged, at party meetings. The allegedly public sphere remained under tight control. The authorities crushed the tiniest attempt at opening up the society. The only public sphere beyond the reach of the regime was the kitchen table; only here could dissenting views be expressed. But, even in one's own home, the state could well be eavesdropping.

On streets and squares, the traditional venues for demonstrations, thus for expressing opposition, it was prohibited to display any conviction— political or religious—or to speak to an audience, whatever the size. Indoor venues for informal gatherings were impossible to come by. Thus, the free exchange of ideas, like the free exchange of goods, was almost completely obstructed. The state maintained a monopoly for the distribution of both. The black market and a flimsy underground network of independent publishing, the *samizdat*, were marginal.

Our daily exchanges have great significance. They allow us to practice our social skills and form our beliefs, according to the French philosopher de Certeau.[12] Everyday life is regulated by thousands of unwritten rules— many of which never reach our conscious minds. For people to feel secure, these rules have to be stable. In Soviet daily life, they were. Life was ruled by the state monopoly of property, by the political and aesthetic domination of the Communist Party, and by the distinct class structure of the allegedly classless society.

The state determined a number of career patterns, educational paths, and professions. Some citizens might choose their own educational or career paths, but they were not allowed to shape their own lives, to invent themselves, in any more meaningful way, as people in other countries are often encouraged to do. Many people were specialists in narrow fields and were neither able nor willing to stray beyond their original education. A majority of the Soviets seemed to accept the view that a person who was not a member of the Writers' Union was not a writer, however well he wrote. For Soviet men, not to have employment was against the law. The police considered an unofficial author who would stay at home and write a parasite and prosecuted him for avoiding working, as they did Joseph Brodsky, who later won the Nobel Prize for literature.

All relevant decisions were made centrally, by the politburo of the party or by any of the lower party branches, whose every step was subject to tacit approval from above. People were not treated as mature citizens, but as petitioners—or as cattle, as some people said. Yet, tight control can be perceived as a weird form of security. Since Gorbachev's ascent to power, however, this stability has been shattered, as the old rules have been abolished but not yet replaced.

People within a society communicate nonverbally; they use signs and signals. A society would not survive if each bit of information had to be verbalized: a far too time-consuming and complicated process. When speaking, people tend to omit what is intrinsically understood. By what they own, what they wear, what and where they eat, and how and when they move around, people convey information about themselves—consciously and unconsciously. They position themselves in order to relate to other members of their society and, in turn, they read others' messages. People who are strangers to a certain society do not fully understand its signs. They are uncertain about the meaning of shaking hands, for example, or they do not know what people communicate by hugging each other or by wearing black clothes. Depending on its context, black attire conveys mourning, bohemian dissent, or the desire to conform. Ivan Grozny wore black when in the mood to drown, strangle, and rob people; he dressed in red to spill blood and kill and in white when he was in the mood for revelry, as Dmitry Likhachev reports.[13]

To strangers, the nonverbal code that helps a society to organize and regulate itself—the fabric of everyday life—is like a foreign language. Its native "speakers" understand it naturally, often unaware that they are using a code. Since most native speakers tend to be unable to explain the grammar of their own spoken language, I presume the rules of a nonverbal sign language are even harder to define. A newcomer may have studied a spoken language; he or she may understand every single word and even be able to explain the grammar. Nevertheless, the more implicit messages are lost. Visual and other nonverbal codes are even more difficult to dissect. The stranger might not even notice that messages are conveyed. My own nonverbal Russian is acquired, hence I did not make the transition from the Soviet to the post-Soviet Russian society like a "native speaker," but had to consciously relearn the changing meanings of signs. I have not immersed myself deeply enough in (post-)Soviet society to read its nonverbal language like an insider, but I have witnessed the dramatic changes in that "language" closely. This work is thus a collection of observed changes rather than an interpretation of particular signs.

The Soviet Union claimed to be a modern, industrialized welfare state. On paper, it provided its citizens with everything they needed. They were pampered—and controlled—from cradle to grave. In reality, though, many services were far from free: physicians expected "presents"; to supply a family, one had to rely on informal networks. In exchange for the benefits of the system, one had to endure waiting in lines for hours or sometimes days. Soviet life required very special skills, avoidance strategies, and tricks. No school could have taught these skills: one learned them by being part of the system. Only a few people were familiar with both the Soviet reality and the outside world. Hence, hardly anyone was "fluent" in both the Soviet and a Western nonverbal code and thus able to "translate" the Soviets' nonverbal language to foreigners. Most Soviet citizens were unaware that they were using a code and that this code might have been different from those of other (European, industrialized) societies—as unaware as most U.S. citizens are of their particular code. Chapters of the Soviet code may even have been singular to the Soviet society: there is no need in a Western society to read other people's bags to find out where to obtain bread and sausages.

This book focuses on city life. Soviet socialism was "created" by cities and in turn created and shaped its own cities.[14] But the socialist cities were no marketplaces for ideas and goods, as European cities have been since the Middle Ages, when the slogan "the city air makes one free" was coined.[15] Soviet cities were sub- or pseudo-urban agglomerations; they lacked any civic quality, despite their city-like appearance. They were look-alikes, big villages that posed as cities. With the weakening of Stalinism, however, some true city life emerged. Cities have since served as a stage for an emerging, unsanctioned urbanity.

Time seemed to move at a glacial pace in the Soviet Union. The last decade of the Brezhnev era was called the period of stagnation. A "no-future-generation" was growing up. Photos depicting everyday life in the Soviet Union are difficult to date. Images taken between the late 1950s and the early 1980s all look almost the same. People's attire did not change much; the Soviets did not follow any fashion trends. They bought coats to last ten years. Only a specialist would have been able to determine the year a car had been manufactured. Unlike in the West, in the USSR the same models were produced for decades, with only the slightest alterations. Time stood frozen.

Journalists and scholars, in general, tend to focus on language: the written and the spoken word, official statements and private conversations. However, Communism had usurped and mutilated the Russian language, turning it into "Newspeak,"[16] a language that made it all but impossible to express independent or nonconformist thought, as the exiled scholar Andrei Sinyavsky showed in his enlightening book *Soviet Civilization*. At the core of the Soviet language, he emphasized, there existed "a specific jargon that the leaders use[d] among themselves and with the people." They spoke "not in words but in . . . word-signals, the implied significance of which . . . not even they [could] explain."[17] Words were estranged from normal human discourse, Sinyavsky maintained. The Soviets thoroughly "bureaucratized" and "standardized" the Russian language, with their clichés permeating the society from top to bottom. This synthetic language was used in the media, as well as in factories, schools, universities, and within the administration; consisting of long strings that tied together Marxist-Leninist keywords, neologisms, stumps, and acronyms, it renamed the world. Words became prefixed or affixed; the "worker" transmuted into a "Soviet worker," a "revolutionary worker," or a "socialist worker." "Men" were made into "Soviet men" or "comrades."[18] Both in language and in real life, the *kolkhoz* replaced the farm. The Soviet language was thus dissembled and mystified, "trying all the while to persuade itself that it [was] right," as Sinyavsky wrote. Moreover, it insisted "on its own interpretation of many foreign terms, such as 'democracy,' 'humanism,' 'human rights' or 'constitution.'"[19] The collapse of Communism made this lingo obsolete, but there is no new, post-Soviet Russian language the society can agree upon; rather, competing jargons have emerged. Thus, to assess the state of post-Soviet Russia, it seems precarious to rely solely on what is said and written there.

Gorbachev was a master of Soviet Newspeak and possibly of Newthink. With his mythical slogans, such as *glasnost, perestroika, democratization,* and *rynok* (market), he tried to lure his fellow Soviets to what he called a new way of thinking, though he never clarified what his incantations meant, putting him very much in line with what Sinyavsky said about the party's language.

With Gorbachev's rise to power, the KGB (Committee of State Security, the secret police) began to loosen its grip, allowing some characteristics of a civic society and a public space for the free exchange of goods and ideas to emerge. Before 1988, a gathering on the street or a public square of more than three people was illegal. In that summer in Armenia, more than one million people rallied and the Baltic capitals saw huge demonstrations—some with several hundred thousand participants. In June 1988, half a million Estonians were present to see off their delegates leaving for Moscow to attend the party conference of the CPSU. In Moscow in the fall of 1988, the KGB tolerated around its own headquarters on Lubyanka Square—and allegedly co-organized in secret—the first commemoration of the victims of totalitarianism.

The period of stagnation finally ended: Gorbachev even demanded that time accelerate. The first catchword he introduced was *uskorenie*, or acceleration. And if he did not succeed in speeding up the transformation of the Soviet economy, as he intended, he certainly managed to accelerate the changes in society—and in its appearances. The stagnation ended; the Soviet Union visibly came to life.

This acceleration of time could be seen, heard, felt, smelled, and even tasted, as I will show. In my chapters on each of the five senses, I explore how they were dampened during the Soviet era and how they have reemerged and evolved. And each of the senses presents the people of the former Soviet Union with a crescendo of impressions of often confusing diversity. Today, the people have choices unheard of only a decade ago.

In the chapters on the "sixth sense"—the awareness of space or proximity—and on time, I attempt to show how the Russians' way of experiencing and dealing with space has transformed dramatically, as has their attitude toward time. The Soviet Union was an apartheid state that tried to contain its people into prescribed spaces, like invisible bubbles. To control the society, the Communists atomized it. Post-Soviet Russians control their own space and organize it as never before. They explore spaces previously inaccessible to them, both at home and, importantly, abroad. Residential and industrial space have become private property. People can buy and sell space; some grow rich as landlords.

In its attitude toward time, Soviet society was schizophrenic: officially, it observed a linear time regime, which was Fordist to the extreme. The economy was to produce according to a centrally issued plan. Even leisure was supposed to be scheduled, so that the citizens would not waste their time on irrational pursuits. In reality, however, most Russians, as well as the other peoples of the USSR, lived in a peasant time—as if scheduled time never mattered. Since the collapse, time for many Russians has become commodified. They schedule their days and use agendas. The first electronic calendars I encountered belonged to Russians and East Europeans, though they possibly owned them as status symbols rather than for practical reasons. The digital watch became popular with the Russians. All of a sudden, time mattered; money began to earn high interest rates.

During the week of the failed coup in August 1991, the transition reached its catharsis. At this turning point, the old system collapsed and fifteen new nation-states were born. Some scholars expected these events to take years to unfold (while others could not imagine them at all), but they were compressed into a few short days. Epic history was made in plain view.

Subsequently, the Soviet republics gave themselves new insignia, new names, and new political structures as independent states; they each recast a coat of arms—except for Russia and Belarus. (Since 1991, Russia has been using new heraldry—the double-headed eagle, the tricolor, and a new anthem, but for almost a decade, those state symbols were not adopted officially, as the State Duma could not agree on them or on a coat of arms. In December 2000, the Duma reinstated the old Soviet anthem, though not its words.)

Despite its shortcomings, Russian society as a whole has made tremendous progress. True, the transition is far from complete, but I firmly believe totalitarianism and central planning will not return. Why, then, is there so much soul searching and finger pointing going on as to who was "squandering prospects for Russian democracy, prosperity and social well-being"?[20] Scholars, journalists, and politicians as diverse as Pat Buchanan (the U.S. right winger), the controversial financier George Soros,[21] and John Lloyd (a senior correspondent with the *Financial Times*) have been debating the question "Who lost Russia?" They all blame Yeltsin and "shock therapy," the sudden transition to a market economy, as well as the Clinton administration.[22]

No one lost Russia, this book tries to show, certainly not the West. Its influence was marginal; it talked more about financial aid than it provided it. Aside from the liberation of the prices, there was no "shock therapy" to speak of; Russia's economic transition has been much slower than in some of the more successful countries, such as Poland and Estonia. First and foremost, however, despite its many setbacks, Russia is slowly growing stronger, more pluralistic, and more open—say, democratic—than anyone could have imagined even one generation ago. The Soviet Union was not what it appeared to be; it was a developing country "posing" as an industrialized state, or "Upper Volta with nukes," as former German Chancellor Helmut Schmidt once memorably described it.

The transition compelled the former Soviet people to cope with tremendous change. The basic set of values they had been taught for decades became obsolete. Soviet life was stable and stagnant. The party determined what was right and wrong. No one had to make any important decision alone. True, the state was challenged by an opposing set of privately held beliefs, but often these consisted of little more than the opposite of the official line. As such, they helped to define the party line. Thus, even dissidents played a role in strengthening the party's monopoly of ideas. With the collapse of the Soviet state, its paternalistic system crumbled, too. The party lost its leadership, and thus its grip on education and the economy, and the ready-made Soviet life patterns became obsolete. Many jobs simply disappeared, while others lost their prestige. There is no longer any need for professional *Komsomoltsy*, the "youth league workers." The hierarchy of careers has been turned upside down. Suddenly, people are forced to invent—not reinvent—themselves. The Soviet role models vanished but were not replaced. The post-Soviet Russians have to shape their futures themselves. People who until recently were barred from any major decision making suddenly had to design their own lives. A society whose future had been monopolized by one institution is now being turned into a decentralized society in which millions of individuals make independent choices, as in any free market of goods and ideas. Ex-Soviet people tend to experience these changes more dramatically than Westerners, who are used to change and plurality, can imagine.

In the Western world at the end of the nineteenth century, the quality of space and time changed. Technical innovations, such as the railroads, the automobile, and the telephone, became gradually accessible to a broader public. Stephen Kern shows how the world has thus become a smaller place.[23] This was said then as it is now in reference to the Internet. Within countries and internationally, one hundred years ago time zones had to be standardized and coordinated. Early Soviet leaders, as well as Russian czars like Catherine II and Peter I, eager to modernize and westernize, introduced state-of-the-art technology to catch up with the West, but they did not allow the technology to change the lives of their citizens. What was made possible by technological progress was prohibited by police methods, for fear of subversion. Soviet modernity was largely a Potemkin-style modernity, a type of modernity with which the Communists tried to fool everyone, including themselves. Theirs was a peasant society glossed over with technology to impress the world, not to make lives easier. In some respects, it was even postmodern *avant la lettre*: words and images were more important than the reality behind them. Appearances mattered more than the content.

Changing values lead to changing behavior and trigger new ways of self-fashioning: since the society has turned to a crude capitalism, one might argue, it is only natural for people to display their affluence. My book tries to go the opposite way. I observed transient appearances and try to deduce a subtext, a rationale, behind the changes. With great respect, I witness how well the Russian society mastered a reality full of insecurities, traps, and deceptions.

Like a soldier's sketch map, in the Soviet Union people's cognitive maps did not show more than one had to know to comply with the state's requests (which contrasted with the richness of people's imagined worlds, those created in writing and reading). Since the collapse of Communism, Russians' cognitive maps have become wider and more complex road maps that allow a choice of routes.

Russia is in turmoil; the old order has crumbled and the central government is hardly in control of its own territory. For a decade, people of dubious reputations, some obviously criminals, others adventurers and profiteers, have been involved in running the economy. There is little transparency, but the Soviet economy was not transparent, either. The post-Soviet economy has been called a virtual economy—based on surreal pricing—and many of its trades are still paid by barters. The laws are not enforced and the country still lacks some basic legislation—that is, on landownership and bankruptcy. The central government is still unable to collect enough taxes. Local authorities raise them in barter deals; some car manufacturers, for example, pay their taxes by providing new vehicles for the bureaucrats. In Chechnya, Russia is waging a war against its own citizens.

Still, Russia has become visibly pluralistic; people have choices as never before, they can express their opinions and live accordingly, they take on more responsibilities than ever, and they can shape their own lives, invent themselves. Whoever wants to can leave the country; some have amassed enormous wealth. Post-Soviet Russia is a far cry from the Soviet Union.

"Westerners stroll through life while East Europeans crawl through history," the Polish writer Kazimierz Brandys once wrote.[24] Having the opportunity to witness the transformation of the Soviet society on a daily basis, I felt as though I had the rare privilege to stroll through history, full of admiration for people who coped so well while their lives were in permanent transition.

NOTES

1. See, for example, Rupert Cornwell, "The Curse of Russia Has Always Been Its Pride in the Motherland," *Independent* (London), August 18, 2000, 4.

2. Stephen Kern, *The Culture of Time and Space, 1880–1914* (Cambridge, Mass.: Harvard University Press, 1983).

3. Arthur Golden, *Memoirs of a Geisha* (New York: Knopf, 1997), 1.

4. Anna Esposito, "Der römische Karneval in Mittelalter und Rennaissance," in *Fastnacht/Karneval im europäischen Vergleich*, ed. Michael Matheus, Mainzer Vorträge 3, Institut für Geschichtliche Landeskunde an der Universität Mainz e.V. (Stuttgart: Franz Steiner, 1999), 11.

5. Mikhail M. Bakhtin, *Rabelais and His World*, trans. Helene Iswolsky (Bloomington: Indiana University Press, 1984), 6.

6. Umberto Eco, "The Frames of Comic Freedom," in Umberto Eco, V. V. Ivanov, and Monica Rector, *Carnival! Approaches to Semiotics 64* (New York: de Gruyter, 1984), 6.

7. Werner Metzger, "Rückwärts in die Zukunft: Metamorphosen der schwäbisch-alemannischen Fastnacht," in *Fastnacht/Karneval im europäischen Vergleich*, ed. Michael Matheus, Mainzer Vorträge 3, Institut für Geschichtliche Landeskunde an der Universität Mainz e.V. (Stuttgart: Franz Steiner, 1999), 129–133.

8. Bakhtin, *Rabelais*, 6–15.

9. Mikhail M. Bakhtin, *Problems of Dostoevsky's Poetics*, trans. Caryl Emerson (Minneapolis: University Press of Minnesota, 1994), 123.

14   Chapter 1

10. *VTsIOM, Informationi byulleten monitoringa* (March–April 1995).

Poll, November 1994: What Does "Democracy" Mean for You?

soblyudayutsa prava tsheloveka [human rights]	29%
vlasti izbirayutsa narodom [elected power]	5%
praviteli sabotyatsa o narode [a government that cares for its people]	12%
vlast v rukakh trudyastshikhsa [power in the hands of the workers]	5%
vo glave strany—partiya, vyrazhayushtshaya [a party at the helm of the country that truly represents the people]	8%
vse eti razgovori o demokratii—obman naroda lovkimi politikami [all talk of democracy is deceiving the people]	20%
zatrudnyayus otvetit [don't know]	21%

11. Nadeshda Azhgikhina, "Myt, mutant, miss" (Myth, mutant, miss), *bang* (a Swedish women's magazine), no. 3 (October 1995): 10.

12. Michel de Certeau, *The Practice of Everyday Life*, trans. Steven F. Rendall (Berkeley: University of California Press, 1984), and Michel de Certeau, Luce Giard, and Pierre Mayol, *Living and Cooking: The Practice of Everyday Life*, Vol. 2, trans. Timothy J. Tomasik (Minneapolis: University of Minnesota Press, 1998).

13. Dmitri S. Likhachev and Aleksandr M. Panchenko, *Die Lachwelt des Alten Rußland (Smechovoj mir)* (Munich: Wilhelm Fink, 1991), 37.

14. Michael Harloe, "Cities in Transition," in *Cities after Socialism: Urban and Regional Change and Conflict in Post-Socialist Societies*, ed. Andrusz Gregory, Michael Harloe, and Ivan Szelenyi (Cambridge, Mass.: Blackwell, 1996), 340.

15. In medieval Europe, city dwellers were not subjected to serfdom, which is the origin of the slogan, "Stadtluft macht frei," or "city air makes one free."

16. George Orwell, *Nineteen Eighty-Four* (London: Heinemann, 1965). Orwell coined the term "Newspeak" for the lingo the party members speak.

17. Andrei Sinyavsky, *Soviet Civilization: A Cultural History*, trans. Joanne Turnbull (New York: Arcade, 1990), 196.

18. Sinyavsky, *Soviet Civilization*, 190–196.

19. Sinyavsky, *Soviet Civilization*, 209.

20. Stephen F. Cohen, *Failed Crusade: America and the Tragedy of Post-Communist Russia*, revised ed. (New York: Norton, 2001), 172.

21. George Soros, "Who Lost Russia," *New York Review of Books*, April 13, 2000.

22. John Lloyd, "The Russian Devolution," *New York Times Magazine*, August 15, 1999, 34.

23. Kern, *Culture of Time and Space*.

24. Kazimierz Brandys, *A Warsaw Diary 1978–1981*, trans. Richard Lourie (New York: Random House, 1983), 165.

2

✛

Carnival or Revolution? When Russia Suspended Time and Space

The tune portraying Tchaikovsky's fleeing swans was a harbinger of news that every Soviet citizen instinctively understood: a tragedy. In 1991, however, the harp called the reform-minded Muscovites to arms. What followed was an aborted coup d'état or, as I read it, a carnival that became serious.

On a sleepy Monday morning on August 19, the Soviet capital awoke to the tune of *Swan Lake*, the music the Soviet people had learned to associate with the death of a Kremlin leader. They had come to know the music as a sign of the passing of an era. But this time the past had returned. The country was scheduled to come back from summer vacation. The so-called New Union Treaty was to be signed the next day; it should have given the Soviet Union a new architecture, granting the republics some autonomy—whether real or sham. President Mikhail Gorbachev had thus hoped to gain breathing space from the union's unsteady republics.

The swans' message, however, was different from the news they usually delivered. Tanks moved into Moscow; Gorbachev was declared sick and was held incommunicado. A group of Communist reactionaries had seized power. They formed an emergency committee, the GKChP.[1] Their goal was to restore "order," as they said, but more important, they wanted to prevent the signing of the New Union Treaty because it was obvious that the treaty was a first step toward a possible dismantling of the Soviet Union.

This time, the swans, the established messengers for mourning by decree, were carrying a declaration of war. Most people ignored it, as they would have ignored the death of a Communist leader. However, a number of Muscovites took to the streets; Boris Yeltsin had called on them to rally "in defense of democracy." Having fortuitously escaped detention, Yeltsin climbed onto a tank in front of the White House, the site of the Russian parliament. He called for a general strike, encouraged the soldiers to engage in insubordinate behavior and the population to oppose the GKChP's takeover. For two months, Yeltsin, the maverick leader of the opposition, had been the elected president of the Russian Federation. Now, Tchaikovsky's subdued woodwinds, the swans, blew him a battle cry. Thus, an established sign of the Soviet state's code suddenly bore new significance.

Signs are ambiguous by nature, different from spoken language, which strives for precision; the signifiers of a nonverbal code modify their significations easily. In the Soviet Union, a sign usually had two different significations, an official one and—juxtaposed against it—an informal one. A joke that circulated during the late Leonid Brezhnev era illustrates this: Every day, a *babushka* stops at a newsstand. She picks up *Pravda, Izvestiya,* or any newspaper, glances at the front page, replaces the paper on the stand, and leaves. After a while, the salesperson asks what she is looking for.

"An obituary," she answers.

"But the obituaries are inside."

"Not the one I am looking for."

Such double meaning has always existed in Soviet discourse. A certain set of codes and morals used officially was juxtaposed in private use, ignoring or opposing the regime's ideology.

The failed coup in August 1991 marked the fall of Communism and the end of the Soviet Union, though it was only the turning point in a slower process. For the first time, the people's informal reading of the swans' flight had become the primary one. For three days, the street set the pace for politics, while the eight men who headed the coup posed as the new government. With Vice President Gennady Yanayev's hands trembling at their press conference, the plotters looked somber, like schoolboys who expected to get punished for a prank. They had appeared increasingly paralyzed— some of them were intoxicated with vodka. Hence, they were subjected to laughter by journalists who attended their press conference, and by ordinary people who saw the conference on television. Still, the swans' message turned into news of death. After three days of a phony revolution, tension, and haggling, three activists lost their lives in an accident. With the subsequent toppling of the statues of Feliks Dzerzhinsky, the father of the KGB, and Yakov Sverdlov, who masterminded the assassination of the czar and his family, the Soviet Union was headed for doom.

The week of the putsch saw the inversion of the Soviet hierarchy. The people took to the streets and barricades were built in front of the White

House. Despite the fear that the army might attack them, the crowd resisted the GKChP's threats. For some two years, activists opposing Communist rule had demonstrated repeatedly, ignoring threats. Now, they became the focus of media attention and many soldiers and their commanders were leaning in their favor.

For carnival, medieval European cities turned the society upside down, although within temporal and spatial limitations and with the guarantee that the inversion of the order would eventually be reversed. Bakhtin called this "second life outside officialdom," following the term of the Catholic theologian Saint Augustine, a "second world."[2] Bakhtin distinguished different kinds of carnivalesque laughter, including circus and other expressions of folk culture, though he focused primarily on literary carnivalizations. Other scholars have identified numerous carnivalesque elements in Russian life. Quoting Bakhtin in her book on post-Soviet life in Omsk, Dale Pesmen recorded "disrespects for money, . . . boundary transgressions, violations of routine, profanation, blasphemy, absurdity, disorder" as carnivalesque genres of behavior. Russians, in interviews with her, identified these behaviors as "very Russian"; to them, she concluded, Russian life is carnivalized.[3] I prefer to use the term "carnival" in the narrow sense of "carnival proper" (Bakhtin), the period in late winter—preceding lent—with its long pageants and processions and the "feast of fools."[4] Carnival proper "does not know footlights, in the sense that it does not acknowledge any distinction between actors and spectators," Bakhtin wrote. It "is not a spectacle seen by the people; they live it, and everyone participates because its very idea embraces all the people. While carnival lasts, there is no other life outside it. During carnival time life is subject only to its laws, that is, the laws of its own freedom."[5]

By theatrically overthrowing the rulers for a finite period, the carnival serves as a social valve. "By making the low high and the high low, [rituals of status reversal] reaffirm the hierarchical principle," the anthropologist Victor Turner emphasized. Turner concluded that, "by making the low mimic (often to the point of caricature) the behavior of the high, and by restraining the initiatives of the proud, [these rituals] underline the reasonableness of everyday culturally predictable behavior between the various estates of society."[6] Foul language is allowed, the potentates may be insulted, taboos are broken, and boundaries are violated. A carnival "liberates not only from external censorship but first of all from the great interior censor" and from fear, Bakhtin stressed.[7] It unites people: there are no outsiders during a carnival; everybody talks to everybody else and all participants are treated equally. Or, as Bakhtin phrased it, carnival allows a "free and familiar contact between people" who are usually separated by social boundaries and hierarchy.[8] Everybody revels in the fact that the emperor has no clothes. Carnival strives to rid people of their dignity; it denies them security. Nobody knows what will happen next. In many ways, a carnival equals a state of emergency.

Historically, European city governments resorted to declaring a carnival when unrest was looming. The Venetian authorities did just that when they felt that their power was being shaken. They aimed to theatricalize the subversion in order to reverse it. Some Venetian carnivals lasted six months; certain cities celebrated two carnivals a year. Yet, some medieval carnivals ended in turmoil. The societies were turned upside down, but reversals did not occur as supposed.[9] Thus, carnival can be seen as a revolution acted out—or, to the laughter of the victorious revolutionaries, one might say each revolution has its carnivalesque elements.

A carnival has to be contained in space and time; it must not affect the land and life beyond its limitations. As with any other exceptional situation, it cannot prevail. Rather, as Turner shows, the status reversal promotes reconciliation between the different hierarchical strata.[10] The lack of rules incites the emergence of new ones. From the first moments, revolution or carnival establishes its own set of prescribed and proscribed regulations.

In Moscow's outskirts, the August coup attempt was barely noticeable. Even in large parts of the city and almost anywhere else in the Russian Federation, life went on as if nothing had happened. Only some monumental places, such as Palace Square in St. Petersburg and the central squares of most of the union republics' capitals, witnessed rallies. Yet even in the unruly Baltics the rest of the cities and the countryside remained virtually untouched by the events.

Away from the White House, the major location where the drama of the failing coup was played out was on the nation's television screens. But even from this ubiquitous virtual space little spilled over. Life went on, the trains kept running, the (empty) shops were open, the mail was delivered, and the people went to work. Hence, can the August incidents, as they are often referred to, have been a revolution, or were they a carnival—an intermediate period during which, in a particular space, the law was suspended? It has been repeatedly claimed that August 1991 did not result in any lasting transformation of the society, despite the personal changes in the hierarchy and the resulting dissolution of the Soviet state. Russia, as the argument goes, is still being run by its established elites. As before in history, they have managed to reestablish themselves under a new system. Thus the changes are mostly cosmetic; one anticompetitive chaos, the Soviet command economy, has been replaced by another, Russia's crony capitalism. The deliberate disorder keeps the ex-*nomenklatura* in control of Russia's wealth.[11] The president, in that view, is just a figurehead, the democratic procedure a farce.

Do the three days in August, as I will argue here, mark a fundamental change in the Russian society? The *homini sovietici*, as characterized by Zinoviev,[12] were apathetic people, pushed around by the government and by each other, an atomized society of willing slaves, content with being in lifelong custody and, hence, with being taken care of. They had learned to not take initiative and to keep a low profile when things seemed to get out of control. They opposed change, since any change in their experience meant change for the worse.

But the people who took to the streets that Monday in August did not act as *homini sovietici*. They took initiative by erecting barricades and organizing food supplies and defense units. They were unusually friendly toward each other, sharing tea, food, blankets, and umbrellas. A growing crowd spent the nights around the White House, the site of the newly created parliament of the Russian Federation.[13] A tentative beginning led to high drama, with the three casualties during the third night and the subsequent victory of the people. The feared so-called Alpha troops, a paramilitary police unit formed to fight terrorists, refused to storm the White House. On the third day, the putschists gave in. Gorbachev returned from captivity in his *dacha* (summer house) on the Crimea, where he allegedly was taken hostage by the GKChP. That evening, a crowd toppled the statue of Feliks Dzerzhinsky, the founder of the Soviet secret police.

The coup was beaten back, yet the final act was still to come. It played out on Friday and Saturday of the same week. During a special session of the Russian parliament on Friday, Yeltsin (on behalf of the people, as he stressed) reproved Gorbachev. Never before had anyone treated the Soviet president the way he used to treat people. Yeltsin did just that: he reprimanded and disparaged him. The Communist emperor had no more clothes. Yeltsin took on a double role: the one of the innocent child, pointing at Gorbachev's nakedness, and another as Gorbachev's powerful successor. On that day, Yeltsin stood for bravery, honesty, morality, and thus, for all of Russia's (seemingly) uncorrupt citizens. Gorbachev had the unfortunate habit of publicly lecturing people, including his fiercest critic, Yeltsin. In 1987, he threw Yeltsin out of office as Moscow's party boss. Subsequently, he did everything to discredit him; by all means possible, he tried to prevent Yeltsin's comeback. Gorbachev obstructed Yeltsin's election to the Supreme Soviet and his rise to the presidency of the RSFSR (Russian Soviet Federal Socialist Republic, the Russian Federation within the USSR). Finally, Yeltsin's turn had come. Live, on the television screens, the nation witnessed Gorbachev's fall and the reversal of power—the climax of the carnivalesque week.

Gorbachev was taken by surprise. In his address to parliament only a few minutes before his symbolic fall,[14] he had vowed to renew the struggle for a modernized version of socialism. But Yeltsin publicly forced him to accept and sign decrees that transferred the power over the economy from the Soviet structures to the prime minister of the

Russian Federation, of which Yeltsin was president. Yeltsin humiliated Gorbachev by making him publicly read out a protocol of the GKChP; it named the leaders—Gorbachev's trusted allies—who had masterminded and executed the plot. There he stood, formally still one of the most powerful men in the world, stripped of all his friends, alone, ridiculed, and appearing foolish—a naked emperor.

The next day, Saturday, the carnivalesque week reached its finale. The funeral for the three young men who had died near the White House attracted more than one million people. Though the deaths were accidental, by calling them saviors of Russia Yeltsin turned the victims into martyrs. He assumed his new role as the benevolent regent, thus confirming the previous day's symbolic transition of power. He found the appropriate warm and fatherly words. He asked the families of the dead to forgive him for not having been able to save their lives. The crowd on Manezhnaya Square silently mourned the three; the subsequent procession of the coffins through the streets of Moscow to the Vaganskovskoye Cemetery lasted all day, the funeral service jointly led by the patriarch of the Orthodox Church and a rabbi. Presumably, for the first time in the Soviet Union, the "religious order," the strict separation of the (oppressed) religions, was suspended—live on television—for the whole nation to see.

The funeral had been organized by Yeltsin's people and policed by veterans of the Afghan war. The police were asked to remain hidden. A Russian tricolored flag, several hundred yards long, was carried by the procession. A new nation had been born, the people believed; or the true Russia had been reborn—a Russia that had never been. A week that began in chaos, with a civil war looming, ended in harmony.

Bakhtin calls carnival the "feast of becoming, change and renewal."[15] This implies purification, death, and reversibility. A carnival concludes by reverting to the old order. Revolution implies a change for the better (for a better life and a better society); those who stage it strive for power. However, the August coup never reached the state of reversal and renewal. The Communist Party of the Soviet Union (CPSU) was dethroned and its power was never restored. August was much more than a spontaneous carnival—but less than a revolution. Yeltsin had already been in office, though the Russian presidency did not entail much power. The country was already in a state of transition when the coup plotters attempted to overthrow the existing order, or as they saw it, disorder. On the Monday morning of the coup, Yeltsin, for his part, rushed to help keep Gorbachev in power. But the latter failed to side with his saviors and to understand the dynamics of the situation. Thus, he found himself on the plotters' side. They ended up looking like fools—and Gorbachev seemed to be one of them.

The victors had not expected to win so soon or so easily. Is that why they hardly drove home their victory? As mentioned above, a small number of

Communist icons fell. However, the city of St. Petersburg still honors Dzerzhinsky with a monument and, at the Lubyanka building, the KGB headquarters in Moscow, a new plaque commemorates Yuri Andropov, the KGB chief turned party leader. For almost ten years after the end of the Soviet Union, Russia lacked a lawfully sanctioned heraldry; the Duma did not accept the replacement of the Soviet state symbols. Many bureaucrats, turncoats shifting their allegiances, have managed to hold on to their positions.

Carnival or revolution? Russia's transition from Brezhnev Communism to its post-Soviet crony capitalism and corrupt democracy was much more than a carnival. Despite many familiar faces remaining at the top, the society has changed dramatically; little remains of the *homo sovieticus*, as Moscow sociologist Yuri Levada's research confirms.[16] However, for a revolution, August 1991 lacked iconoclastic vigor. Instead of dismantling the party apparatus to see the end of Communism through, the victorious Yeltsin remained absent from the scene for weeks, thus paralyzing politics. He missed a golden opportunity to destroy the secret police and introduce a new constitution—in the immediate aftermath of the coup, he might have had enough popular backing for such drastic measures.

Carnival unifies people against the powerful suppressor they have always feared; it cracks the threatening yet diabolical order. It has a univocal social or political meaning and provides a space in which activities and symbols can be inflected in different directions. Everything is fluid; signs can adjust very quickly. During a carnival, the rabbit chases the hunter, the bishops sin, and the fools are crowned, Umberto Eco has taught us.[17] Carnival enables the child to say that the emperor has no clothes. The laughter of carnival is subversive, but primarily it is the laughter of those liberated from angst. And, since fear is a cause for corruption, the end of fear is perceived as the end of lying, a purgatory.

The medieval carnival was political by implication. However, in the fifteenth century, in the Swabian-Alemannic region, it lost its antiauthoritarian character and thus its subversive thrust.[18] A revolution passes through its main carnivalesque moment when fear turns into scorn, when the dreadful potentates are reduced to clowns searching for an exit—when fear changes sides. At times, the mood outside the White House was festive, happy, and vigorous.

During the medieval carnival, as during a revolution, the order of time is suspended, just like the partitioning of the society. People live in carnival time and in that time only. Their "second life" (Bakhtin) does away with their usual rhythms of life. They do not eat at the usual times and they sleep little. Borders and laws are violated and the violation must be felt as such. Carnival, however, is authorized; it lasts only for a short time and is limited in space. "Nothing satisfies as much as extravagant or temporarily permitted illicit behavior," Turner noted.[19] At its end, the law is reenforced, the social valve has worked, and the steam has been released. Umberto Eco goes even further by seeing the comic as a "form of social control," not as "a form of social criticism." He sees carnival as an "authorized transgression," a *contradictio in adjecto,* and therefore a typical double bind. An unexpected carnivalization is usually read as a rebellion. "But even revolutions produce a restoration of their own," according to Eco, "in order to reinstall their new social model. Otherwise they are not effective revolutions, but only uprisings, revolts."[20] The August putsch, or the people's reply to the attempted coup, was not a transitory disturbance nor did it precede the installation of a new social model. It dismantled the old order, but did not succeed in imposing a new one. It encouraged the break with the old laws, but the new leaders failed to impose their own set of laws. Rather, they have introduced laws, but neither they nor the population respect them—hence, the lawlessness.

Russia since 1991 has not been in a permanent revolution, as Trotsky would have had it. Rather, with hardly any restoration of order going on— if this process has not begun with the election of President Putin—Russia is in a permanent state of a carnival, or in a continuing chaos. Or, one might say, Russia is stuck in a revolution that began half-heartedly with perestroika and remains unfinished. With the violation becoming the rule, the political joke has disappeared. In hindsight, many people see the week in August as a turning point. They date things before or after it. Thus, the failed putsch was more than a revolution reduced to its carnivalesque moments, but less than a carnival turned into a permanent condition. The dissolution of Communism is unfinished business, with a good part of the Soviet elite remaining in power, without any iconoclastic fervor.

Another way of reading the carnival metaphor into Russian history is controversially discussed among Bakhtin scholars. "The whole book is best read as a coded attack on the cultural situation of Russia in the 1930s under Stalin," the British scholar Simon Dentith wrote. He perceived Bakhtin's theory of carnival as (partially) prompted by Lunacharsky, the Bolshevik commissar of education who had called laughter the "merest safety valve for social tension."[21] Although they concede that *Rabelais and his World* "presents, inter alia, a critique of contemporary Soviet ideology," the Bakhtin biographers Katerina Clark and Michael Holquist dissuade the scholarly community from writing "off the work as an anti-Bolshevik or anti-Stalinist tract." They emphasize Bakhtin's enthusiasm for revolution, "some sort of permanent revolution in society or culture," implying a "dramatic thrust for perpetual renewal."[22] Dentith remains skeptical; he accuses Bakhtin of utopianism and calls carnival "a mixed blessing."[23]

Can the whole Soviet period be read as a heinous carnival, an interlude of trouble that began in 1917 (or in 1905) and that is finally coming to an end? Stalin, then, and his successors, would be the "Lords of Misrule" of that carnival, Bakhtin's fool's kings.[24] Gorbachev's tentative opening up of the society was not meant to terminate the red lords' rule. He was loosening the party's grip on power to put a human face on Soviet Communism. But the society took him at face value, it began to transform itself, and he lost control. The August plotters hoped to reverse this process. They pulled the human mask off the party's face, but the diabolical mask behind—the somber face of Communism—had lost its power of deterrence; a protracted period of turmoil, with the society turned upside down, with the civic rules and laws suspended, promised to come to an end. Was this the reason Yeltsin and his fellow reformers did not resort to iconoclasm? Did they see themselves as engineers of the return to order? After 70 years of nightmare, some people hoped to return to the pre-Communist order. Soon, advertisements took up the issue of czarist Russia; the Bank Imperial, one of the first commercial banks, used footage of everyday life in Russia around the turn of the century, hoping to evoke reassurance and trust.

A carnival creates a sense of community; it allows "free and familiar contact between people" who would usually remain separated, as Bakhtin put it.[25] In the Soviet Union, this was particularly effective, as I witnessed during the many rallies preceding the August coup. The Soviet society had been highly atomized; hence the experience of a crowd, a spontaneously forming community, was especially powerful. Despite that, August 1991 was no popular uprising; a minute faction of Soviet society, and only a small part of Moscow, took to the White House. More Russians followed the events at home in front of their television sets. The carnival or revolution became a reported one: what was presented on the television screens was more important than what actually happened.

In their excellent essay "Televorot," Victoria Bonnell and Gregory Freidin identified three "scripts" of the coup, stressing its theatricality.[26] All three scenarios were publicly known before August 19. Earlier that summer, twelve Soviet leaders published an appeal to the Soviet people to resist the breakup of the USSR. Their article, together with appeals and decrees released on Monday morning, the first day of the coup, defined a U-turn toward the reestablishment of Soviet power. The alleged purpose of this U-turn was to avoid imminent chaos. The second script was the one for which Yeltsin and his fellow democrats stood; it was indisputably the most powerful scenario. It aimed to re-create a democratic Russia—as a country and particularly as a culture—and to sever Russia from the ill-fated Soviet legacy. This script was widely published; it enjoyed the acceptance of the most active segment of the society. The third script, the "*perestroika* script," as Bonnell and Freidin called it, was Gorbachev's idea of a soft and gradual transition to a new form of socialism. Even after his return to Moscow from captivity, Gorbachev insisted on it, but it attracted "fewer and fewer good actors, not to mention an increasingly sparse audience." After the coup, it became "a solo performance in a nearly empty theater." Yeltsin's script was the only one that enjoyed relevant backing from the society.

In their declarations, the emergency committee resorted to the old, shallow language of pre-perestroika Communism. People did not have to listen to what was being said; the vocabulary and intonation signaled a return to the past and so did the changes made to television's entertainment programs that Monday afternoon. It reminded viewers of the Brezhnev era. This was a deliberate part of the putschists' script, but it might have further decreased their chances for success. The GKChP attempted to control the media and to impose censorship.

Nevertheless, the television directors managed to sneak pictures of the democrats' script into the major news program *Vremya*. Among these images, two were particularly powerful: the first saw Boris Yeltsin standing on the tank, framed from below, the final shot of a reportage from the streets of Moscow. Tanks were rolling and the soldiers' expressions were confused. Yeltsin, quite the daredevil, belied these images by calling on the people to defend the just cause. He was surrounded by supporters, a picture reminiscent of Lenin arriving at the Finland Station in 1917, an icon of Soviet culture. At the time, the crowd in front of the White House was small; the camera exaggerated its size and resolution. The other picture that burned itself immediately into the memories of millions of people was taken during the press conference of the GKChP. Here, the camera focused on Yanayev's trembling hands. His arrogant voice did not betray his agitation, but the hands did. Thus, the framing of the camera conveyed to the whole country that Yanayev was feeling uneasy, that he might be lying about Gorbachev being ill. He and his fellow plotters were not as reassuring as they tried to appear—in fact, just the opposite. Yanayev's hands revealed his vulnerability. And the cameraman exposed his bluff, triggering the nation's laughter—a laughter on the threshold between fear and relief.

The Soviet people were prepared for these pictures. They had seen television footage of the fall of the Berlin Wall. January 1991 showed the tanks attacking the television tower in Vilnius. They had heard how brave, unarmed Lithuanian civilians fought them off. Civil disobedience was on all activists' minds. In Vilnius, the people barricaded the parliament building; in Riga, with the support of what seemed to be the whole Latvian nation, the historic center of the city was cordoned off. Everybody knew that Yeltsin was no stranger to those actions. He had rushed to the Baltics to support their fight. Although these nations had not won independence yet, they had successfully resisted the Kremlin's attempts to bring them back into line. By the summer of 1991, the reform-minded Muscovites had learned the lesson. They had seen enough barricades to know how to defy the Soviet tanks, at least symbolically.

During carnival, people do not read decrees. Nor do they do so during a revolution. They know what they are fighting for, or they believe that they do. Their future, and at times their lives, are at stake. They react emotionally to signs, signals, and icons—particularly to the strongest—and they react collectively. A carnival's comic does not allow any gradation. A minor signal may change the mood and direction of the crowd and the crowd acts as one. The choice of angle made by a single cameraman, the decision of a director to cut out neither Yanayev's trembling hands nor some scornful questions and the subsequent laughter in the hall—seemingly small incidents—may well have changed the course of history. The director's decision heavily favored the Yeltsin script, triggering the subversive laughter and thus emphasizing the carnivalesque aspects of the putsch.[27] Also, many people learned only from *Vremya* that the White House was where to go if they wanted to join the protest against the coup.

Carnival suspends the conventional sense of time and space. Usually, different activities are assigned to different periods of the day. In times of a carnival (or revolution), there is no set lunchtime, teatime, dinnertime, after-work time, or bedtime. Carnival continues around the clock, as does revolution, and more often than not the crucial moments occur in the dead of night. In everyday life, spatial and temporal order are taken as givens. Their very suspension marks a state of the extraordinary. When time and space are altered, nothing appears to be taken for granted anymore. And with these central frames of the previous order gone, everything is open to examination.

Exceptional situations cannot prevail; the sheer absence of any rule provokes the emergence of new rules and, almost immediately, the crowd begins to observe unwritten laws of its own. After August, the Soviet Union did not manage to reestablish its previous rules nor did the newly emerging Russian state succeed in reinstalling Russia's prerevolutionary framework of values and principles—an act that might have been part of the "democratic script" during the coup.

Perestroika brought the concept of civic space to Russia. Until Gorbachev came to power, there was no space for public exchange. A phony civic space existed in the Potemkin-style form of the Soviet democracy, with its fake representations, party meetings, committees, and votes. And civic space existed in some homes, reduced to the kitchen table. Only there were opinions freely exchanged. Before the putsch, the conquest of civic space, as I will show later, happened tentatively. Since the summer of 1988, the Soviet regime had tolerated some demonstrations. For a limited time and in a restricted area, normally a route for a procession and a square for the final rally, the free expression of dissent was allowed, yet contained by the police and by troops of the interior ministry. On March 28, 1991, for the first time, this situation was inverted. Gorbachev had called 50,000 troops into Moscow to prohibit a planned demonstration against the CPSU. The army barred all access streets to the Kremlin, with the result that Gorbachev suddenly saw himself enclosed by dissent. His power did not reach beyond Moscow's inner ring. On the other side of the military's barriers, speech was free. For one day, and in full view, the Soviet Union had become pluralistic: that is, a dualistic society, with at least two voices, though the voice of the Communist Party was barely audible. In an almost festive mood, hundreds of thousands of Muscovites defied the Kremlin's orders. For a few hours, the power structure was turned upside down, a carnival was in rehearsal. Gorbachev finally backed off. Although no one had called him naked—powerless—he obviously no longer controlled the nation's public voices.

In hindsight, that chilly Thursday in March 1991 looks like a dress rehearsal for the popular response to the coup in August. It was arguably the first time that non-Communist Russia had taken control of the streets of the capital. Intuitively, many people understood what had happened.

All major Soviet institutions, without exception controlled by the CPSU, Gorbachev's own people, supported the coup or remained indifferent, and thus loyal; these included the government, the Supreme Soviet, the army and the troops of the interior ministry, the youth organization Komsomol, and the bureaucracy. They were all represented in the GKChP, including the government in the person of Prime Minister Valentin Pavlov. This made it easy for Yeltsin to morally separate Russia from the Soviet Union.

In the aftermath, Yeltsin praised the heroic Russian nation and thanked it for defying a deadly threat. He himself stood out as a selfless leader who risked imprisonment and possibly execution by the GKChP. However, he avoided talking about himself. Gorbachev, by contrast, used the first press conference after his return to Moscow to complain that he and his wife Raisa had been treated harshly, as if his personal fate was more important than the country's. He barely mentioned the people on the barricades and had little praise for his saviors. The difference in the attitudes of the two men was not lost on the Russians. Gorbachev represented the self-indulged party bureaucracy, Yeltsin a happier future. Indeed, Yeltsin celebrated the days of the putsch as the birth of a new Russia. He punished the culprit, banned the CPSU, and humiliated Gorbachev by publicly calling him "naked." The putschists were detained; two committed suicide.

A carnival is a time outside time, "a second life of the people, who for a time enter the utopian realm of community, freedom, equality and abundance," Bakhtin wrote.[28] A carnival does not look forward to a distant utopian future; its activists perceive it *to be* this bright future, if only for a limited time.

A fierce adversity within a society cannot prevail; the nation has to be consolidated. Carnival is exhausting; its activists eventually understand that this is not the bright future. Thus, a carnival must end on a conciliatory note, with the people being relieved that an order—possibly any order—has been reestablished. However, with no set of rules to revert to and no new social contract, the former Soviet Union has remained in a permanent turmoil for more than a decade. Laws exist, but they are rarely observed and, generally, no convention of manners is accepted anymore.

With the funeral procession for the three victims of the coup and the ecumenical service, Yeltsin and his allies succeeded in obtaining the clergy's blessing for their carnival-revolution, that utopian period of time. Despite the lack of a new order, or any order, the putsch ended in reconciliation and a symbolic transfer of power. Yeltsin acquired the role of father of the new Russian nation. When addressing the mourning crowd on Manezhnaya, he asked the families of the three victims to forgive him—"your president," as he called himself—for not being able to save their sons. True, he had been elected president by the population of the Russian Federation, but the country was still the Soviet Union and Gorbachev was its president. Thus, by calling himself "your president," Yeltsin again implied the transfer of power from the Soviet Union to Russia and to the other republics. He placed Gorbachev in the position of a president without a land.

Technically, the transfer of power was to be completed in December 1991, when the presidents of Ukraine and Belarus, Kravchuk and Shushkevich, agreed to dissolve the Soviet Union. On December 25, 1991, Gorbachev formally resigned and the USSR was dismantled.

The new year, and with it a new country and a new government, arrived. However, the new country looked much like the old one, only less orderly. The inversion of the society had just begun; the longer it lasted, the harder it would be to reestablish order. The carnival was far from over; to this day, the overhaul of the Russian society has not been completed. Post-Soviet Russia, one might say, remains in and suffers from a chronic state of transition—the signs are fluid and the society is in turmoil. In part, Vladimir Putin's surprising popularity as president can be explained by the Russians' being tired of their carnival; they are longing for order and stability.

The collapse of the Soviet regime, as I will argue later, can be read as a step toward modernity, or away from the USSR's nonliberal, Potemkin-style modernity. When this transition finally comes to its completion, the result will be a more open, liberal, mobile, and industrialized society that respects the individual.

NOTES

1. GKChP, Gosudarstvennyi komitet po chrezvychainomu polozheniyu (State Committee on the State of Emergency).
2. Mikhail M. Bakhtin, *Rabelais and His World*, trans. Helene Iswolsky (Bloomington: Indiana University Press, 1984), 6.
3. Dale Pesmen, *Russia and Soul: An Exploration* (Ithaca, N.Y.: Cornell University Press, 2000), 239.
4. Bakhtin, *Rabelais*, 5.
5. Bakhtin, *Rabelais*, 7.
6. Victor Turner, *The Ritual Process: Structure and Anti-Structure* (New York: de Gruyter, 1969), 176.
7. Bakhtin, *Rabelais*, 94.
8. Mikhail M. Bakhtin, *Problems of Dostoevsky's Poetics*, trans. Caryl Emerson (Minneapolis: University of Minnesota Press, 1994), 122.
9. For example, in 1478 during the Saubannerzug, in wide parts of today's Switzerland, and in 1529 during the Basler Bildersturm.
10. Turner, *Ritual Process*, 190.
11. Gregory Feifer, "Deliberate Disorder: A Report from Moscow," *World Policy Journal*, no. 1 (1999): 69–75.
12. Aleksandr Zinoviev, *Homo Sovieticus*, trans. Charles Janson (Boston: Atlantic Monthly Press, 1985). According to Sonja Margolina, the term dates back to Giorgy Smirnov, a member of the Central Committee's ideology department. In the late 1970s, he published a book, *The New Soviet Man*, which stated that, in the state of socialism, the people developed a new sense of community; Zinoviev's novel was intended as a reply to that. Sonja Margolina, *Rußland: Die nichtzivile Gesellschaft* (Russia: The noncivil society) (Reinbek, Germany: Rowohlt, 1994), 155.
13. The Supreme Soviet of the USSR, by contrast, was located within the walls of the Kremlin, symbolically out of reach of the people.
14. Formally, Gorbachev resigned on December 25, 1991.
15. Bakhtin, *Rabelais*, 10.
16. Yuri A. Levada, *Sovetskii Prostoi Chelovek*, from the German translation, *Die Sowjetmenschen, 1989–1991: Soziogramm eines Zerfalls* (Munich: Deutscher Taschenbuch Verlag, 1993).
17. Umberto Eco, "The Frames of Comic Freedom," in Umberto Eco, V. V. Ivanov, and Monica Rector, *Carnival! Approaches to Semiotics 64*, ed. Thomas A. Sebroek (New York: de Gruyter, 1984), 2.
18. Werner Metzger, "Rückwärts in die Zukunft, Metamorphosen der schwäbisch-alemannischen Fastnacht," in *Fastnacht/Karneval im europäischen Vergleich*, ed. Michael Matheus, Mainzer Vorträge 3, Institut für Geschichtliche Landeskunde an der Universität Mainz e.V. (Stuttgart: Franz Steiner, 1999), 129.
19. Turner, *Ritual Process*, 176.
20. Eco, "Frames of Comic Freedom," 7.
21. Simon Dentith, *Bakhtinian Thought* (New York: Routledge, 1995), 71.
22. Katerina Clark and Michael Holquist, *Mikhail Bakhtin* (Cambridge, Mass.: Belknap, 1984), 300–307.

23. Dentith, *Bakhtinian Thought*, 76.

24. Bakhtin, *Rabelais*, 5.

25. Bakhtin, *Dostoevsky's Poetics*, 124.

26. Victoria Bonnell and Gregory Freidin, "Televorot: The Role of Television Coverage in Russia's August 1991 Coup," in *Soviet Hieroglyphics: Visual Culture in Late Twentieth-Century Russia*, ed. Nancy Condee (Bloomington: Indiana University Press, 1995).

27. The images of Yeltsin on the tank were taken by cameraman Vladimir Chechelnitsky, the reporter was Sergei Medvedev, and the director who did not edit out Yanayev's trembling hands was Elena Podzniak, according to Bonnell and Freidin, "Televorot."

28. Bakhtin, *Rabelais*, 9.

3

Sight: The First Sense

Russia looks different from the way she used to. Her smells have changed, as have her sounds. Her inhabitants' eating habits, and thus her tastes, are changing. And Russia's texture is undergoing a transition, too.

The former Soviet cities have become noisier, faster, livelier, and much more variegated. They used to appear gray and monotonous; nothing but dullness met a foreigner's gaze. These same cities have turned loud—acoustically and optically. Passersby are bombarded with music, with announcements, with visual screams, billboards, and fashion extravaganzas. For Russia, this is new. The level of the semiotical background noise has grown enormously. It required and still requires an extra effort by the people, so used to stability, to adjust.

Thus, everyday life in Russia and the former Soviet Union appears to have been revitalized, enameled, pushed to extremes, and therefore it has become complicated. It has transformed dramatically, especially in the cities. People dress differently, they behave differently, they own different objects, and they enjoy pleasures unheard of only a decade ago, for example, gambling in casinos. Moscow these days looks almost like a modern Western city. When one wonders if Russia has become democratic or if she continues to be a backward authoritarian country, when one asks if the transition toward capitalism can be reversed or if the move away from the centrally planned economy can be undone, when one is frightened by the unreformed rhetoric of Russian politicians, the Duma (parliament), or the president, then one should perhaps bear in mind these changes, which are so obvious that one tends to overlook them. One forgets them since one has become accustomed to them, since they can be seen everywhere. The human eye has a short memory and adapts easily to changes.

Whenever I traveled from Switzerland to West Berlin, I was surprised how dimly lit the streets were—almost as dark as in the Soviet bloc, East Germany, Poland, or the Soviet Union. When I traveled in the other direction, I found the streets of West Berlin to be brightly lit, almost as light as Zurich's. Passing from Moscow through Estonia to Sweden, I felt that the Estonians looked almost Scandinavian; in the other direction, Estonia seemed "Soviet." Similarly, when arriving in the Soviet Union or in Eastern Europe, I was struck by the people's impoverished appearance. However, after spending a month or two in the Soviet sphere, I began to view the people—especially the women—as attractive and elegantly dressed. My eye had adjusted.

The Soviet Union looked different from other countries, particularly those of Western Europe. It also sounded, smelled, tasted, and felt different. However, this chapter does not aim to compile the differences between Russia and the West; rather it attempts to document the conversion from the appearances of the Soviet Union to those of Russia today.

A country that looks different from another country is most likely a different country. Hence, a Russian society that is dramatically distinguished in its looks, sounds, scents, tastes, and textures from its Soviet predecessor is most likely a new society, even if its verbal self-stylizations, the faces of its politicians, and its state symbols have not changed much. Symbolically, the Soviet Union was preserved long after its demise: for example, on the currency bills with Lenin's portrait, on Russian passports, on official forms, that is, on paper read by millions every day.[1]

Russia's new diversity exists not only in fashion, advertisements, cars, food, and entertainment, but also in architecture. Since 1991, the big cities have witnessed a construction boom; their newly erected buildings display a great and often confusing variety of styles. As in the latter half of the nineteenth century, and for only the second time in Russia's history, clients appeared who were independent of government authority. They started commissioning works from independent architects, thus causing a diversity of styles previously unheard of. This pluralization occurring toward the end of the nineteenth century has been interpreted as "total decay," as the current trend has been by many conservatives in post-Soviet Russia.[2]

A society that experiences an outbreak of sudden visual plurality most likely will shed its uniformity in other fields. A society that changes its hygiene and eating habits might also change its views of the human body and the individual inhabiting that body. This also has occurred in Russia. Thus, the Russian society, having undergone such change, is not the same society that existed in the Soviet era, even if it happens to be the successor of the Soviet society. This is all the more true because Russian society no longer perceives itself the way it once did.

The distinct visual appearance of a society is usually the first thing a visitor notices when encountering another culture: a dissimilar architecture, peculiar types of cars, and foremost, a different style of clothing. If the visitor were a Soviet citizen from the 1970s, traveling through time to arrive in contemporary Russia, he or she would barely recognize his or her own country. By contrast, if a Soviet time traveler were visiting the different postwar decades of the Soviet Union, he or she would barely notice the differences; the Soviet Union of the 1980s looked much like the Soviet Union of the 1970s and the Soviet Union of the 1970s was not so different from the country of the 1960s.

In the following pages, using all five senses, I try to demonstrate how fundamentally Russia's appearances have transformed, to what extent they have become multifaceted and, in some cases, refined. In its appearance and scents, the Soviet Union has been turned upside down in a truly carnivalesque manner. The previous order has been suspended; new rules have not yet been made. A wild plurality has replaced Communism's uniformity; disorder has become the order of the day.

Naturally, the changes in appearances are the ones most likely to be grasped initially, with no records of past scents, textures, tastes. Only the sounds of music, not society's noises, are preserved. Our senses adjust quickly, forgetting how the disappearing once looked, smelled, or felt. Were it not for photography, one could not gather to what extent visual appearances change over time.

The Soviet public space was free of advertisements. Along with slogans, such as "Long live the CPSU" or "*trud istochnik bogatstva*" ("Work is the source of wealth"), in white capital letters against red backgrounds, the central squares of the Soviet cities, especially on state holidays, were dominated by images of a few faces: Karl Marx, Friedrich Engels, and Lenin. The three men together, often on red cloth, or Lenin alone, stood for the regime and its alleged ideology. With the exception of some monuments, these faces have all but disappeared, replaced mostly by those of young women such as Cindy Crawford and Claudia Schiffer, and also by the "Marlboro men" (taken from the Western cigarette advertisements) and many other flawless models. The old, seemingly wise men, as well as the sturdy letters of the slogans, stood for propaganda talk, for a dull and outdated theory that had little meaning in real life, and for privation and discipline. The earthy style of the old images and slogans was part of *Sots*-art, or socialist realism. It promoted an ideology of scarcity and sacrifice and was a design allegedly in accordance with nature and technology. The style of the new advertisements, by contrast, could be characterized as "pop art," promoting consumerism, hedonism, fun—in short, dreams and emotions.

Hence, in the public realm, Cindy Crawford and Claudia Schiffer can be seen as Marx and Lenin's successors. They symbolize youth, wealth, and success. Not that the Russians believe that buying a particular brand of watch would bring them happiness, but neither did they take Marx's and Lenin's messages seriously. Implicitly, Marx, Engels, and Lenin stood for stability—or stagnation. Their faces remained static over decades; the models advertising goods and services, by contrast, change constantly, with new faces appearing on billboards almost weekly, with the changing fashion seasons.

There were no fashion cycles in the Soviet Union like the four annual collections thrown onto Western markets, a crucial characteristic of Western culture. Changes in style occurred incrementally. Westerners rarely took notice of a Soviet way of dress or that Soviet women cared about their appearance. The correspondent Hedrick Smith once spoke of a "cloth-coat proletarian respectability" and ascribed "a petit bourgeois instinct for appearances" to the Muscovites. Soviet women sewed their own dresses and sought tiny accessories to distinguish themselves. Their dresses were plain and men wore simple suits, Smith reported.[3] Bright colors were incompatible with state employment and no other jobs were available. In the summer, most men wore short-sleeved polyester shirts. The *apparatchiks* had their gray, ill-fitting suits. Adolescent men preferred nylon tracksuits—Adidas or Nike—worn so that the brand name and sign, Adidas's easily identifiable three stripes, for example, were visible. The young rebellious urbanites longed for blue jeans to convey nonconformity with the older generation; they tried to mark a slight deviation from Soviet society. Anything American stood for what was better and "other" and provided contrast. However, a number of items never failed to betray one as a Westerner: my metal-rimmed glasses, for example. Only a few horn spectacle frames were available to Soviets.

Uniformity more than anything else dominated the picture of Soviet life and clothing was no exception. Fashion seemed remarkably absent, despite many Soviet women's attempts to add discreet personal features to their clothes, subliminal to us Western correspondents, as Smith showed. Men did not seem to care.

Fashion shows did not exist before the Gorbachev period; the first ones made headlines in the most "serious" newspapers. Photos that depict life in the West can be dated automatically by the viewer. According to people's clothing, hairstyle, and glasses, there is a 1950s look and a 1960s look, while the 1980s experimented with the punk image. The Soviet Union, however, experienced relatively little change in appearance. For twenty years, the clothes, like the cars, looked almost the same. A sharp eye was required to distinguish the so-called fifth model of the Zhiguli from its predecessor, the fourth model, or from the third. To me, they all looked like the late 1960 Fiat upon which they were based.

Many people who had served time in the gulag or in prison wore tattoos. The tattoo conveyed a special type of information that transferred from the invisible world of the labor camps to the everyday reality of Soviet cities. Less powerful tattoos were and are those of soldiers, seamen, and other people on the fringes of society. A tattoo signified membership in a special group of insiders, one of the rare signs that conveyed someone was different. These groups did not want to be or could not be part of the Soviet petty bourgeoisie. As elsewhere, to have oneself tattooed was an act of subversion and initiation. Its irreversibility required courage in a society where people avoided clear stances. In post-Soviet society, however, these tattoos are a sign of the past, a uniform of yesteryear, like a noble title in a (counter)world that has abolished its aristocracy.

There were no commercial advertisements in the Soviet Union and hardly any design elements. The few attempts to tout consumer products were either meant to steer consumption away from articles that were in limited supply or absent, or to launch new products. Completely absent was Western advertisement's main purpose—to create need by exhibiting the product temptingly. Since there was always a demand for goods and no competition among comparable products, there was no need to present goods in an enticing manner and thus no need for design.

In general, change was unwelcome in the Soviet Union; it was considered neither politically nor economically advantageous. People tended to believe change was always for the worse. The media fostered stability; they sketched a country where change, by decree, was focused on improving the status quo, on technological progress, on record harvests, and on other achievements of the Communist system. They were slow to report changes, particularly spontaneous social changes, and they deliberately ignored unexpected occurrences, such as catastrophes. The Soviet media hardly ever portrayed individuals. While Western and post-Soviet media search for the exception, while they dig for scandals or even fabricate them, their Communist counterparts used to advertise a Soviet-style normality, painting a picture of how life should be.

Yet, social change happened visibly, if slowly and tentatively. Since the early 1950s, a minute counterculture has existed. On the fringes of Soviet society, some youths dressed differently, thus expressing their discord with society. However, they remained at the periphery, basically contained to clubs, gatherings, and informal hangouts.

Leonid Brezhnev's reign (1964–1982), the period of stagnation as it was called, was very much a period of visual stagnation, too. Packaging, the few existing logos, signs, and other emblems remained the same. They had to. And the Soviet people did not object; they were afraid of any new development. They stayed in the same flat for years, even decades. The time of stagnation was a tedious period, especially for young people.

Many expressed a hunger for diversity and a world beyond militaristic Soviet life.

Joseph Brodsky once expressed the fantastic idea that major Soviet newspapers should have printed excerpts from the works of Western modernists such as James Joyce, Marcel Proust, or Robert Musil on their front pages to make the Russian readers understand that "life is basically an unhappy thing, anyway, anywhere, in the West, too."[4] Could this have impressed *Pravda*'s average reader? Probably not, since many people did not believe what the papers said, but read them for signs. In Estonia, where a higher proportion of the population had access to modern Western literature and to Finnish television, acceptance of the Soviet *byt* ("being"), the burdensome everyday life, did not increase—the opposite occurred.

Posters celebrating the "friendship of the nations" of the Soviet Union used to portray the non-Russian ethnicities in their national costumes; only the Russians wore Western clothes. This invoked a reading that the other nations were uncivilized people not fit for a life under the conditions of the scientific-technical revolution, although, if enlightened by the Russians, they would gradually transform into Russians.[5] The propaganda related similarly to the West—full of awe when it came to technology, but otherwise condescending. I often encountered a sense of superiority in Soviet Russians. Even dissenters were proud of the space program, happy when the USSR's *Sputnik* and *Soyuz* beat the Americans in the space competition. When they finally understood that the Communist regime was not as formidable an adversary as they had believed, they felt a great loss.[6] It is therefore hard to imagine how any kind of literature would have influenced the Soviet identity, which was complex but positive.

When I first embarked on researching the visible fallout of the transition, or on the visible effects of perestroika, I hoped to compile a type of concordance of signs in order to juxtapose the old Soviet codes—both formal and informal—with their post-Communist equivalents. This project proved flawed because, in times of transition, meanings are too fluid.

The most obvious feature of the Soviet deficit economy were the lines in front of stores, a visible indicator that there was something to buy. The store windows, for those that had them, were decorated with simple plastic pictograms displaying what the store was supposed to sell. That gave rise to many jokes: a store's clerk tells a customer that his is not the shop where he or she could not get meat, but the shop where the customer could not get vegetables—the shop not to get meat was next door. A queue was a signifier that there was something worth waiting for, albeit something that one might have to trade for something else later.

With the advent of private enterprise, the lines disappeared. The few that remained seemed to meet a social need. Since 1992, the bread store on Bolshaya Yakimanka Street in the center of Moscow has rarely suffered from shortages. One can go there a few minutes before closing and get a loaf of dark bread or a baguette. For three years, I lived opposite the bakery. Almost every afternoon before the store reopened after its lunch break, a line of pensioners formed. They knew each other and seemed to meet for a chat, as they had when they were forced to stand in line for bread. This had obviously become a habit and an opportunity to socialize.

Other lines only emerged after the introduction of the market. In 1997, a line of several hundred mostly elderly women on Nevsky Prospect in St. Petersburg reminded me of the worst days of the Soviet Union. Yet the women were queuing for a free sample of a new brand of perfume. At MTS, the Moscow cell phone company, a symbol of the new times, people have to queue for long periods. As in the Soviet Union, clerks sit behind desks, ignoring the customers.

Surviving in the Soviet Union meant constantly searching for items that were unavailable or at least not seen in stores. People relied on informal networks, *blat*, or they simply roamed the stores, hoping for a lucky discovery.[7] Soviet people never left home without a bag, in case they encountered an item worth buying or queuing for. Everybody was constantly bargain hunting; the women wandering the stores recognized each other, as the scholar Olga Vainshtein observed: "If one of them noticed something of interest in another one's bag, she immediately asked where her fellow huntress had bought it." This extended the complex virtual web of queues that covered the Soviet Union. Women wore a "coat for standing in line," which helped them "to protect [themselves] from bad weather, constant shoving, and excessive curiosity."[8]

The bags people carried were usually canvas; however, Western plastic bags served the same purpose. In fact, they were desired objects in themselves. People used them over and over, conveying a longing for worldliness, marking the bearer's yearning for the outside world of consumerism, a world constantly denounced by Communist propaganda. The logos of Finnair, Coca-Cola, or Marlboro had become familiar sights long before the soft drinks or cigarettes were made available to the average Russian. In fact, Marlboro cigarettes were accepted as an unofficial (hard) currency. Western blue jeans, Adidas garments, jackets with the logos of Western companies, sweatshirts of U.S. universities, and anoraks with the St. Moritz ski resort logo held high positions in the hierarchy of clothing.

Appearance mattered more than content; in Otar Dugladze's film, *Nevesta iz Parizha* (The bride from Paris), set during perestroika, the father, who represents the old Soviet values and their subsequent breakdown, pours his homebrew vodka into a Gordon's Gin bottle.[9]

With the introduction of market mechanisms in 1992, the stores began decorating their windows, as they had done before the revolution—nineteenth-century Russia was famous for its beautifully painted *affiches* displaying the goods on sale. Written signs appeared only around the turn of the century, with the advent of literacy.[10] Imperial St. Petersburg, the French writer Theophile Gautier noted, was the city with the highest density of advertising.[11] The Communists abolished this richness in favor of those poor pictograms (suitable for illiterates).

Post-Soviet advertising appears strikingly similar to its Western counterpart. This is no surprise; many Western ad campaigns were simply adapted, often superficially, for Russia. The Russian ads might be more slogan dependent, as Svetlana Boym points out in her book on everyday life.[12] Boym sees Russian ads as reflecting a "peculiar *ménage a trois*"; in Russia's post-Communist romance with the West, the Western goods compete with mystified Old Russia. In the latter 1990s, ad campaigns became more original. Some began to mock Western campaigns; a cigarette brand played on its U.S.-style billboards with the slogan *otvetny udar* ("retaliatory strike"). Similarly, in Krasnoyarsk, the soft-drink company OAO Pikra created "Crazy Cola," using loud green and red labels. Crazy Cola parodied Coke and Pepsi and its market share soared.[13] Eventually, new Russian brand names were introduced. Domestic fast-food chains Yolki-palki and Bistro made it difficult for some U.S. companies, such as Burger King, to sustain their operations in Russia.

Labels provide the consumer with a sense of security and reassurance, and possibly status, as Anne Hollander emphasized in her book on fashion, *Sex and Suits*.[14] This is in itself not a Russian peculiarity. But many Russian men keep the labels on the sleeves of their jackets. Volodya, deputy director of a regional Russian bank, buys all his clothes at the same Hugo Boss store. The sales assistant literally dresses him. When I complimented him on his good taste, he admitted that he simply wore what the Hugo Boss clerk told him to. In 1997 on Apraksin Dvor in St. Petersburg, a merchant sold shirts labeled Gianni Armani, as if the last name Armani sufficed, even if it was an unknown Armani, not the famous Giorgio. Some people might have been fooled by the fake brand name; for others, any Armani label served its purpose, especially if it remained visible. Ten years earlier, hardly anyone would have recognized the name Armani or any other designer brand. Now people pride themselves on the ability to identify them.

In Soviet schools, a unitary aesthetic was promulgated. Students were supposed to learn "discipline"; they were told that an outfit had to adhere to the law of "three colors." If a fourth color intruded, the wearer was guilty of an impermissible liberty or sheer bad taste. A monotone range was mandatory. "Vestimentary specificity had great significance for official surveillance over the individual: each person had to be clearly classified, and ideally she had to represent her place in some group, whether it was based on age, gender or social standing," Russian-born scholar Olga Vainshtein recalls from her own days in school.[15]

By telling the population what to wear, the Communists aimed to dictate what to think—not the least what the people should think about themselves. The CPSU leaders were not the first to try to reach Russian minds by ruling their appearances. Peter the Great introduced hairstyles and clothes through legislation—"trifles [which he had] better left to hairdressers and tailors," as his biographer Klyuchevsky thought. Klyuchevsky concluded, "These caprices aroused much hostility among the people. These petty annoyances explain the disproportion, which is so striking, between the sacrifices involved in Peter's internal reforms, and their actual achievements."[16] This sounds familiar to any observer of the Soviet Union. The Western European countries abolished their dress laws and their bans of luxury during the seventeenth century, as England did in 1621, for example. Montesquieu stressed that luxury was necessary for the economy to work. The German sociologist Werner Sombart saw capitalism and modernity emerging from the desire for beauty and luxury (and sex).[17]

Seeing is believing. In the Soviet Union, people were not supposed to see what was happening. They were shown what ought to happen. The Kremlin did not inform anyone about its resolutions, actions, and reasonings. This was a society of closed doors, walls, and fences. The television news presented a perfect world of victorious wars. The daily struggle for a record harvest was won by model *kolkhozniki*, depicted as iron men; swarms of red tractors worked the fields without a soul around. The fight for technological progress was the state's priority; the authorities pretended to battle for hard-to-procure apartments—living space—for the population, but never really tried to attain this goal. The world at large was the turf for the contest with the other superpower. Sport was a war of the systems and, as if the world was not large enough, the competition expanded into space.

For the average citizen, too, daily life was a constant battle: for places in lines to get food, clothing, shoes, tickets, good jobs—in short, to survive. Yet the existence of this struggle was not officially acknowledged or even recorded as a fact of life. Hence, everyone knew that the media did not reflect reality. The barrier between truth and lie was blurred, as Frank Ellis argued: "The idea of truth itself is discredited."[18] Life was presented according to the so-called class struggle, or its then-current version. Soviet truth did not have a long shelf life, being temporally limited. When politicians fell from grace, the group photos were subsequently retouched, with the disgraced politician being airbrushed into oblivion.

The Soviet media lulled their audiences. By easing censorship, Gorbachev hoped to restore the media's credibility, but it was too late. The Communist propaganda had reached the point when dulling the audience did not work anymore, and revealing its failings of seventy years would not help either. The media did not cover the perennial shortage of apartments, the flaws of the Soviet industrial products, or the losses during harvest. People knew better, of course. They waited fifteen years for a car and twenty for an apartment; as students (and as soldiers), most had been sent to the countryside to collect potatoes. My Russian friends recalled how much they disliked this job, so they left most of the crops in the fields.

The darker side of life—accidents, corruption, criminality, the poor state of the health care systems, alcoholism, physically and mentally handicapped people—just did not exist in the portrait that the Soviet state media sketched, and no other media existed. When an earthquake or train accident occurred, one had to guess what happened by reading about other regions' "brotherly care," as Brodsky noted.[19]

The Soviet TV news looked like a news program, it sounded like a news program, and it was called a news program, but it did not convey newsworthy information, with the eventual exception of certain international news. TV news was pure propaganda, even purer than what was reported in the print media.[20] It mimicked news, the way Soviet life imitated an industrialized society. The print media were less severely restricted to propaganda; local and youth newspapers had some leeway. For them, other standards were required to keep in touch with their readers. Plus, newspapers could always be read between the lines. With TV, this seemed much less of an option.[21]

As late as October 1989, when journalists already seemed to enjoy a certain freedom, as long as they supported "socialist pluralism," Gorbachev introduced Ivan Frolov as *Pravda*'s new editor in chief to the *Pravda* workers by saying, "We are pinning great hope on Comrade Frolov and on our joint work with him." Gorbachev reiterated that *Pravda*'s task was "to be actively involved in . . . propagandizing and explaining the ideas of perestroika,"[22] thus he emphasized that *Pravda*'s editor in chief was still a subordinate of the Central Committee and that it was the Kremlin who decided what people might see and what was to be suppressed.

In general, the Soviet people did not watch the news for what it reported, but for what it hinted at, for how it distorted facts and for what it omitted. Or they watched the news out of habit, and for sports coverage and weather reports. They knew their lives were full of lies, as the psychologist Leonid Gozman repeatedly emphasized.[23] For the majority, accepting fabrications and ignoring falsifications was a strategy for survival. The public, to a certain extent, was aware of the misrepresentations to which it was subjected. It experienced the deficiencies of the economy every day. The media's Soviet Union did not have much in common with the real Soviet Union. What was reported from the capitalist world was watched with ambiguity, too. On the one hand, people assumed that the reports from abroad were distorting the facts, while on the other the constant negativity had a certain effect. Joseph Brodsky stated that, as early as the 1950s, Western films—basically the trophy films captured in the course of World War II and that the Soviet theaters played without paying royalties—were consumed as documentaries about Western life. They were the only images that depicted the West. "In every frame we tried to discern the contents of the street or of an apartment," Brodsky recalled in an essay.[24] He wrote that he had grown up watching the actress Zarah Leander, who appeared in many of these films. The Tarzan series alone, the poet believed, did more for the de-Stalinization of the Soviet Union than all of Khrushchev's speeches.[25]

To most people, life in the Soviet Union felt safe and stable. Brodsky spoke of a culture of consolation. Its people experienced the Soviet empire, he said, as well as its egalitarianism, as a comfort.[26] The state was a powerful father, intensely loved by most people, as Leonid Gozman believes.[27] Soviets—especially men—were made to think that they were soldiers of a titanic quest, of which the whole world would eventually be a part. Their affection for the fatherly state allowed them to ignore the true nature of the Communist regime. In return, the state regulated their lives from the cradle to the grave, providing everyone, although in scarce quantities, with the basic necessities. The Soviet state allowed its people to feel secure by making all the necessary decisions for them.[28]

The propaganda worked. Therefore, people were shocked when crime finally made it to the television screens, when the violence that had always existed began to be reported. People, unaccustomed to free and factual reporting, were suddenly afraid to take the train, thinking that it would be derailed.[29] Mikhail Gorbachev understood that the gap between reality and pretense, both in the economy and in the media, had grown too wide. Extensive falsification of industrial and agricultural output rendered Soviet statistics useless; the Soviet economy was a Potemkin-style economy. People pretended to work and the state pretended to pay them, it was often said. But it did not stop there. The cars produced by Soviet factories looked like cars, they even sounded like cars, and it was pretended that they worked like cars; the shoes looked like shoes, some foodstuffs merely looked like food. But this could not continue indefinitely; something had to be done. Gorbachev allowed the media to reveal a bit more of the gloomy reality. At the same time, he introduced his incantations, first *uskorenie* (acceleration), then *glasnost* (transparency), *perestroika* (restructuring), and finally, *rynok* (market). To implement his amorphous ideas, he reached out to the media, the Soviet power's seasoned tools for propaganda. He used the weekly newspaper *Moskovski Novosti* and the magazine *Ogonyok* as his mouthpieces, regularly summoning their editors in chief to the Kremlin for briefings. As the heads of important Soviet publications, they had direct phone lines to the general secretary. Until the fall of 1990, *Ogonyok* received two to three letters a week from the Central Committee with orders on what to publish. Finally, in 1990, Vitali Korotich, the editor in chief, told his secretary to return them unopened. That's how *Ogonyok* won its freedom, said Korotich.[30]

Ogonyok was in the vanguard in the transition of the Russian media from the painters of a bright future to reporters of the gloomy reality. In its early years, people scorned perestroika as "all words and no vodka." Yet, gradually, with the help of *Ogonyok*, more people began to wonder. They started to actually *read* the newspapers; lines formed in front of the newsstands—the most common indicator of public demand in the Soviet Union. Some of the dailies and the weeklies, such as *Argumenti i Fakti*, *Moskovski Novosti*, and *Ogonyok*, were sold out quickly. What did people read? And what did they *see*?

Many authors have stressed the primacy of the sense of sight. As every newspaper editor knows, an article accompanied by a photo receives much more attention than one without illustrations. If the text contradicts the picture, it is generally the picture's message that gets across. A picture is worth a thousand words, as they also say in Russia.

The Russian language—more than English—has an aspect of incantation. Gorbachev employed that device in his attempts to mobilize the populace. Photography, however, appears to carry the truth. People view photos less critically than the written word. *Ogonyok* has been compared to *Life*, an American magazine, or *Stern*, a German magazine, in which the text follows the pictures, not vice versa, as in news magazines or newspapers. Susan Sontag speaks of photography's "virtually unlimited authority."[31]

Hence, the sense of sight is often viewed as carrying the sense of truth. The Soviet public had hardly ever been subjected to images of atrocities and suffering, of photos displaying pain inflicted on fellow citizens by its own government. Compared with Western societies, therefore, most Soviets' thresholds of shock were very low. Thus, photos showing the dark side of Soviet life, virtually nonexistent in the Soviet media to that day, shocked many readers. For this reason, it seemed relevant to review *Ogonyok*—from 1987 to 1993—with particular attention to the photos. The volumes read like a compilation of everyday Soviet life's taboos, hardships, and evils.

From its inception, the opening up of the media toward the more somber walks of life had a spatial dimension. Opening all sorts of spheres for the first time and bringing them into public consciousness enlarged the Soviet Union portrayed by the media. *Ogonyok* expanded its coverage to the venues of informal culture, the *dom kultury*, where rock groups could perform; to the realm of spirituality, basically the churches and monasteries; and to communal apartments, backyards, basements, and the waiting areas of railway stations. The secret empire, the gulag, prisons, and psychiatric clinics, came to light. The poor state of hospitals was revealed: due to a lack of rooms, patients were sleeping and dying in the corridors of the clinics. That had been common knowledge all along, but it was never officially admitted—and the misery was much deeper than people realized. *Byt*, meaning "being" or, more accurately, the burden of life, including poverty, death, crime, and abortion, became a central subject of the magazine, which previously had devoted its pages to painting the bright future of Soviet society.[32]

The television bridges between Soviet and Western cities, live connections between two TV audiences, one in the USSR and the other one in the United States or Western Europe, lifted the iron curtain briefly.[33] This opened up yet another space to the Soviets—life abroad—through direct television encounters with Americans, Canadians, or Germans, who seemed to be "normal people." Their questions reflected subjects still untouched by the Soviet press. *Ogonyok*, by reinforcing the TV bridges, added permanency to the brief gaze behind the iron curtain.

No doubt with the general secretary's consent, the magazine began to tackle major ecological disasters, such as the "project of the century" (the plan to divert the Siberian rivers) or the extinction of the Aral Sea, which was shown by a photo of a boat falling apart in the sand, with no coastline in sight.[34] Another photo essay featured the dying of the Volga River, showing its sturgeons rotting.[35] That same summer, a section called "Retro Vernissage" which presented previously banned and lost photodocumentaries, was introduced. After extending the space it covered, the magazine also began to broaden its time frame to take on the taboos of Soviet history. *Ogonyok* displayed the more somber and often ironic side of Soviet life: demonstrators handing in their banners after an official rally, chairs unoccupied during the wake for the dead Leonid Brezhnev, a voting Soviet assembly with everyone sleeping.[36] It recapitulated the destruction of the Christ-the-Savior cathedral in Moscow, a closely guarded taboo, and it recounted the Kronstadt mutiny, the 1921 sailors' rebellion against the Bolshevik regime. One must keep in mind that these stories were revelations and that they were received as sensational. Thus, *Ogonyok* transcended the limits that the country had lived with for so long regarding history and other areas previously out of bounds. By doing so, it expanded the time frame and space that the Soviet Union officially was willing to recognize as its own. At the same time, it started to explore the private sphere, the living space, of its readers, with its first story on a *kommunalka*, a communal apartment, where several families, each living in one room, shared the kitchen and bathroom.[37] "A Night at the Yaroslav-Station," about the train station serving Siberia where stranded passengers slept on the ground, some for many days, was another exploration of the dark side of Soviet life.[38] The Soviet media had never portrayed individuals, the rare exception being socialist heroes, such as Yuri Gagarin, the first cosmonaut, or some artists faithful to the regime. Even the leading politicians were never treated as private individuals.

On the pages of *Ogonyok*, 1988 was to become the year of the individual. Artists, sports stars, and beauty queens made it to the cover, such as Miss 10,000 Meter, the winner of a Miss Vosdushnii Okean (Miss Air Space) contest, convened in Budapest. Mirror, mirror on the wall . . . a Soviet woman was the fairest of them all. Such contests had been held in Poland and Yugoslavia since the early 1980s; only 1988 saw the participation of Soviet citizens. Subsequently, the beauty contests reached the Soviet Union. In March, it was Vilnius's turn; in April, Riga's. Leningrad, Odessa, and Kiev followed suit.[39] Even two capitals of Muslim union republics, Tashkent and Baku, saw their versions. Miss Air Space, crowned in more liberal Hungary, may have been the first such contest to enter the minds of the Soviet people. But time was progressing quickly. Only three months later, the first Miss Moscow made it to the cover of *Ogonyok*.[40]

Individual beauty had been taboo; it then became semiofficially sanctioned. A report of the Miss Photo '89 pageant was headlined, "Beauty Will Save the World."[41] Around this time, the Soviet Union's sole clinic for cosmetic surgery was featured favorably by *Ogonyok*.[42] The nineteenth party conference, held that summer, changed the country, approving semifree elections. In a less noted move, it also passed a resolution to increase the production of consumer goods, specifically fashionable clothes.

"A child is always first of all an aesthete: he responds to appearances, to surfaces, to shapes and forms," Brodsky wrote.[43] This might be true for adults, too; it certainly was for what the Soviets called the "masses." And it works with advertising. Communist propaganda tried to celebrate the party's own glory through appearances, architecture, rituals, and symbols—symbols that were poorly designed, sloppily maintained, and rarely changed. One might ask, what if the regime had been advised by Western image makers? It was only during the demise of Communism that the media begun to focus on individual appearance. The aesthetics of the individual took the place of the aesthetics of the state.

However, not all those featured were glamorous; the worker-politician Nikolai Travkin was shown as Mr. Average. Individuality was also bestowed on the disadvantaged, the sick, the addicts, and the physically disabled, for example, a man in a wheelchair who traveled the Moscow subway regularly. His story explored for the readers the special hardships of a handicapped life in a society that had chosen to ignore its disabled.[44]

September 1988 saw the first Estonian flag on the pages of *Ogonyok*, although the flag was a small part of the photo, and not central.[45] Technically, displaying a republic's national flag was still a crime, yet, by violating this law, the magazine reflected the popular mood, as it did with the picture of a ruble note in a trash can.[46] More and more, *Ogonyok* mirrored life and became a "normal" magazine, as both Russians and Westerners were saying. The earthquake in Armenia provided the media with a dreadful opportunity to show how much its treatment of bad news had changed, as did the intensifying war in Nagorno-Karabakh. Both were covered extensively, often with horrifying pictures.

Slowly, the Soviet press began to act like the media of an open society, pursuing subjects that were of interest to its readers or of political importance. The media set out to reflect the everyday experience of the readers. Because of that, the people slowly began to trust the media—soon to an extent that surpassed reason. In many Russians' perceptions, virtually overnight, Moscow, a cozy and dull metropolis, turned into a crime-ridden urban jungle, despite the fact that the crime rate in 1990 still was very low. But for the first time people read about crimes happening in their vicinity and they even saw it on television. Aleksandr Nevzorov, a sensationalist Leningrad journalist, launched his innovative program *600 Seconds*. Night after night, he confronted his audience with the authorities' abuse of power and their secret, privileged lives; he hunted criminals and exposed the negligence of officials. Often, with his camera crew, he arrived at the scene of a crime before the police, allegedly tipped off by the KGB. In his somber, intimidating style, he documented arrests and interrogations and showed off the confiscated guns. Except for hunting rifles, private gun ownership was unheard of in the Soviet Union. Because crime began to appear in media reports, people suddenly became aware of its existence. In her book *Russian Talk,* Nancy Ries recorded people speaking about the "complete disintegration" of society, when in fact not much had changed.[47]

In May 1989, finally, the reality painted by the media reflected the political truth. The People's Congress convened for its inaugural session. Its debates were televised live; factories all over the country stood still. The workers watched the proceedings of the new semi–freely elected body. They obviously believed that what was going on inside the Kremlin mattered to them. Endless talk shows discussing the proceedings of the new parliament followed in the evenings and those, too, were watched. Politics became a part of everyday life; for a time, this was true for almost everyone, especially in urban areas.

In many ways, the media began to be religiously believed. On TV, the healer Kaspirovsky cured people thousands of miles away. The audience took him seriously: had they not *seen* it? To some, it sufficed to put a bottle of water in front of the TV set while Kaspirovsky was on the air, because the water would assume magical powers. His show was canceled after he was unable to wake up a young girl he had "hypnotized" over TV. Meanwhile, one of his imitators sanctified an issue of the daily *Vechernyaya*

Moskva. The newspaper sold out within minutes. For months, copies were traded for up to one hundred times their newsstand price.

While the educated, urban people seemed to believe what little they could hear from Western media—basically on short-wave radio—many did not trust the domestic media. This changed dramatically. Suddenly, these same media became credible and were even considered by some to bear magical powers.

Since the early 1950s, one of the main sources for information about the West was movies. As mentioned previously, Brodsky believed that the films looted from Germany did more to de-Stalinize the Soviet Union than Khrushchev's speeches. Toward the end of the Gorbachev years, foreign soap operas began to appear on state television programs. The Mexican-produced *The Rich Cry, Too*[48] literally cleared the streets; everybody watched. Apart from the drama, this Mexican serial and all the subsequent ones were watched as documentaries and social models of Western life. Interestingly, Latin American soap operas held more appeal for the Russian audience than did U.S. ones. This might be explained by the fact that the Mexican programs were more dramatically emotional and reflected a stratified society, with a thin layer of very privileged people and many levels of poverty. Ironically, television, the main instrument for Communist propaganda, unwittingly became the main tool of propagandizing an equally unreal image of life in the West. And this one was believed. Dress patterns and even role models were copied from Western movies.

In the course of the perestroika years, the picture presented to the Soviet public by the media became more complex and began finally to reflect what was happening in the country. The bad news outweighed the good news, as in real life, not the least in Russian lives. The media began to cover whole realms heretofore carefully avoided, thus sketching a fuller, more complex picture of the country and the world. For the first time, the press's agenda was set by what happened, not by what was supposed to happen.

By both applying Western standards in editing and printing and by including advertisements, the Soviet media began to look more like their Western counterparts. This could only have added to their perceived credibility.

As long as the CPSU was firmly in control, most people complied with the imperatives of Soviet society. They dressed accordingly and behaved generally well; that is, they observed the written rules and the unofficial customs. For decades, the magazine *Rabotnitsa* (The woman worker) advertised a dress code for women. However, many conformed with those norms against their will, with the sheer objective of being left alone, while some parts of the society, especially the youth and the opinion leaders, engaged in a code of signs to express their muted disagreement with the state, Masha Lipman recalls.[49]

The human eye is dangerous, being the most susceptible to seduction of all of our sensory organs. However, the more our eye is deprived of pleasure, the quicker it is at detecting hints of joy. The Soviet power deliberately stripped the society of many references to pleasure. A pleasing view was treated as a source of subversion. In particular, any kind of erotic imagery was banned, including paintings of nudes. Only with perestroika did this begin to change. Erotic and crudely pornographic imagery conquered Russia with a vengeance, in both art and publishing—a carnival for the eye, the previously hidden "lower body," to use Bakhtin's phrase, appeared virtually everywhere. New magazines were launched—many with "how to" sections and, most remarkably, numerous illustrated sex primers. This kind of publication had not existed before. By pushing the most private aspects of life into the spotlight, the media was again expanding their scope and extending the space of coverage into the bedroom.

During the Soviet era, the media were ignored, disbelieved, or read against the grain. In the first years of post-Communism, however, the society was inclined to trust the media beyond reason and to conform with the social norms advocated by them. This was a huge change that, in its effects, cannot be overestimated. Moving from being indifferent or in opposition to what the media propagated, many Russians and people of the former Soviet republics trusted them and followed their advice, especially when it came to lifestyle and fashion.

Clothes make the person. Or, as Virginia Woolf wrote, it is the clothes that wear us, and not we them. We may form them to take the mold of an arm or breast, but they mold our hearts, our brains, and our tongues to their liking.[50] In the Soviet Union, the social, mystical, and erotic origins of clothing were all but forgotten. Now, people are rediscovering these characteristics. The New Russians try to hide their social shortcomings by dressing up, often to extremes. For Western individualists, altering dress styles (or the hair) is a tested and easy way to indicate a change in self-perception or attitude. However, a society that thinks little of individualism consequently lacks appreciation for the individual's means of expressing himself or herself through fashion. One basis of fashion lies in people's insecurities; they dress according to the rules of the group they want to belong to and even more so if they do not belong to it, as Anne Hollander noted.[51] That's basically why the young, the hyperambitious, and the nouveau riche tend to uniform themselves.

Despite the shortages and going against official ideology, many Soviet women developed an obsession with clothes. "The tiniest detail—a collar, the shape of buttons or pockets—was to be reproduced at home by self-taught tailors," Masha Lipman wrote.[52] This preoccupation was not illegal, but not condoned either.

Perestroika changed that. It rendered fashion acceptable. In 1987, as one of the first steps toward opening up the society, Gorbachev allowed the publication of a Russian edition of the German fashion magazine *Burda Moden*. Women enthusiastically greeted the arrival of this Western do-it-yourself fashion periodical, pioneered by the German publisher Burda.[53] With its German edition, in publication since 1949, the company had made a fortune in the postwar years selling dress patterns to women. In Russia, for obvious reasons, Burda repeated its success. It even sponsored some of the beauty contests. Soon, back copies of both the German edition and the new Russian edition were traded for exorbitant prices. At the emerging independent newsstands, even single dress patterns, ripped from the magazine, were offered. One might say, in its discovery of fashion, the crumbling Soviet society paralleled the social developments of early postwar Germany.

Soviet dress seems "to have lacked coherence and meaning, and so elude[d] customary symbolic rubrics," Olga Vainshtein wrote.[54] Indeed, to a Western eye, the majority of Soviets dressed with little taste; many Russians do so to this day. However, most messages conveyed through dress codes are indecipherable to an outsider. In Western Europe, black is the color of mourning; in parts of Asia, it is white. Worn casually, black stands for a bohemian lifestyle, art, and intellectualism, dating back to the existentialist movement. It was also the color of fascism. In Soviet Russia, black met the Soviet dress code's requirement for modesty among men and women. Not exclusively, though. In 1989, when wearing a rather fancy, long black coat on a Moscow street near the Kiev railway station, I was stopped by an elderly man. "You ugly German," he said. Why did he think I was German? I asked. Because I wore an SS coat, he said. A few years later, the same black woolen coats had become the outerwear of choice of the new business elite and the mafia.

Black skirts were "a symptom of the incomplete presence of the female body in culture," as Vainshtein has written.[55] Soviet women were walking a tightrope act; they struggled to attain feminine elegance without breaching the decreed modesty, and despite the ubiquitous shortages. For that reason, as mentioned above, many women sewed their own clothes. Men did not and to this day do not seem to care about fashion. Despite the scarcity of fashions, both prerevolutionary Russia and the Soviet Union went through "battles of tastes." Everyone seemed to fight bad taste, banality, or *poshlost,* as Svetlana Boym recounted in *Common Places.*[56] However, bad taste was always the other's taste. The official Soviet society fought against a slowly emerging culture of the fringes, of youth culture as *poshlost.* For their part, the young dismissed the state's official aesthetics as banal. The first to deliberately deviate from the sanctioned Soviet aesthetics were the so-called *stiliagi.* They manifested their disenchantment with the society by fashioning themselves as colorful outsiders. As with other protest movements, the *stiliagi* can be traced back to the children of the elite. What had begun as "a fad among elite children" by 1953 had developed "into a full-scale revolt by alienated Soviet youths," Frederick Starr noted. The historian of Soviet jazz argued Khrushchev's own children had founded the "style hunting" movement in the 1940s; the children of Gromyko and other prominent Communists were their early peers.[57]

The *stiliagi* are remembered as jazz fans. Yet initially their movement was not about jazz but about being different. They found their way to jazz to defy the Stalinist ban against it, Starr contended: "Jazz, with its emphasis on individuality and personal expression, became the *lingua franca* of dissident Soviet youth, the argot of jazz the verbal medium."

The *stiliagi* wore short hair, sunglasses, Hawaiian shirts, narrow slacks, and pointed shoes. By being arguably the first to violate the aesthetic norms after World War II, they were the first to implicitly advocate a pluralism of styles. "How I run my private life does not concern anyone else. One's way of life is a private matter," *Komsomolskaya Pravda* quoted a *stiliagi* in 1950.[58] Starr wrote: "They revolted with the deed, not with the word. They shirked work, dressed strangely and spoke little, withdrawing into rude silence or private argot. In the spirit of classic bohemians, they took delight in the fact that they struck others as deviant." They conveyed their orientation toward the West through clothing. Early on, they sported long jackets, often checkered black and white with broad shoulders; wide-striped or black shirts; white ties; and narrow trousers. Artemy Troitsky, the first and only rock columnist of the USSR, remembers that during his time as a *stiliaga*, the shirts were white and the ties bright and long, with palm trees, monkeys, or girls in bathing suits on them.[59]

The *stiliagi* uniform—especially the hairstyle—can be traced back to jazz musicians and to Tarzan, played by the American actor Johnny Weissmuller, who combed back his hair and smeared it with grease. For a time, the *stiliagi* even called themselves Tarzanians (*tartsantsi*). In the 1950s, the *stiliagis'* appearance provoked the guardians of (Soviet) style to periodic raids of *stiliagi* hangouts. Armed with scissors, Komsomol activists stormed *stiliagi* assemblies, pressed the *stiliagi* against walls, and cut off their hair or pant legs.[60]

In the 1960s, the hippies replaced the *stiliagi*, though that did not change anything fundamentally. The hippies were "almost an exact copy of the *stiliagi*, only the scale was hundreds of times greater and different names for things appeared," Troitsky wrote, stressing that Western images, for example, the cover of the Beatles' album *Abbey Road*, served as models.[61] The majority of the *stiliagi* were young men. The few female *stiliagi* tried to mimic the British model Twiggy, an extremely slim, girlish-looking woman usually depicted in a miniskirt, with a child-like haircut and make-up that made her look wide-eyed and innocent.

In the 1970s, rock and roll replaced the hippie movement. Jeans and leather jackets became fashionable and American labels were preferred. Some young men wore their hair long. The symbols and countersymbols of the West preceded the arrival of the West's values—a liberated press, free enterprise, and multiparty elections—as if looking like a Westerner was a precondition of becoming like a Westerner. And who did not want to become a Westerner? Over and over again, young Soviets told me proudly that someone had mistaken them for a Westerner. One was served differently in the USSR, depending on whether one was dressed in casual Soviet outfit or in a styled Western suit.

Blue jeans, for their part, represented the world behind the iron curtain. Young Soviets tried to obtain pairs of the American-made denim pants. The jeans were supposed to help them act the way they thought Western-ers did. The masquerade seemed to work, since some of my young Moscow friends succeeded in eventually being mistaken for foreigners. This was a situation of genuinely carnivalesque ambiguity: the Russian wearing Western clothes acquired a double personality. At the same time, he or she was aware of being Russian, despite the disguise. This possibly affected the person's sense of self as well, allowing the indulgence in two parallel personalities. One must bear in mind that the prime audience of a cross-dressing act is the cross-dressers themselves, not least because they experience a treatment not meant for the person they actually are.

Soviet society was thoroughly militarized, that is, thoroughly hierar-chized. Uniforms played an important role, as did other signs of rank, such as medals, which were convenient substitutes for uniforms. Some uni-forms provided the wearers with the legitimacy to rule other people; oth-ers provided easier access. Law allowed army veterans to bypass certain lines. However, a uniform places the wearer's function above his or her personality and strips away individuality. In the Soviet Union, in one way or another, all uniforms represented the state. Thus, for the average citizen, uniforms were either awe inspiring—like an extension of the Soviet flag, as in the case of generals' uniforms or the national sports teams' dress—or a symbol of hated power, as represented by the policemen on the street col-lecting fines. Some uniforms stood for both simultaneously; young army officers were well respected as the rank and file of the military and were also despised as soldiers, the dirty, black-marketeering privates. The Com-munist Party, through the state, held a monopoly over uniforms: whether workers, waiters, railway conductors, cleaning brigades, everyone was a state employee.

The collapse of the party brought an end to this monopoly. All sorts of uniforms emerged; private companies began to sport uniforms, pioneered by McDonald's, with its caps and aprons. Security services were formed, with newly created uniforms or camouflage gear. With its monopoly of uniforms gone, the state also lost its monopoly of violence. Many of the new uniforms imply a readiness to apply force. Some of the newly founded security firms are relaunched privatized paramilitary units of the state security apparatus. Other emerging groups shaped themselves as heirs of the Cossacks; they sported colorful uniforms that reflected the style of Russian soldiers of the late nineteenth century. On St. Petersburg's Nevsky Prospect, in front of the Gostiny Dvor department store, the new Russian fascists began to recruit members. In black shirts, symbols of the German SS and of Mussolini's party, they handed out their somber leaflets. During the process of de-Sovietization, the society also underwent a demilitarization; thus the state-sponsored uniforms lost much of their relevance. Even the habit of young Westerners' mocking the army by wearing military outfit as an antifashion has reached Russia.

A person wearing a uniform is usually serving—whether it is the country, the party, a company, or a superior person. When the service ends, people get rid of their uniforms. Those at the helm of an institution often display their power by violating the dress code. However, the demilitarized Russian society, opposed to any ruling from above, displays a surprising tendency to reuniform itself. The bosses of the groups, involved in shady or criminal businesses, seem to observe a strict dress code, just as the cadre of corporations. The bosses wear long black cashmere coats and white silk scarves. Their black shoes are carefully polished. In the evening, they used to wear burgundy jackets, though now these have all but vanished. The bosses' lieutenants and drivers sport black leather jackets.

Women gradually began to dress more Western, or what they believed to be Western. Their main sources of fashion were television and glossy Western magazines, such as *Cosmopolitan* and even *Playboy*. This resulted in overly eroticized dress styles. These days, even for the office, many Russian women dress the way only streetwalkers, party goers, or rebellious teenage girls would in a Western city. Thus, the new standards were set along a perceived Western reality that does not exist. Soon, job opportunities for secretaries began to be advertised with the requirement of wearing sexy clothing, often along with the willingness to perform what the ad openly called sexual services. Many working women reshaped themselves as sex dolls, inflating and thus parodying the erotic signals they thought they should emphasize.

Pictures of (erotic) nudity were unheard of in the Soviet Union. Today, they have become omnipresent and a major tool of the advertising industry. The beauty contests are sexualized to the limit. The newspaper *Moskovsky Komsomolets* elected a Miss Hair, Miss Bust, Miss Legs, and Miss Erotic. Even the contestants for the title of Miss Hair had to remove all their clothes but the slips. One Moscow nightclub has cages hanging from the ceiling in which naked dancers perform; another invites young female guests to undress while dancing on the bar.

However, fashion entails more than clothing. In the West, shoes, accessories, handbags, and glasses are designed in ever-changing styles, as are telephones, kitchen utensils, and stationary. All these are supposed to emphasize the wearer's personality. In the Soviet Union, people were not supposed to stand out as personalities. The number of frames available for glasses was extremely limited, while shoes were so hard to come by that nobody considered choices. Ten years later, many city dwellers in the former Soviet Union use clothing as an extension of their personality, just like Westerners do.

Sneakers, baseball caps, and T-shirts with logos have also become popular. Teenagers loiter around the city centers. Somehow, they echo the so-called hooligans of prerevolutionary Russia or the teenage gangs in Western cities. As elsewhere, some people see this as a threat to public order and the authorities try to contain it, but young adolescents who hang out in noisy groups are natural occurrences of a living society.

Western brands and department stores moved in, Benetton and Karstadt being among the first, allowing the emerging urban middle class to dress according to their newly acquired status. The average city dweller in Moscow, St. Petersburg, and the capitals of the former republics dresses more and more like a Westerner. Some women might exaggerate their styles, although many people—mostly men—do not care yet and others reuniform themselves. A part of the society simply cannot afford to dress lavishly and remains unaffected. Nevertheless, the gap between Russian and Western dressing habits is narrowing.

Some politicians have refused to comply with the new requirement in being styled; Yegor Gaidar, for example, sought to persuade people with his words, not his looks. For years, his suits suggested the attire of a party functionary, as did his office furnishings. Eventually, Gaidar understood that, because he looked Communist, he did not persuade people at all; he even contradicted his own message in his dress. Anatoly "Chubais was much more presentable," Janine Wedel wrote. Western financial supporters tended to identify Chubais with market reforms because "he possessed the personal attributes that Westerners respond to favorably,"[62] that is, he looked and behaved Western. The Western donors might not even have been aware of the reason for their preference. Therefore, if it is true that clothes make the person, one has to conclude that many minds were gradually being Westernized, too.

Under Communism, it was unusual to display wealth or any personal characteristics. Soviet egalitarianism did not strive for the same degree of affluence; it leveled downward to a common denominator: people did not aim at becoming rich and success was not measured in material prosperity. Luxury provoked suspicion, not awe; everyone knew that it was impossible to obtain material goods legally.

Everything that becomes a sign, every item that bears significance, purports an ideology—and possibly its counterideology. Long lines conveyed shortages, but promised a rewarding bounty. In today's Russia, they normally stand for bad organization, just as in the West. The availability of sausages and vodka was the recognized sign of well-being—Communism's bread and water[63]—in stark contrast with the official propaganda, according to which there ought to have been an abundance of food and a variety of sausages. In post-Soviet Russia, sausages and vodka are no longer scarce; thus, they have lost their significance (with the possible exception of some remote parts of the country).

If success and influence could not be represented by material prosperity, they had to be detectable in other ways, especially informal influence. The number of telephones on his desk indicated the power of a Soviet bureaucrat to the visitors. The more telephones he had, the more closed circuits he had access to. High officials usually sported six or seven phones on a special table to their left; some even had a switchboard. At least one phone did not have a dial. By lifting the receiver, the bureaucrat was connected to his superior or to the front room. In the spring 1990, Yegor Gaidar, then *Pravda*'s economics editor, jokingly, although not without pride, demonstrated his six or seven phones to me. The one without the dial connected him with the Number One, as people used to say, with General Secretary Mikhail Gorbachev or his office. The visitors may not have been aware of the meaning of the number of telephones a bureaucrat had, but they read it subconsciously.

Cellular phones and computerized switchboards should make the row of telephones on a desk obsolete—indicative of backwardness even. Yet, many Russians, including open dissenters with the late Communist system, still make the nonverbal statement of having many phones. In the headquarters of RAO-UES (Russia's Unified Energy System), the all-encompassing energy company, run by former reform premier Anatoly Chubais, the system of the closed phone circuit is still in use. Chubais's top advisers have a switchboard-like telephone on their desks, next to a phone with direct access to the boss. Meanwhile, they talk on their cell phones.

What dresses might represent to women, cars might represent to men. As with clothes, the choice of cars was minimal. A person who got one was fortunate and, as women did with dresses, many car owners altered minute details, to individualize the object and extend their personality.

In Soviet times, official cars could be categorized into three basic classes: (1) higher party or government officials and top brass military officers were driven around in black Volga sedans; (2) other bureaucrats, including factory managers, clerks, and journalists, used Volga sedans of different colors, mostly white, beige, light blue, or gray; and (3) top government figures were driven around in the well-known ZIL limousines. Additional indication as to who was sitting in a car could be read from the license plate, though almost all drivers used their cars during slow periods as unofficial taxis to earn some extra money. Thus, for the equivalent of two U.S. dollars, one could and still can enjoy a ride in the middle lane, with a driver flashing the blue light and ignoring traffic rules.

In the USSR, private cars were not used to convey status. True, minor variations could be seen among the Zhiguli, the Moskvich, and the more recent Samara. The small and rickety Zaporozhets was subjected to much ridicule. Russian eyes could distinguish models, but the differences were far too insignificant to allow the owners to distinguish themselves from one another. Soviet men often asked me about the Western brands. They knew the technical details of an Opel, a Mercedes, a BMW, or a Volvo, but they were puzzled upon learning that the brands stood for different lifestyles rather than for their technology. How could an Opel be a boring car, a Mercedes upper class, a Volvo "politically correct," and a BMW of slightly ill repute, the car of reckless young men? Yet, within a few years, the former Soviets learned this language of cars.[64] BMWs have become popular among organized criminals.

With the opening up of the country and with Russians earning foreign currency, people began to import used cars from the Western countries of Finland, Germany, and Belgium and from Japan in the Far East. Increasingly, imported cars became symbols of affluence. First, any used car sufficed, but many Russians soon learned to distinguish. Moscow's streets are crammed with Mercedes and BMWs; in other places, Vladivostok, for example, Japanese sport utility vehicles are the cars to show off. A number of Russians who succeeded in profiting from the economic transition drive around Moscow in black Mercedes 600s, a car normally used by top government officials; the police, for a substantial amount of money, license their owners to use a flashing blue light and a siren to travel the middle lane, reserved for emergency vehicles. They are allowed to violate the traffic rules. By implication, a class society is thus implemented on the street. For the motorcade of a state visit, the streets are temporarily closed; for the presidential convoy, traffic is briefly stopped. Ministers rush along the middle lane—and so do the richest of the newly rich. The so-called mafiosi and businessmen share a common space with the top executives of the government and display their status with the same signs, thus rendering the two groups virtually indistinguishable.

The Soviet-era criminals, just like the party powerful, were hiding their privileged positions. Their post-Soviet counterparts, however, are showing off shamelessly. At the same time, some of Moscow's foreign residents walk in the opposite direction. They use (Western) cars with Russian number plates, mostly by registering their cars under their Russian (girl)friends' names and so are stopped less often by the police for fines.

Delivery vans—neither privately nor officially owned—did not exist in the Soviet Union. All goods, including bread, meat, and vegetables, were delivered by trucks. The absence of any small-scale economy was reflected by the absence of the cars used by shopkeepers. Only the advent of small businesses brought about a need for small delivery vans. First, small Japanese panel trucks were imported; then the VAZ auto plant launched its own model, the Gazel (gazelle). Thus, the street reflects the changes in society and economy, the increasing gap between rich and poor, the new scale of production, and the new ways of distribution.

Social changes are also reflected by architecture, although more slowly. Architecture is to cities what fashion is to people: a necessity turned into a way of expressing perceived characteristics. Architecture is not necessary for survival. Shacks are sufficient and Soviet-constructed housing was not much more than that. The regime had virtually abolished architecture by reducing the discipline to either artistic theory—paper architecture—or to the management of the assembly of industrially prefabricated concrete modules. The architect's latitude was reduced to ornamentation. Architecture students knew that, most likely, they would never work as "real" architects in their lives. Instead of promoting their students' creativity, the Dutch architect Goldhoorn alleged, the Soviet schools of architecture trained them to "conformity through a system of imitation: known fact and skills could be drummed in. It was a matter of imposing discipline. He who was best at the art of imitation had most chance of reaching the upper echelons. An inevitable concomitant of this disciplinarian system was the elimination of disruptive factors, those very factors that, in an open society, spark renewal."[65]

Architecture was thus reduced to the assembly of prefabricated concrete elements organized by the ministry of construction. Housing projects looked identical over the eleven time zones—countryside or city. There were no architects as such in the Soviet Union; they were reduced to being a managerial cog in the construction machine. Architecture critic Ilya Utkin wrote: "The art of architectural design turned into the imbecilic arrangement of boxes on a plan and counting of panels on facades. . . . Thus the New Harmony was put together, forming the New Man. The [Soviet] leaders themselves, though, were not quick to leave the area of the old city."[66]

Buildings were planned by the construction authorities; "all problems, including aesthetic ones," were solved by bureaucrats with little or no architectural skills, Olga Kabanova alleged. Yet the execution was done by professional architects.[67] The further the industrial production of prefabricated parts was taken, the simpler the building structures had to become. The single elements became bigger and their number was gradually reduced. Construction is a complex process; a certain quantity of different materials has to be brought together at a given time and place on a one-time basis. This cannot be centrally planned by a ministry. Too many different jobs, too many different parts and pieces are required. It was impossible to get the right elements to the right place in time. In the absence of competition, deadlines were not met; therefore, construction had to be simplified further and the number of modules reduced. There was no space for an architectural designer to shape anything; his or her job was to coordinate the assembly of the elements. Accordingly, the laborers' craftsmanship disappeared. Hence, not surprisingly, when the Soviet Union rediscovered its stock of historic buildings as physically constructed history or as tourist attractions, the companies assigned to renovate them were Polish. Nobody within the Soviet Union could do the job.

Soviet cities looked gray and faceless and the buildings were shoddy, with flaking paint. Despite central planning, the cities seemed put together by accident. After Stalin, there was little city planning of note. Gaps, vacant lots, and vast empty spaces marred the city centers, or rather the cities looked as if the original master plan had been abolished, with no intended structure to replace it. In addition, since the final years of the Soviet era, the cities, as well as the countryside, have become full of debris. Skeletons of cars, boats, and trucks were left in the streets and gradually dismantled by human vultures. Some airports look like graveyards for airplanes that are scavenged for spare parts. This "techno-cannibalism," as it was called, has become the way of provision for parts. In the countryside and at the beach, people enjoy the summer among abandoned factories, rusty parts of cranes, or tanks. People seem not to notice. Visiting Moscow, the six-year-old Swiss daughter of a friend asked if there was a war in the city.

"Why?" I asked.

"Because everything is broken and smashed things are lying around everywhere," she replied.

Prerevolutionary houses sported yellow, pink, light blue, and light green—pastel hues that were perceived as painted Russianness. The Stalin era, after a brief period of modernism in the 1920s, turned to a phony classicism, a sort of *Heimatstil*. The streetside facades of buildings in this style are in granite and impressive, while the courtyard sides are shabby. Stalinist architecture's megalomaniacal constructions and immense bleak squares were supposed to humble the passersby, to make them understand how small and helpless they were. Almost everything more recent, including many monuments, was of naked concrete. Traces of creativity were hard to glimpse and, after the late Brezhnev years, little construction was undertaken.

The collapse of Communism changed that drastically. A construction boom took Moscow, as well as other cities. The renewal of the capital took off at a dizzying pace and obviously without any thought for a coordinated concept. Instead of one single client—the government, that is, the party—a multitude of companies and even individuals began to commission construction of their own taste, or lack thereof. Ilya Utkin calls the dismal architectural quality of the new buildings a catastrophe; he blames the new money for dictating the direction.[68] Yet, as Kabanova rightly argues, the New Russians, raised in communal and narrow Khrushchevka apartments, had little concept of luxury or business headquarters. It was the Russian architects' frustrated imagination that contributed to the many exaggerations one sees today. Thus, the new plurality of architectural voices amounted to a Tower of Babel, a true heteroglossy of styles, to use Bakhtin's term; and yet it was built pluralism. For the first time, city space could be owned privately by practically anyone and every owner did practically anything he or she liked in that space. Suddenly, thousands of different people, with different tastes and different goals, began to shape the city's space. Kabanova identifies twelve "styles," among them Tsereteli's "pop-monumentalism," Glazunov's "anaemic neo-classicism," and a "Euro-overhaul" style. Each stands for a different political, aesthetic, and economic conviction.

Basically, however, post-Soviet architecture can be divided into two main directions: (1) a "Russian" style of richly decorated brick buildings with towers, bay windows, ornamentation, and columns and (2) the "Western" style glass box. These styles coexist in contemporary Moscow; in some new premises, they have even blended together. Yet their representatives despise each other. The Russianists embark on a hollow historicism. They advocate the reconstruction of lost prerevolutionary structures, such as the Church-of-Christ-the-Savior, implying a breach with the pseudomodernist Soviet regime. But this is an empty gesture; no one would think of returning to the values of prerevolutionary Russia.

Both corporate and private clients understand architecture as a means of showing off: the newly rich commission huge estates, villas with marble entrances, porticos, bay windows, columns, rotundas, porches, peaks, and turrets. The houses reflect their owners' taste, or what they perceive as being the Western idea of luxury. No house, no matter how large, is considered large enough. Freshly privatized companies, such as Sperbank (the "Savings Bank") or Gazprom (the gas monopoly), rushed to build new headquarters, tall castles in steel and glass, some with little bell towers, to display the influence of the companies or their new masters.

Everything has to be big, beautiful, and often referential to a history that Russia never had. This can be compared to the Russian empire associating itself with ancient Egypt by building sphinxes and obelisks or to

St. Petersburg's baroque architecture, which claimed a European tradition
for Russia's newly founded capital.

Soviet cities did not reflect class differences; there were no rich or poor
districts. Judging from its architecture, nineteenth-century St. Petersburg
could be seen as a city of the upper-middle class and the aristocracy, not
the melting pot of classes and nations it actually was, with hundreds of
thousands of impoverished peasants, former serfs, an industrial proletariat, tens of thousands of peddlers and beggars. The poor lived in the
basements and courtyards, the slightly better off in the wings of the bourgeois mansions. The class division seeped through the buildings, as James
Bater showed.[69] The city, since Peter had founded it in 1703, was supposed to fool both its visitors and its own population. A fortress, a naval
base, a port, and the most important industrial city of the country were
hidden behind the beautiful facades of the czar's residence.

Stalin reshaped Moscow to make it a major capital of the world. Tverskoy (Gorky) Boulevard, with impressive metropolitan facades, became
the main artery leading to Red Square. The quarter in front of the Kremlin was flattened to become Manezhnaya Square and the gate to Red
Square was torn down. Yet most facades on Tverskoy Boulevard were
nothing but that. As can be seen from the backyards, the houses are much
less stately than they seem from the street. Their rears are shabby, their entrances narrow, leading to the typical Soviet staircase, somber and humid.
Huge, anonymous office buildings—for example, Gosplan's headquarters, now the site of the Russian Duma—sported entrances twenty feet
high to intimidate people. After World War II, Stalin commissioned the
construction of the "tall buildings," the seven wedding-cake skyscrapers
dominating Moscow's skyline. They were supposed to impress the world,
"the influx of foreign visitors" that would come.[70] But Khrushchev halted
the grand plans. He abolished the idea that the Soviet state should try to
project its power through architecture. His pets were heavy industry and
the space program.

Russia has traditionally adopted European styles and often mixed the
unmixable, not dismissively or with irony, but naively or with pathos, Kabanova says.[71] Almost ten years after the collapse of Communism, in fashion, architecture, and design, the former Soviet Union has become a
Tower of Babel of nonverbal codes. Old and new, Soviet and Western languages of signs mingle. Many of the implicit Soviet signs have faded, being overwhelmed by the loudness of the new visual enticements. Others
remain, such as the red stars on the Kremlin towers and some slogans and
monuments, but they are for the most part ignored.

The disintegration of Soviet society was accompanied by a breakup of
the traditionally codified language of signs, which had been much more
stable than any such system in the West. However, the old signs were not

replaced by new ones; one can instead observe the appearance of a visual polyphony. This should not distract one from noticing fundamental changes. The visual landscape of ex-Soviet cities has become much more complex and diversified. The subtle informal signs and the vulgar Soviet propaganda have given way to a constantly changing blend of old and new. Remaining Soviet habits and Western-style advertisements coexist and the "state of emergency" in appearances persists. The population came to trust the media; people learned to believe what they see. Now, gradually, they are beginning to understand that what appears to be is not all true.

By shaping their appearances, people convey messages, involuntarily or on purpose. In the Soviet Union, the means to emphasize one's personality through clothing, accessories, and property were very limited. A person either complied with the regime's aesthetic precepts or opposed them; to display individuality was discouraged. With the collapse of the Communist system, this has changed fundamentally. Appearances, even to appear not as what one is but as one wishes to seem, have become crucial. This, however, has a long tradition in Russia, as I will show in the following chapter.

NOTES

1. Banknotes with Russian emblems were first introduced in 1993; domestic passports bore the Soviet heraldry to the end of the 1990s.
2. Olga Kabanova, "The End of a Starry-Eyed Era," *Project Russia*, no. 11 (1998): 28. Kabanova emphasizes parallels between the reemergence of architecture, independent of the authorities before 1917 and in the 1990s.
3. Hedrick Smith, *The Russians* (New York: Ballantine, 1984), 54–55.
4. Joseph Brodsky, conversation with the author, September 9, 1994.
5. Leonid Gosman (Gozman), *Von den Schrecken der Freiheit: Die Russen— ein Psychogramm* (The scare of freedom: The Russians—a psychogram) (Berlin: Rowohlt, 1993), 51–55.
6. Leonid Gozman, interviews with the author, November–December 1999.
7. For a discussion of *blat*, see chapter 8. Ledeneva defines blat as "acquiring desired commodities, arranging jobs and the outcome of decisions, as well as solving all kinds of everyday problems." Alena Ledeneva, *Russia's Economy of Favours: Blat, Networking and Informal Exchange* (Cambridge: Cambridge University Press, 1998).
8. Olga Vainshtein, "Female Fashion, Soviet Style: Bodies of Ideology," trans. Helena Goscilo, in *Russia, Women, Culture*, ed. Helena Goscilo and Beth Holmgren (Bloomington: Indiana University Press, 1996), 67.
9. Otar Dugladze, *Nevesta iz Parizha* (The bride from Paris) (St. Petersburg: Lenfilm, Diapazon, 1992), film.

10. Alla Powelichina, *Das russische Reklameschild* (Leningrad: Aurora-Kunstverlag, 1991). The Soviets' return to pictograms was thus not accidental.

11. Theophile Gautier, *Voyage en Russie* (Paris: Charpentier, 1867).

12. Svetlana Boym, *Common Places: Mythologies of Everyday Life in Russia* (Cambridge, Mass.: Harvard University Press, 1994), 274.

13. Betty McKay, "Local Flavor: Russia's Crazy Cola Beats Coke, Pepsi at Their Own Game," *Wall Street Journal*, August 23, 1999, 1.

14. Anne Hollander, *Sex and Suits* (New York: Viking, 1976), 10–13.

15. Vainshtein, "Female Fashion," 66.

16. Vasili Klyuchevsky, *Peter the Great*, trans. Liliana Archibald (New York: St. Martin's, 1958), 268.

17. Werner Sombart, *Liebe, Luxus und Kapitalismus: Über die Entstehung der modernen Welt aus dem Geist der Verschwendung* (1922; reprint ed., Berlin: Wagenbach, 1983), 137–140.

18. Frank Ellis, "The Media as Social Engineer," in *Russian Cultural Studies*, ed. Catriona Kelly and David Shepherd (Oxford: Oxford University Press, 1998).

19. Joseph Brodsky, *Less Than One* (New York: Farrar, Straus & Giroux, 1986), 15; Gozman, *Schrecken*, 70.

20. Elizabeth Linn Pearl, "Semiotics and Politics: An Encounter on the Pages of Pravda" (Ph.D. diss, Harvard University, 1990), 4. Pearl reminds us that the Bolsheviks developed "a system of linguistic convention that shapes the verbal communication of the official Soviet establishment. This convention dictates almost every aspect of articles that appear in official Soviet publications such as *Pravda*. It mandates what *Pravda* journalists write about and how they write about it, both the content and the style of their articles, and is endemic to Soviet authors."

21. This is a European point of view. American TV news also shows a tendency to avoid hard news, not because of political censorship but for commercial reasons. Where the Soviet TV covered harvests, in the United States, it is crime, traffic jams, consumer information, and *faits divers*.

22. Pearl, "Semiotics and Politics," 5–9.

23. Gozman, *Schrecken*, 61.

24. Joseph Brodsky, "Spoils of War," in *On Grief and Reason* (New York: Farrar, Straus & Giroux, 1995), 12.

25. Brodsky, *Less than One*, 8.

26. "The Soviet culture was a culture of comfort; the empire was a comfort, as was egalitarianism." Brodsky, conversation.

27. Gozman, *Schrecken*, 20. To paraphrase Gozman, only people who honestly loved the system could have been blind to its obvious criminal policy and could have allowed these rogues to lead a great country into the abyss for seventy years.

28. Gozman, *Schrecken*, 33–35.

29. "But it was not the fall of murky idols such as Stalin, Lenin, or Brezhnev or the discovery of the Communist regime's crimes that hurt people's sense of national identity most; it was the smaller blows. For example, it was publicized that the Soviet Union's child mortality almost reached the level of Barbados's. Hence, . . . it was impossible to perceive oneself as a proud Soviet national, because the Soviet Union was no more; 'soviet' turned into something one had to be ashamed of." Gozman, *Schrecken*, 70 (translation by the author).

30. Vitali Korotich, editor in chief of *Ogonyok,* interview with the author for the German radio station RIAS, February 1991.

31. Susan Sontag, *On Photography* (New York: Farrar, Straus & Giroux, 1977), 158.

32. On abortion, see *Ogonyok,* no. 25 (1988).

33. *Ogonyok,* no. 40 (1997).

34. "The Siberian Rivers," *Ogonyok,* no. 40 (1997), and "Kogda umeraet more" (When the sea is dying), *Ogonyok,* no. 1 (1988).

35. *Ogonyok,* no. 35 (1988).

36. "Retro Vernissage," *Ogonyok,* no. 26 (1988).

37. *Ogonyok,* no. 41 (1987).

38. "A Night at the Yaroslav-Station," *Ogonyok,* no. 47 (1987).

39. Elizabeth Waters, "Soviet Beauty Contests," in *Sex and the Russian Society,* ed. Igor Kon and James Riordan (Bloomington: Indiana University Press, 1993), 117.

40. "Miss Moscow," *Ogonyok,* no. 28 (1988).

41. "Beauty Will Save the World," *Ogonyok,* no. 48 (1989).

42. *Ogonyok,* no. 10 (1988).

43. Brodsky, *Less than One,* 466.

44. *Ogonyok,* no. 9 (1988).

45. *Ogonyok,* no. 38 (1988).

46. *Ogonyok,* no. 47 (1988).

47. Nancy Ries, *Russian Talk: Culture and Conversation during Perestroika* (Ithaca, N.Y.: Cornell University Press, 1997), 47.

48. *Bogatye tozhe plachut,* or *Los Ricos Tambien Lloran,* a Mexican telenovela from the late 1970s.

49. Masha Lipman, "Fade to Red? Letter from Moscow: Style in the Land of Anti-Style," *New Yorker,* September 21, 1998, 106–110.

50. Virginia Woolf, *Orlando* (London: Vintage, 1992), 120–122.

51. Hollander, *Sex and Suits,* 174–189.

52. Lipman, "Fade to Red," 106.

53. Burda Verlag started publishing its Russian edition of *Burda Moden* in 1987. The Russian edition's launch received strong support from Raisa Gorbacheva, the Soviet leader's wife. The first issue was greeted as a major cultural event by Western media. See, for example, Celestine Bohlen, "Russian Dressing? In Moscow, a Fashion Mag Import," *Washington Post,* March 5, 1987, B1.

54. Vainshtein, "Female Fashion," 64.

55. Vainshtein, "Female Fashion," 74.

56. Boym, *Common Places,* 63.

57. S. Fredrick Starr, *Red and Hot: The Fate of Jazz in the Soviet Union, 1917–1991, with a New Chapter on the Final Years* (New York: Limelight, 1994), 239.

58. *Komsomolskaya Pravda,* September 20, 1950, quoted from Starr, *Red and Hot,* 236.

59. Artemy Troitsky, *Back in the USSR: The True Story of Rock in Russia* (Boston: Faber and Faber, 1987), 14.

60. Troitsky, *Back in the USSR,* 17.

61. Troitsky, *Back in the USSR,* 30.

62. Janine Wedel, "Rigging the U.S.-Russian Relationship: Harvard, Chubais, and the Transidentity Game," *Demokratizatsiya*. 7, no. 4 (Fall 1999): 473.

63. Simon Dentith, *Bakhtinian Thought* (New York: Routledge, 1995), 23.

64. The only non-Soviet cars were the ones owned by Western expatriates, diplomats, journalists, and companies. Representatives of "friendly" Communist countries drove Soviet cars. All foreigners' cars had special license plates: a three-digit number code identified the country of origin, such as 001 for Great Britain, 004 for the United States, and 072 for Sweden; a letter indicated the owner's business, such as "K" for correspondent, "D" for diplomat, and "T" for technical staff. Diplomatic cars' plates were red, other foreigners' yellow. In the 1980s, the state introduced a car rental service and its cars bore yellow plates with an "H." Eventually, some Russians who wanted to convey their inclination toward a Western lifestyle found ways to obtain cars with foreigners' number plates; they either drove foreign representatives' cars or managed to get an H plate for a joint-venture cooperative. Driving a car licensed to someone else required a special registration with the traffic police.

65. B. Goldhoorn, "State and Market: A Polemic View," in *Rotterdam Moscow: Architectural Training at the Academy of Architecture and Urban Design*, ed. M. Provoost and J. Duursma (Rotterdam: 010 Publishers; Rotterdam and Moscow Architectural Institute, 1995), 18–20.

66. Ilya Utkin, "The Hour of the Monster," *Project Russia*, no. 11 (1998): 101.

67. Olga Kabanova, "New Moscow Architecture in a Compulsory Search for Cultural Identity," *Project Russia*, no. 3 (1995): 25–28.

68. Utkin, "The Hour of the Monster," 102. Implicitly, the author shows his Europeanness—in some areas of the world, such as some Asian countries, buildings are treated much more like commodities.

69. James H. Bater, *St. Petersburg: Industrialization and Change*, (London: E. Arnold, 1976).

70. Nikita Khrushschev, *Khrushchev Remembers: The Last Testament*, trans. Strobe Talbott (Boston: Little, Brown, 1974), quoted from Timothy Colton, *Moscow: Governing the Socialist Metropolis*, (Cambridge, Mass.: Belknap, 1995), 239.

71. Kabanova, "New Moscow Architecture."

4

✛

To Fake Is to Make Believe

Russia has a long history of make-believes, such as the infamous Potemkin villages, if they ever existed. Grigory Aleksandrovich Potemkin (1739–1791), at the time the governor of the Crimea, allegedly erected false-front villages along Catherine the Great's travel route when she toured the newly incorporated territory, to impress the passing empress with the wealth of her newly conquered territories. There is, as James Billington notes, a deeper truth behind the legend. The unbroken, seamless facades prescribed for new cities were supposed to give an "unreal impression of imperial elegance" or, with their seamlessness, simply an exaggerated air of urbanity.[1]

The most important make-believe was the city of St. Petersburg, the capital, a Potemkin-style metropolis and Russia's "window to Europe."[2] But was this a window open to Europe so that the Russians could learn about a different lifestyle and rehearse their own European future? Or was this a window into Russia, so that the Europeans could study Russia—not how she was, but how her emperors wanted her to become? Visiting Nikolai I's court, the French traveler Marquis de Custine was reminded of a theater rehearsal. From its very beginning, St. Petersburg was designed to look like a Dutch-style naval city and a trading center, with the imperial residency and a center for culture and the sciences, although it served as much as a fortress against the Swedes and as Russia's main site for manufacturing. But the latter purposes were not supposed to be detectable.

The Petrine revolution caused a *visible* transformation of Russia's elite, of official Russia, as James Cracraft showed in his book on Russian imagery. That revolution, most obvious in the realm of architecture, reflected "the rulers' and elites' new perceptions of themselves." The new system claimed to be European and it was committed "to Europeanize as much of Russian life as could be involved in the project."[3] Thus, not only did the changes of appearances mirror the basic transformation of society, as can be expected, but also the appearances were deliberately modified to Europeanize Russian society. The same was true for Peter's church reform. In this chapter, I try to show how before and after 1917, and today, appearances have been altered to change society.

The Marxists inherently criticized the superiority of appearance over content. Feuerbach in 1843 observed that "our era prefers the image to the thing, the copy to the original, the representation to the reality, appearance to being."[4] The Bolsheviks, building their ideas on historical materialism, pretended to eliminate the bourgeois obsession with appearances and make-believe. Lenin explicitly did not believe what he could not see,[5] but he made his party create make-believes to win over the populace, as I will show below.

Big cities are theaters where city dwellers, as political movements and parties, play out their own desires for attention and status, as if they were their own theater directors, a topic extensively discussed by Richard Sennett.[6]

One may argue that some Communist leaders originally believed in their project, that indeed they tried to build the scientific socialism about which they spoke. They thought their plan was flawless. Thus, if things did not work out as they had expected, they suspected sabotage. However, one can assume that the majority of the party bureaucrats did not care. The managerial class, as Wittfogel[7] calls the lower ranks of the party apparatus, did not profit in any way if the economy worked smoothly or if the plan was implemented successfully. Therefore, the interests of these bureaucrats, and thus the party as a whole, were collectively vested in staying in control. The lower bureaucrats faked success; the higher ones were willing to buy the deception, to also look efficient and thus keep their positions. To safeguard its grip on power, following Wittfogel, the managerial class recruits only the most reliable replacements—people whose loyalty exceeds their competence. No member of the apparatus had much to lose if things did not work out the way they were supposed to, as long as they *seemed* to work. Appearance was more important than reality.

Competence was dangerous, since it might have been cause for disloyalty. Thus, over time, the Soviet apparatus became a class of extremely loyal people who lacked the basic ability to run the country. The gap between reality and appearance widened; therefore, loyalty mattered more and more. Eventually, the sole purpose of the apparatus's dealings was to act "as if," to keep up appearances—to make people believe that the economy was working, that the society was forging ahead, and that the emperor was not naked. People pretended to work and the government pretended to pay them.

Soon after coming to power, the Communists rewrote their own history. They created a heroic revolution as the founding myth of the Soviet Union, the so-called October Revolution, which climaxed with the "Storming of the Winter Palace," an event that never took place. In 1920, for the third anniversary of their putsch, they commissioned the theater director Nikolai Evreinov to stage what was described as a reenactment of history, but what was in fact a construction of a past that never was. They aimed to alter the collective memory and the memories of the individual participants. Already in 1912, Evreinov claimed to have discovered "the instinct of theatricalization, a pre-potent, pre-aesthetic will to play." He characterized it as the desire to be different, to do something that was different, to imagine oneself in surroundings that were different from those of everyday life.[8] He believed in "transformation through imagination." By influencing the exterior, one transforms the interior of a human being; Evreinov called this "autobiographical reconstruction" or "theater therapy." It reflected what Peter the Great had attempted two centuries earlier and Stalin a few decades later.

Repeating an experience is impossible, Evreinov maintained. If it is replayed, memory will confuse the two—the original experience and the reenactment—and, if the reenactment is more recent and more impressive, the human memory will be more than willing to accept the staged version as the truth. In his short work on masks, Evreinov went even further, stressing that a person who acts while wearing a mask can transform his or her persona for good.[9] For that matter, he recruited for his "Storming of the Winter Palace" as many soldiers as possible, especially Red Guards, who were present in Petrograd during the Bolshevik takeover in 1917. He cast them to participate in his construction of history, in order to change their memory as witnesses; and he succeeded.

On a drizzling night in November 1920, in a meticulously planned spectacle that lasted six hours, a few thousand Red Army soldiers stormed the palace. This became the widely accepted version of history, both in the Soviet Union and in the West. The official Soviet historiography and even some Western historians use photos from the rehearsal of Evreinov's spectacle as historic.[10] In its credits, Sergey Eisenstein's film *Days of October* claims to be true to the original events. He is right, though his film is not true to the 1917 "October Revolution," but to Evreinov's spectacle.

Socialist realist culture, both in literature and film, was a hybrid of antique, aristocratic European and proletarian culture, avant-garde rhetoric, and Victorian morals, based in nineteenth-century realism, as Svetlana Boym has said.[11] By adopting classical styles, Soviet culture claimed a history for itself different from the recorded one, as did imperial Russian culture before. The great Russian opera, for example, had been a recent import from Italy. Thus, perhaps more than in any other European country, the arts were used to invent a history for Russia and to engineer a cultural identity for the Soviet Union. Art served to create the impression of civility, to make both the Russians and the world believe that the Communist society was a superior state of a social development.

Soviet institutions were not created to match the people's needs; they were not supposed to reflect the Soviet reality, but to create a new one. This is true for the political institutions and for industry, and it is true for the administrative structure of the country. In Belarus villages in the 1920s, people were forced to become Belarus nationals because the plan from Moscow foresaw a Belarus nation. Many villagers resisted being deprived of their Russianness, yet within ten years a Belarus nation had been firmly established. But the Belarus nationality's representation in Soviet politics preceded its existence as such. The Soviet state imposed identities upon people. If the people wanted to survive, they had to comply.[12]

The most common way for a regime to influence appearances is architecture. The city of St. Petersburg successfully evoked the impression that it was much older than it actually was. More than once, Western European tourists asked me for directions to the "old town," meaning the medieval center. Their home towns had taught them to read earlier centuries of preceding history into a baroque city. Hence, they found it hard to believe that baroque St. Petersburg was founded almost a century after New York (1624). The deception worked: Russia thus adopted a past quite different from the one it really had.

The Communist imperial *Heimatstil*, implying a history that never existed, confuses its visitors. Visiting Moscow, St. Petersburg, or any other ex-Soviet city, a layperson tends to date buildings earlier than their actual time of construction. Dozens of columns decorate the buildings around the Haymarket in St. Petersburg, but only one of the premises, the old Guard, dates from pre–World War II.

Not only did the Soviet leaders reach out for an imaginary past by commissioning historic-looking facades, they also set up a model of the utopian future they had imagined: Magnitogorsk, the steel city in the Urals, was to become a showcase, both for internal and foreign consumption. "We are becoming a country of metal, an automotive country, a tractorized country," Stalin declared in 1929. "And when we have put the USSR on an automobile, and the *muzhik* on a tractor, let the esteemed capitalists, who boast of their 'civilization,' try to overtake us. We shall see which countries may then be 'classified' backward and which as advanced."[13] Stalin was obsessed with overtaking the West, as were Russia's other self-styled modernizers, such as Peter the Great, Khrushchev, and Gorbachev. "We need Europe for a few decades; later we must turn our back on it," Peter said.[14] To some observers, Stalin's deception worked. The German philosopher Heidegger called Bolshevism "only a variation of Americanism."[15]

In November 1987 in Togliatti, Gorbachev proclaimed that by 1990 the Soviet automobile industry would build the world's most advanced car. They would not attempt to catch up with the Western automobile producers, but overtake them, he told the workers of the VAZ-plant.[16] He expected the Soviet Union to "gain attractiveness" and become "the living embodiment of the advantages that are inherent in the socialist system," while that very system was unable to meet its population's basic needs.[17]

Beating the West was a titanic task that demanded sacrifices from everyone. The production of steel might have been crucial to the modernization of the Soviet Union, and it was certainly more important than building a socialist society, but it was done so ineptly that one has to conclude that Magnitogorsk first and foremost was built as a metaphor, a window into the future. For the production of steel, its site was far from ideal. Stephen Kotkin speaks of the city as the "encapsulation of the building of socialism" and asserts that it "embodied the Enlightenment dream." According to Kotkin, that was "reason enough for the world attention it received."[18] The utopia was what mattered, that is, the image, not the steel that was to be produced. This becomes even more absurd when it is considered that Magnitogorsk, allegedly a pioneer settlement, was actually built by the victims of that dream—Christians, *kulaks*, and (political) prisoners—thus, by slave labor, much like St. Petersburg some two centuries earlier.

Kotkin, in his monograph, gives evidence of how effective Magnitogorsk was as a propaganda tool. He ascribes to the steel city "a direct and profound influence on the rest of the world's industrialized countries." Magnitogorsk, that doomed venture of city construction, was considered by the Bolsheviks to be their model project of "progressive modernity." Kotkin misreads it also as a project of urbanity, meant to "exemplify the unique benefits supposedly derived from the advance of urbanism."[19] However, there is no urbanism in places such as the industrial giant Magnitogorsk. There never was. It was a sub- or pseudo-urban desert.

Many large agglomerations do not qualify as cities, as the early sociologist Oswald Spengler emphasized. For a settlement to truly be a city, he wrote, it has to have a "soul" and "intellect." "'Geist,' 'esprit'," he stressed, "is the specific urban form of the understanding waking-consciousness."[20] City air makes one free, goes a medieval European saying. Cities are marketplaces for merchandise and ideas. They centralize wealth as places of exchange. But for the city to function successfully, this wealth has to be mobile. Cities are pluralistic: different groups coexist and interact with each other. The whole of a city is simultaneously engaged in a multitude of activities; it speaks in many voices and displays many faces. A city is a melting pot, as the American urbanist Louis Wirth wrote.[21] It is the metropolis that drives a society forward, as Spengler, Lefebvre, and Harvey show.

In the Soviet "cities," or the USSR's large agglomerations, including Moscow and St. Petersburg, the regime attempted to suffocate both material and intellectual exchange. To create a classless society, it leveled all differences. What could not be flattened was segregated. Soviet cities did not provide space for exchange. The authorities closed places that seemed to serve as spheres for intellectual exchange and persecuted anyone who attempted to trade goods or ideas openly. City dwellers innovate and speculate; hence, a city's development includes a degree of unpredictability. Dictatorships, however, fear the unexpected, since it might, if only implicitly, point to their lack of legitimacy. In reconstructing their cities, therefore, they follow Baron Haussmann's recipe; they carve wide boulevards to segregate and partition. Stalin emptied and leveled Moscow's chaotic, highly fragmented quarters. Red Square was once a lively marketplace; Manezhnaya Square used to house rows of shabby shops. But gigantic houses and arteries for circulation are easier to police.

By moving the government site to Moscow from Petrograd, imperial Russia's capital and the pinnacle of early-twentieth-century modernism, the Soviet government entrenched itself behind the Kremlin Wall.[22] The space around the Kremlin, the center of absolute power, was emptied of city life, of any life. The area immediately north of its wall was fenced in and turned into Aleksandr Garden, a park. During the day, people strolled here; at night, the park was closed. Manezhnaya Square became a large, empty asphalt field, serving as nothing but a preparation area for large parades.

The Soviet authorities sealed themselves off with a moat much larger than any ditch around a medieval fortress. Power thus was, quite visibly, beyond the people's reach. The state authorities' dealings remained invisible behind the Kremlin Wall, more secret than those of the czars, who could be approached and whose family appeared in public. Literally, the distance between the rulers and the ruled had never been bigger. And this distance implied fear—on both sides. The Bolsheviks were never going to allow any urbanism, as sketched above. They feared a civic society and its attendant unpredictability and degree of disorganization—the melting pot. Their idea of a city was a dense agglomeration—a chicken pen for humans—with heavy industry and a movie theater. Paraphrasing Brodsky, one might say that this is a peasant's dream of urbanism—just enough to resemble a city, to fool a chance visitor and, more importantly, the Soviet citizens who did not have any frame of reference.

Appearances are important. The Soviet Union gave itself a federal structure, a seemingly democratic constitution, and basic laws. For all the terror Stalin applied, he was always keen to work within formally legalistic procedures, and so were his successors. Even during the purges, records were kept. The laws were just not observed literally. When Leonid Brezhnev in 1977 was about to introduce a new constitution, a joke went: Why did the Soviet Union need a new constitution, since the old one had been used so little? And as for the new constitution, on paper it seemed reasonably democratic.

After World War II, the Soviet Union went to great lengths to shape itself as an industrialized society, again mimicking the West. Khrushchev, Brezhnev, and Gorbachev all tried to boost the production of private cars, arguably the single most important symbol of affluence. At the same time, they neglected city planning and architecture.

Communist cities looked gray and dirty and at night were badly lit. There were no commercial advertisements. But since the streets and squares of Western city centers were decorated with billboards and flickering logos, the Communist cities accordingly had to have party slogans similarly displayed. In Eastern Europe or the USSR, whenever I had meetings as a journalist with Communist officials, they tried to convince me that life in their country was the same as in the West, but without the flaws of capitalism. Or they claimed their country was on its way to becoming just the same as a Western country; it only needed time to catch up. People were free to leave their country, but they did not want to, many officials maintained. Obstacles such as travel restrictions were explained, for example, by the necessity to repay the free education people had enjoyed. There was a free choice of consumer goods, but who cared for ten different brands of detergent, anyway? By name, the Communist states had all the institutions that a democratic Western state had: a parliament, elections, courts, and trade unions. The state's vocabulary reflected this. Some countries—the German Democratic Republic and Poland—even had several parties. Yet, these institutions, including the federal structure of the Soviet Union, were merely for appearance. The USSR was highly centralized and all important decisions were made centrally.

Rarely did any Communist official attempt to justify the peculiarities of the socialist totalitarian regimes to me: they all denied them. And Gorbachev, with the creation of the People's Congress and the Supreme Soviet, went further, trying to imitate the proceedings of a Western parliament. The people were to be involved; multicandidate elections were held. However, Gorbachev carefully attempted to control them by an electoral law that gave the CPSU one third of all seats, and by flagrantly and secretly obstructing the election campaigns of dissenters, not the least of which was Boris Yeltsin's. By adopting Western methods of relating to the people—for example, public appearances, including the legendary walks among the crowd, which he learned from foreign leaders—Gorbachev created the illusion of taking the population seriously. While the CPSU propaganda aestheticized ideology, with the bright new world as the final goal, Gorbachev was the first to indulge in the aestheticization of Soviet politics—or should one say the first since Stalin? He was coating his public appearances with a democratic gloss. I believe that he did not distinguish between appearances and reality. However, when faced with opposing opinions, such as when he visited Lithuania in January 1990, he revealed a different attitude; he interrogated and lectured the complainants, asking them for their names and workplaces, almost like a police officer. In line with its tested strategy, which is to infiltrate what cannot be suppressed, the KGB co-organized political demonstrations, as has been alleged by numerous political groups.[23] Even Vladimir Zhirinovsky's Liberal Democrats, parroting an opposition party, were rumored to have been initiated by the KGB.

Appearances matter. They mattered during the Communist time and they matter in post-Communist Russia. However, before 1991 they were manipulated to disguise reality, to hide facts, or to teach the population how life should be. The regime lectured its observers—domestic and foreign—or tried to fool them. The elites hid evidence of their status and success; they sheltered their privileges from the gaze of ordinary people. Post-Soviet Russia is the opposite. People shamelessly display their wealth—acquired, borrowed, stolen, fake—there are no limits. Politicians, reticent until recently, have begun to play to their audiences.[24] They invite TV cameras into their homes and take them to church, despite having once been diehard atheists. One of the first to publicly "convert" to orthodoxy was Anatoly Lukyanov, the speaker of the Supreme Soviet and Gorbachev's right hand. Soon after Lukyanov's conversion, the newly pious string puller became the mastermind behind the coup. In July 1990, television screens showed Gorbachev and the German chancellor Helmut Kohl in sweaters and hiking gear, strolling through the Soviet president's home region, Stavropol. There they sealed the deal that allowed the reunification of Germany. The image of the Communist leader entertaining a foreign dignitary in casual attire had been as inconceivable only a few years earlier as the reunification of Germany.

The public portraits of the Communist leaders, hanging in every office and classroom, were retouched. To his last day, the doddering Brezhnev was pictured as a youthful sixty year old. Accordingly, Gorbachev for several years was shown without the birthmark on his forehead. His drive for openness eventually made it possible to display his face imperfectly, but soon after, his time was up and his portraits were removed. Yeltsin stopped the practice; he did not have his portrait decorate the government offices. Surprisingly, of all rulers, Vaclav Havel, the fervently anti-Communist Czech president, kept the "tradition" alive. Within a few months after his ascension to power, the Czechoslovakian post office issued stamps carrying his portrait.

Gorbachev was the first Soviet leader to have his wife appear in public and to openly grant her influence on his decisions. This was well received by some Western media, and perhaps was meant for them. Most Russians were uneasy about Raisa. Yeltsin, for his part, pioneered the campaigner's biography, which was aimed at potential voters.[25] In 1990, he had recast himself as the daredevil he turned out to be in 1991 and the following years. However, after the standoff around the White House, when the country craved stability and on the eve of the 1993 parliamentary elections, he fashioned himself as a good father and grandfather for the TV cameras. Returning home from work, he took a seat at the family's modest kitchen table; he joked with his grandchildren and chatted with his wife, who was preparing dinner. Other contenders invited the media into their houses, too, so that the TV stations could air their home stories.

For Yeltsin's reelection in 1996, a second autobiography was crafted.[26] Other presidential hopefuls, such as General Aleksandr Lebed and Grigory Yavlinsky, followed suit. Political autobiographies of Mayor Anatoly Sobchak of St. Petersburg, former prime minister Yegor Gaidar, Governor Boris Nemtsov of Nizhni-Novgorod, and Yeltsin's dismissed bodyguard Aleksandr Korzhakov became available, all reversing the customary secretiveness of Soviet politicians. One might argue that the politicians had not opened up their private lives because they did not have to face elections. Displaying the human touch is a well-known campaign tool in the West and is sometimes referred to as showing "character." Yet it conveys the supremacy of the appearance over political content. "Character" is doctored by image makers.

The Soviet Union used to be a country with few celebrities. Socialist heroes were the exceptions. In post-Soviet Russia, however, even the politicians aim to become celebrities. One learns how they live, what they read (if they read at all), what they eat—although not how—and who their relatives are. Regularly, some are denounced as being Jewish or as hiding their Jewish heritage. Not only are the messages of these images politically irrelevant, but they are also carefully fabricated. Deception is never far away. When covering Victor Chernomyrdin, then prime minister, on his country estate near Moscow in 1996, a film crew wanted to show him driving a car. The prime minister, however, did not own any humble Russian model; hence, the cameraman's *Zhiguli* was used.

Status symbols make a society legible; they emerge as a matter of course. If a previous set of signs vanishes, new ones replace them naturally. With the Soviet class markers becoming obsolete, and in the absence of any other accepted status markers, money became the only reference for social power, and subsequently the newly available luxury goods—expensive watches, clothes, trips abroad, and foremost, imported cars—became its signifiers. The New Russians' wealth is there to be displayed. An expensive vehicle upgrades its owner; therefore, even people who cannot afford to own one attempt to show up in one. Thus they are treated as richer and more influential—and thus more credit worthy—than they actually are.

Clothes make the man. Soviets did not dress up. They dressed discreetly, attempting to not stand out, especially men. Women enjoyed slightly more leeway. In post-Soviet Russia, fashion has become a field of competition for young women. Men have turned to suits. One behaves differently when wearing a suit; formal attire can feel like a straitjacket, yet it implies status. And people treat the person wearing a business suit differently. To this day, a suit can work as a *propusk,* a permit to enter the hall of an expensive hotel, while a track suit invariably provokes the guards into checking the wearer's documents. With American-made blue jeans, some of my young Moscow friends were eventually mistaken for foreigners and treated as such.

Post-Soviet Russian men's dressing patterns can be loosely classified into four categories, with a fifth, for those who do not care how they dress, composing perhaps the majority. First and most obvious are the men in Western business attire. They attempt to look affluent and professional, some modestly, others showing off. The former succeed in conveying a degree of seriousness. They wear Hugo Boss suits and Patek Philippe watches, or they overdo it with black cashmere coats, a silver tie, white silk scarves, and abundant jewelry. This aping of the West's pinstripes came to be the uniform of the bosses of illegal businesses. In the evening, when touring the nightclubs or casinos in burgundy jackets, some had bundles of U.S. dollar bills stuffed under their belts. Too blatant even for New Russians, the burgundy jackets' popularity has gradually diminished. Crude or subtle, the self-fashioning of a businessman or of a criminal gang's white-collar leader was to convey power, influence, and a degree of civility. During the early years of post-Soviet Russia, jewelry-laden thugs in expensive yet ill-fitting suits were a common sight in Moscow's and St. Petersburg's opera theaters. They played with their cell phones or chatted during the performance and then left during the intermission, their purpose having been fulfilled. They had come to be seen and to prove to themselves their culture.

A second category consists of the first group's lieutenants, the men who exert power on behalf of their leaders, when necessary. Mostly, it suffices for these contract enforcers to be present, threatening violence. Almost without exception they sport flawless and shiny black leather jackets, sunglasses, and sporty watches. Whatever the men belonging to these two categories do, it has to convey their (buying) power. In front of everyone, they waste money. They pay high sums in cash and refuse to accept change. They prefer not to fly over flying economy and they are loud and condescending. These men enact a fantasy they harbor of themselves, and while ordinary Russians joke about these New Russians, the former seem to believe the message conveyed by the latter's antics.

A third category could be called the wrestlers, or boxers. The attire of choice for these angry young men is sporting gear, which some of them already wore during Soviet times. As peddlers, taxi drivers, scientists, and small-time extortionists, they clearly do not care about form or etiquette, but meet the counteretiquette of their old boys' network. They behave like drinking buddies, bullying everyone, including each other.

The fourth group might be named the "tourists." Mostly young intellectuals, they try to distance themselves from the Russian reality. They claim to be disgusted by Russia and prefer to think of themselves as living in the wrong country. They would like to leave the country, but they do not know where to go and often they lack the means to emigrate. Their dress code is copied from what they see when traveling to the West or when watching foreign tourists. As a group, they do not stand out.

Of course, the distinctions between these groups are blurry. A *mafia* lieutenant wearing a black leather jacket might suddenly transform himself with a pinstripe suit or sports gear. Common to all these men is their provisional, amorphous identity. They attempt to be somebody they are not, or are not yet. And if no one else can be persuaded, they persuade at least themselves. By trying to act in a way consistent with their attire, and by being treated as who they look like, some might gradually grow into the persons they try to imitate. Those who fail are met with scorn, although they might be unaware of it, or adopt even more exaggerated attire to stress their identity. "Costly thy habit as thy purse can buy," says Polonius in Hamlet. "But not expressed in fancy, rich not gaudy; for the apparel oft proclaims the man."[27]

In Moscow in the 1990s, one could observe how the newly well clad had their way with their self-assured appearance, overwhelming the poorly dressed bureaucrats. This became particularly evident when people interacted with the police. Back in Soviet times, foreigners were regularly stopped for alleged violations of traffic rules. The man in uniform, which represented the state, usually lectured them and, eventually, issued a fine. Most officers gave long-winded explanations for the fines. By then asking if the foreigner needed a receipt, the officer hinted that he was willing to discount the fine, since, for him, not issuing a receipt meant that he could pocket the cash. During the years of transition, with the gradual opening up of the society, these men changed their behavior. Initially, they bullied drivers, Russian motorists even more than the foreigners. Those who drove imported cars had to pay higher bribes to get off without a receipt. With the arrival of more Western cars and with Russian municipalities being short of money, the drivers began to look more well-heeled, while the officers' uniforms seemed to become shabbier. If the policemen were supposed to represent a powerful state, they could no longer convince anyone of that state's power. All of a sudden, the officer stopping the car looked like he was soliciting a handout. Later, officers even let the drivers set the amount of their fines, usually the equivalent of one to three U.S. dollars.

Thus, during the early years of post-Soviet Russia, even though they were aggressive, the policemen seemed to convey inferiority toward the drivers of expensive foreign cars. In 1996, however, both Moscow and St. Petersburg furnished their police force with new uniforms. Subsequently, the officers adjusted their behavior to fit their new appearance. They began to intimidate drivers again with authoritarian behavior, as if they embodied a general refortification of the Russian state. The relation between the drivers and the officers had come full circle. In the Soviet era, the drivers begged for mercy; after the collapse, the policemen practically pleaded for money; later, they got the upper hand again. The behavior of the policemen apparently reflected their change in appearance. When better—or at least adequately—attired, the police seemed to feel that they were in control. And by acting as if they were in control, they asserted control.

Indeed, appearances can change behavior. The Moscow sociologist Lev Gudkov considers the imported soap operas to have a positive effect on Russians, because they reassure the TV audience that things can be done differently: dealers in the programs care for their customers, homes are clean, and deliveries are on time. While the intelligentsia dismisses the serials as American (or Mexican) junk, the population at large absorbs the values they feature, such as morality, scrupulousness, responsibility, a work ethic, professionalism, and success. Some people might even feel encouraged to read the figures of those serials as role models. A part of the intelligentsia, however, seems to stick to its Soviet values, still treasuring mobilization, heroism, asceticism, and patriotism. It enjoys its self-imposed isolation. Still, according to Gudkov and as shown by the devotees of the serials, the display of American mass culture affects Russia much more than does Russian politics. A serial situated in a hospital, the sociologist believes, demonstrates that a clinic can be clean and orderly, that people can be on time, and that physicians can care for their patients. The audience can see that such clinics do exist.[28]

In January 1992, when liberalizing prices, then acting Prime Minister Yegor Gaidar and his team justified their plan by arguing that full shelves would change the mood and behavior of people. They would be motivated to search for ways to earn money, since they saw that money could buy the yearned-for goods, and would accelerate the economy's development. The almost Potemkin-like idea was to replicate a market, to make the stores look like those in a market economy. If people could be made to believe that the change was permanent, they would act accordingly. Thus, a make-believe market economy should gradually transform itself into the real thing, just as St. Petersburg, the replica of a European city, was supposed to gradually transform itself and its inhabitants into what they appeared to be. Indeed, Grigory Yavlinsky has called the post-1991 free market economy a Potemkin village.[29]

Already in 1839, Marquis de Custine saw the Russians as half-hearted imitators: They "have everything in name, nothing in reality." To Custine, Russia was a theatricalization of its elite's ideas.[30] He speaks of a "burlesque style of modern decoration."

It might be an exaggeration to call the new Moscow Russia's third Potemkin-style city, after St. Petersburg, the first one, and Magnitogorsk, the second.[31] Those cities were built from the ground up, as windows to a future as envisioned by the autocrat, with the declared purpose of becoming a model for a new order and thus changing Russian society. This time, there is no master plan, no Peter the Great, Potemkin, or Stalin. Nevertheless, the whole city embellishes itself, thousands of entrepreneurs commission new facades, and millions of individuals dress up to seem what they wish to become. And Mayor Yuri Luzhkov's restyling of Moscow's center must be read as a program. The kitschy, pseudoclassical monuments of *Okhotny Ryad* and the former Manezhnaya Square and its malls imply a future perfect, a late imperial Russian consumer society in plastic. Boym calls it "Kurortny Styl," holiday resort style—a space for consumerism disguised as a return to historic Russia, an "imperial Russia-light" or a "fat-free imperialism." The city is turned into a pseudocontemporary metropolis, an eclectic mixture of Western imagery and historic quotes. Eventually, this fake identity will affect the self-perception of the people, as yet another of Russia's many missed chances to come to terms with her history.

Some of the tycoons who made fortunes stealing property from the state fashioned themselves as Russian Rockefellers by sponsoring cultural events and supporting charities. Aleksandr Smolensky, then the owner of SBS-Agro-Bank, Russia's biggest commercial bank until its crash in August 1998, donated fifty kilograms of gold for the cupola of the reconstructed Christ-the-Savior cathedral.

As with the designer clothing and fancy cars, the New Russians' new homes—castles, with turrets, porticos, and parapets—are attempts to create a pretense of aristocracy. In his book on fashion, Stuart Ewen observed how "the power of aristocratic imagery persevered among various parvenus of the new market economy" in early modern Europe.[32] For nineteenth-century New England, the newly rich "[got] together to display their monetary power, and hence their industrial might." Their "class position was determined by the ability to purchase." Those "with money could buy the look of history," the American economist Thorstein

Veblen wrote one hundred years ago.[33] This is exactly what is happening in post-Soviet Russia.

It has been argued that the oligarchs, even before the collapse of the ruble in 1998, had much less power over the economy than the press, which they owned, led their readers to believe.[34] With donations such as Smolensky's, the oligarchs certainly enhanced their partly fictitious leverage. Appearance also outdid reality for them. And they grew richer by exaggerating the wealth they had already acquired. The image of being rich was more valuable than the riches themselves; the image of power is superior to power itself.

Potemkin created only facades of villages. St. Petersburg and Magnitogorsk are Potemkin-style cities, with real people living in them. These residents have to assume their city's fake identity is real and thus create a reality that never was. St. Petersburg came alive in the nineteenth century—and grew out of the authorities' control. Magnitogorsk is finally succeeding in vitalizing its economy. For the first time since its founding, real people live real economic lives in the former "model city."

Swiss historian and diplomat Carl-Jacob Burckhardt once wrote that cities, distinguished from some large, pseudo-urban agglomerations, are individuals. Cities are mortal, too, but they can rise from the dead.[35]

NOTES

1. James H. Billington, *The Icon and the Axe: An Interpretive History of Russian Culture* (New York: Knopf, 1966), 708.
2. The term was coined in 1739 by the Italian visitor L. Réau, as cited by Billington, *Icon and Axe*, 181.
3. James Cracraft, *The Petrine Revolution in Russian Imagery* (Chicago: University of Chicago Press, 1997), 294.
4. Ludwig Feuerbach, preface to the 2d ed. of *The Essence of Christianity*, quoted in Susan Sontag, *On Photography* (New York: Farrar, Straus & Giroux, 1977), 153.
5. Vladimir Ilich Lenin, *Collected Works*, Vol. 14, 4th ed. (London: M. Lawrence, 1960), 232. In a bizarre attack, Lenin disparaged Machism (the school of thought based on the works of philosopher Ernst Mach) as a fashion.
6. Richard Sennett, *The Fall of Public Man* (New York: Knopf, 1976).
7. Karl A. Wittfogel, *Oriental Despotism: A Comparative Study of Total Power* (New Haven, Conn.: Yale University Press, 1957).
8. Spencer Golub, *Evreinov: The Theatre of Paradox and Transformation* (Ann Arbor, Mich.: UMI Research Press, 1984), 54
9. N. N. Evreinov, *O Novoi Maske* (Leningrad: Tretya Strazha, 1924).
10. See, for example, P. N. Sobolev, Y. G. Gimpelson, G. A. Trukan, *The Great October Socialist Revolution*, trans. David Skvyrsky (Moscow: Progress, 1977).

11. Svetlana Boym, *Common Places: Mythologies of Everyday Life in Russia* (Cambridge, Mass.: Harvard University Press, 1984), 106.

12. Francine Hirsch, "Towards an Empire of Nations: Border-Making and the Formation of 'Soviet' National Identities," *Russian Review* 59, no. 2 (April 2000), 201–226.

13. Stephen Kotkin, *Magnetic Mountain: Stalinism as a Civilization*, (Berkeley: University of California Press, 1995), 29.

14. Vasili Klyuchevsky, *Peter the Great*, trans. Liliana Archibald (London: St. Martin's, 1958), 263.

15. Martin Heidegger, quoted in Björn Lindell, "Sovjetusa," *Moderna Tider*, no. 3 (March 1999): 27.

16. Roy Harry, "Motoring: The Russians go Ladida," *Guardian*, November 16, 1987.

17. Mikhail S. Gorbachev, *Perestroika and the New World Order* (Moscow: Novosti, 1991).

18. Kotkin, *Magnetic Mountain*, 18.

19. Kotkin, *Magnetic Mountain*, 21. In a footnote, Kotkin wrote, "Few scholars have taken up . . . the influence of the USSR on Western Europe and the United States." Could it be that there was none, not when it comes to industrialization, at least? The existence of the USSR supposedly helped the socialist movements and unions in Western Europe to exert pressure. Western capitalists, however, have not been impressed by the Soviets' ill-guided attempts at creating an industrialized society.

20. Oswald Spengler, *The Decline of the West*, Vol. 2 (New York: Knopf, 1928), 92.

21. Louis Wirth, "Urbanism as a Way of Life" in *Reader in Urban Sociology*, ed. Paul K. Hatt (Glencoe, Ill.: Free Press, 1951), 38. A city is a "melting pot of races, peoples, and cultures, and a most favorable breeding-ground of new biological and cultural hybrids."

22. The Kremlin Wall is an anachronism itself; it was erected in the sixteenth century, when other European cities began to dismantle their fortifications.

23. There is strong evidence to such allegations: "activists" infiltrated the Karabakh movement in Armenia, while Kazimiera Prunskiene, a former Lithuanian prime minister and a leading member of Sajudis, the Lithuanian movement for independence, was exposed as a KGB agent.

24. There were exceptions in the Soviet era. One was the publication of mediocre poems and novels by some party leaders, including Leonid Brezhnev, who seemed to believed that he would thus acquire the acceptance of the intelligentsia. In the winter of 1990–1991, when the battle for the future of the Soviet Union was at its fiercest, Anatoly Lukyanov found time to publish his dilettante collection of poems, *Harmony*, under the pseudonym Anatoly Ossienov.

25. Boris N. Yeltsin, *Against the Grain: An Autobiography*, trans. Michael Glenny (New York: Summit Books, 1990).

26. Boris N. Yeltsin, *The Struggle for Russia*, trans. Catherine A. Fitzpatrick (New York: Times Books, 1994).

27. William Shakespeare, *Hamlet*, act 1, scene 3.

28. Donath, *Die Tageszeitung*, February 1999. Gudkov was the cochairman of the VTsIOM (All-Union Center for the Research of Public Opinion).

29. Grigory Yavlinsky, *The Connection*, WBUR, Boston, National Public Radio, December 14, 1998. Yavlinsky spoke of "Potemkin villages of radical economic reforms."

30. Astolphe de Custine, *Empire of the Czar: A Journey through Eternal Russia* (New York: Doubleday, 1989), 13, 88.

31. David J. Nordlander, "Origins of a Gulag Capital: Magadan and Stalinist Control in the Early 1930s," *Slavic Review* 57, no. 4 (Winter 1998): 781–812. Nordlander argued that Magadan was a secret Soviet capital, or the capital of the secret gulag empire, arguably an important part of the Soviet empire.

32. Stuart Ewen, *All Consuming Images: The Politics of Style in Contemporary Culture* (New York: Basic Books, 1988), 114.

33. Thorstein Veblen, quoted from Ewen, *All Consuming Images*, 117.

34. Clifford G. Gaddys and Barry Ickes, "Russia's Virtual Economy," *Foreign Affairs* (September–October 1998), 53–67. Anders Åslund, "The Myth of Oligarchy," editorial, *Moscow Times*, January 29, 1998.

35. Carl-Jacob Burckhardt, "Städtegeist," in *Gesammelte Werke*, Vol. 6 (Bern: Scherz, 1971), 13.

5

Sound, Scent, Taste, and Touch

Vision is arguably the most important of the senses, since humans are predominantly visual animals.[1] We are more consciously dependent on sight than on the other senses. Without hearing, without a sense of smell, even with a very reduced sense of touch, it is still possible to navigate one's way through the world. Accordingly, there is less standardization in the description of these other sensations.

However, one's gaze is not vigilant when it comes to gradual changes. It grows accustomed to the specificities of what one sees, so that one does not distinguish them after a while; for example, one does not note how a person is aging if one sees that person every day. More often, seeing is reduced to merely recognizing, rather than observing details. The Soviet grass was gray, as was Soviet snow and the Soviet people, but after a time in Russia my eyes grew used to the gray. The Western calibration melted into the thin air of memory.

If one wears green sunglasses, after a period one perceives the brightest green as white. Similarly, after my gaze had adjusted to the Soviet reality, the light that was least somber seemed bright; the spot that was least dirty seemed clean. After I had adjusted my scale, the Soviet world looked colorful. The first few times I returned from the Soviet Union to the West, everything seemed too bright, too loud, too rich, and the people were amazingly beautiful. Upon returning to Russia, the grayness hit hard. Soon, however, I grew accustomed to switching back and forth, as I grew able to apply different standards to perceive my surroundings.

Accordingly, despite the pace of the transition, for those living permanently in Russia the changes have been difficult to notice. Of course, one became aware of the appearance of a certain advertisement; one of the earliest, for example, was the Samsung sign on the square in front of the Belarus railway station, Belorussky Voksal. New shop windows and brighter lights were easy to spot, but the transformation occurred like the light of dawn, or like increasing noise. All of a sudden, one notices it and it feels as if it has been there for a while already. One morning, Moscow, or St. Petersburg for that matter, looked different—more Western—and one could barely recall how dark and gray those cities had been only a few years earlier or when a certain innovation had emerged. What was greeted as a sensation when it first appeared, McDonald's on Pushkin Square, for example, soon felt as though it had always been there.

The imperceptibility of gradual change is even more true for the other senses. Despite the Soviet Union's looking and smelling different, and its food tasting different, as a foreigner living there, I had grown accustomed to these sensations—even to the different sounds and textures.

SOUND

There is an old Russian saying that men love the eyes and women love the ears. Soviet propaganda often read like poetry; the slogans—"*slava trudu*," "glasnost," "perestroika"—sounded like incantations. In Russia, poets were more than poets, as Yevgeny Yevtushenko once said. If anywhere, Lacan's idea of "the world of words creating the world of things" is true for Russia[2] and could there be a darker verdict than that of Gogol, who asks in *Dead Souls*, "Where do you rush, Russia, answer! You keep silent."

The Soviet power wanted to reach its subjects anywhere, anytime and so created a system of loudspeakers and radios. Elderly Russians remember the moment when, at noon on Sunday, June 22, 1941, the war was announced over speakers all over the cities, towns, and villages. On Communist holidays, marches blared from the system. While it is possible to ignore the media, for example, by switching off a radio, it was practically impossible to not register what was broadcast by that system. Soviet hotel rooms were furnished with a fixed-wire receiver that could not be turned off, only turned down, and it carried a limited number of stations. On Soviet trains, *Radio Mayak,* one of the all-union radio programs, was permanently turned on, long before any Western train offered audio service. With its light classical music and its hourly newscast and commentaries, the program was considered to reflect the dull state of the official society. Stamped into everyone's memory is the time signal, followed by a sonorous voice, "v Moskve, odinnadzat chasov utra" (in Moscow, it is 11 A.M.).

Rumors persisted, though, that these radios, especially those in hotel rooms, were a two-way system, devices to eavesdrop, as the telephones were also alleged to be, even when the receiver was put down. It is difficult to imagine that the Soviet authorities could master a technology sophisticated enough on such a mass scale, yet it does not matter whether this was true because people believed it and acted accordingly. In conversations touching on critical matters they usually turned up another source of noise—the TV, a tape recorder, or a record player—or they asked their confidante to go for a walk. A critical matter did not necessarily mean political dissent; in the last decades of the Soviet Union, when it had become possible to vent privately, political dissent was the exception, but to make ends meet almost everyone had to violate the laws restricting economic activity.

Soviet citizens, particularly those living in communal apartments, lacked acoustic privacy. Their neighbors were constantly overhearing them. People were aware of the likelihood of being listened to wherever they were; therefore, in the subway, streetcar, or bus, most people remained silent. They did not talk to strangers, or to friends for that matter. A private car, however, or the compartment of a train provided the illusion of privacy, enough for many Russians to reveal their whole lives, even to me, a chance acquaintance. Hence, not only did the Soviet power control the media and try to influence visual appearances, it dominated the acoustic environment of its citizens. This included a strong grip on music.

As late as 1987, the frequencies of Western radio stations such as Radio Liberty/Radio Free Europe, the Voice of America, and the BBC were jammed.

The Communist regime had mutilated the Russian language. Its utterances, however, were lyrical rather than factual—a myriad of empty keywords like "worker," "socialism," and "soviet." What was said could be the subject neither of agreement nor rejection. Instead, it resembled incantations and heroic legends, the sounds accompanying Communism's rituals.

The collapse of Communism drastically changed Russia's acoustic environment, including the language. The party lost its monopoly over Russian. New jargons emerged, some full of English words; today, many different lingos coexist. Private radio stations were founded. The first, Ekho Moskva, turned into the only reliable source of news during the Baltic crisis in January 1991. Today, Deutsche Welle and the BBC, with their Russian as well as their German and English programs, are retransmitted by local AM transceivers. Radio Liberty is rebroadcast by dozens of FM stations all over the former Soviet bloc. Thus, within a few years Russia and the former republics went from barring Western news sources and music to embracing them. At the same time, many genuine Russian stations imitate and reinvent the different genres of radio, such as talk shows, game shows, news programs, and of course, music programs.

Russia's cities have grown increasingly noisy. The Communists observed strict business hours. Some stores closed at 6 P.M., the latest at 9 P.M. There was no such thing as late-night hours. Theater performances started early; the restaurants closed at 10 P.M. Night traffic was scarce and bus traffic stopped before midnight, even in Moscow, the capital, with a population of ten million; the subway ran until 1 A.M. During the day, Moscow and St. Petersburg did not look and sound like the large cities they were. At night, they resembled small, Western European towns—sleepy and quiet. In this regard, they have changed beyond recognition. On Moscow's main arteries, such as the Leninsky Prospect, Leningradsky Prospect, and Kutuzovsky Prospect, traffic rumbles around the clock. However, the sound has become more of a buzzing. The Soviet streets once roared with heavy trucks and unrefined Soviet engines. Today, there is also the quiet humming of well-trimmed Western and Japanese machinery. And the sound of construction is never far away, even during the evenings and on weekends.

In the city centers, the sounds of new bars and casinos, open until dawn, are ever present. Some stores operate around the clock; people shop and play at any hour. These activities generate noise. Gangs of youths fooling around in the dead of night have become a common occurrence, as have cars blasting music. There is no night and no hour in which a car alarm might not be blaring. On Palace Square in St. Petersburg, clacking skateboards have become elements of the white noise. Meanwhile, many a downtown factory, formerly dominating a whole block with its noise, has turned oddly silent. At the same time, with the advent of private enterprise, many small workshops, such as those of carpenters and blacksmiths, have newly opened. For a few years, their noises, such as the distant clanging of a forger, woke me up in the morning—in the center of Moscow.

Music, ever present in Western cities, was rarely heard in the Soviet Union, except for a few places it was confined to, such as the concert halls, the *dom kultury* (culture houses), and most restaurants. It was not until the end of the 1980s that street musicians appeared; jazz and rock musicians began to get together in underpasses, for example, under Nevsky Prospect in St. Petersburg, in front of the Gostiny Dvor department store. On winter nights, they still gather there for jazz sessions. Nowadays, music is everywhere. Players of all sorts have turned up in the streets. Some are accomplished artists; others are simply beggars. They play in underpasses, on the main boulevards, and in subway stations. The department stores play muzak. Kiosks on markets, at street corners, and around subway stations sell CDs, cassettes, and video recordings; they blast their merchandise into the air, with other kiosks competing with their volume. There is no boundary to noise pollution in the post-Soviet world, nor is there any awareness of it. Still, compared with a Western city, the Moscow subway is quiet. Some people chat and whisper, the headsets of personal stereos crackle, and occasionally a gypsy, a child, or a war veteran solicits money, or someone who's been treated badly by the authorities bemoans his or her fate, searching for solidarity.

The cities have become noisier, more diversified, acoustically more aggressive, and sometimes violent. Electronically amplified music is everywhere; Moscow and St. Petersburg sound like any other metropolis.

Historically, the earliest deviation from the officially dictated Soviet culture occurred in music. Jazz in the 1950s and rock and roll from the 1970s on were widely enjoyed. By listening to jazz or rock, young people distanced themselves from the Soviet cultural establishment, which was perceived as boring and provincial, as Fredrick Starr shows in his excellent history of Soviet jazz.[3]

Jazz was not always banned in the USSR. During the 1920s, American jazz orchestras, so-called Negro bands, toured the Soviet Union. Soon, Soviet copycat groups turned up in the cities. Many had their origins in the Jewish community of Odessa. In 1929, Maxim Gorky denounced jazz as belonging to the realm of homosexuality and bourgeois eroticism. The police confiscated saxophones, the instrument that seemed to embody jazz.

Attempts were made to domesticate jazz, to "increase its artistic quality." In 1934, a competition was launched for "red jazz" compositions. No less a composer than Dmitri Shostakovich was assigned to write a model suite of "red jazz."[4] Soviet jazz was to be composed, not improvised. Accordingly, Shostakovich's suite sounds pleasant, but an uneducated ear would not recognize it as jazz; it echoes film scores, or sounds like a blend of Johann Strauss and Glenn Miller, and uses the saxophone as its leading instrument. In 1938, after the purges, Shostakovich wrote a second jazz suite for the USSR state jazz band. The composition is lost, contrary to other information. The piece often mistaken as Shostakovich's second jazz suite is actually a compilation of arrangements, as Laurel Fay stressed in her Shostakovich biography.[5] This misidentified "red jazz" sounds like Johann Strauss readying himself to go to war. The saxophone weeps over impending deaths. Thus, the militarized Communist party establishment had absorbed jazz.

After World War II, Andrey Shdanov, Stalin's chief ideologist, purged Soviet culture of Western influences. "Expressionistic exaggerations, nervosity, and a tendency toward degenerate, disgusting pathological issues" were alien to Soviet culture, he said. The young generation was to be educated as the constructors of Communism. Jazz was banned, including specific musical elements, such as typical chords; diminished fifth, for example, the so-called "blue notes," and too much percussion were censored, Starr writes. Troops of Komsomol activists, the Communist Youth organization, stormed clubs where jazz was being played and the bandleaders were arrested. In 1949, all saxophones were confiscated.[6] Considering the level of education of most party functionaries, one can easily imagine that genuine Russian folk music played on a saxophone would have drawn the attention of authorities, while a jazz piece played on a violin would have gone unnoticed.

The first Soviet jazz fans and the first movement to deviate from the official cultural doctrine were the *stiliagi*. However, they found their way to jazz not for the sake of the music, but as a means of dissent. Jazz became the medium of an emerging subculture and eventually the Komsomol tolerated it. Since the 1960s, it has been allowed again, mostly in dining halls and the *dom kultury*. As a culture of disagreement shaped from below, however, jazz had lost its sting by then. Rock, first in the form of the Beatles and the Rolling Stones, replaced it. In the Baltics, in St. Petersburg, the young listened to Western shortwave stations, not the political ones such as Radio Liberty, but Radio Luxemburg, one of the first commercial stations in Europe.

The tolerated music gatherings in the *dom kultury* were confined to the few bigger cities: Moscow, St. Petersburg, Sverdlovsk, and Riga. In the early 1970s, some 250 rock groups were known in the Moscow region.[7] Free jazz, the less melodious, more intellectual variant of jazz, remained banned, although it flourished in several cities. Frederick Starr asks, is it coincidental that, in the free jazz cities, some of the strongest movements for urban autonomy and, later, democracy were to develop?[8] He speaks of a "second revolution" of the twentieth century, in reference to F. Scott Fitzgerald: "In the cultural sphere . . . the Soviet Union had collapsed from within long before it fell apart as a political system."[9]

In the last years of the Soviet Union, rock music suffered the same fate as jazz had a generation earlier. Absorbed by the state culture, it lost its potential as protest and was slowly crushed—not through police action, but through the loss of its special status, and thus its appeal. The music never mattered that much, anyway, but the lyrics did. Soviet musicians basically copied their Western models, although this was less true for the free jazz scene, where according to Starr the Russians had found an intellectually independent approach. Russia's rock has never succeeded in creating its own style. Its mission lay beyond the music, as Artemy Troitsky, the Soviet Union's first and only rock columnist, confirms in his book, *Back in the USSR*. Rock forced "people to think independently," Troitsky wrote.[10] Boris Grebenshchikov once called his band, Akvarium, "a lifestyle, not a rock band."[11]

Generally, the authorities left amateur rock groups alone, though their attempts to play were regularly hampered. Professional bands were systematically harassed; their members were detained and often jailed. As recently as 1984, particular rock groups were banned. The last musician to be released from prison was Aleksandr Novikov, who was released in Sverdlovsk in 1990.[12]

Similar to the *samizdat*, the clandestine publishing of prohibited literature, a movement called *magnizdat* emerged. During the rare rock concerts in the *dom kultury*, people held tape recorders over their heads to record the music. Even video recorders could be seen. The recordings were later duplicated tens or hundreds of times. Thus, despite the authorities' attempts to contain nonofficial music, it reached a wide audience—and so did its lyrics. In youth culture, pluralism had been achieved long before the regime was aware of its implications.

In the 1980s, the cultural authorities began to embrace some rock music, an action that divided the subculture into sanctioned and nonsanctioned wings. During perestroika, rock music received its own "rock laboratory" in Moscow, with recording studios, a record label, and the chance to invite Western groups to perform. Some members of the rock movement responded to the approaches by the political establishment; a benefit concert for the victims of Chernobyl enticed many artists into the sanctioned rock music. "We established rock as a positive social force," Troitsky wrote, celebrating glasnost and perestroika.[13] "All our old stereotypes are obsolete."[14] He and his fellow musicians were ready to believe that the Communist Party and the society had finally fused. Together with the bureaucrat Olga Opriatnaya, the columnist was entrusted with the leadership of the Moscow rock laboratory, which subsequently monopolized rock music, much like the Komsomol had monopolized jazz some twenty years earlier. Independent groups were again stopped from playing. If the rock laboratory did not recognize them, their music was not tolerated, though this did not last long: Soviet society had begun to open up and it became increasingly difficult to enforce state monopolies. In short order, the Soviet Union was to fall apart, and so was the Soviet society.

Independent (or underground) rock thrived in Leningrad, in Sverdlovsk, in other Siberian cities, such as Chelyabinsk, and in the Baltic republics. DDT and Akvarium, two of the most popular bands, became known abroad. The musicians had their own networks; they organized festivals and even a monthly underground magazine, *Urlait*. Originating as an illegal student paper, *Urlait* was first published in 1980. Full of political satire, with essays, cartoons, poems, and pamphlets attacking the military and the conservatives, *Urlait* sported absurdist slogans, such as "anarchy is just another word for order."[15] The March 1990 issue ran a broadside attack against Nina Andreyeva, the Leningrad Stalinist who in

1989 had made an appeal to stop the reform process. *Urlait* was more a mouthpiece of the young protest movement's next generation, the last one of the Soviet Union, than an underground music magazine. It arrived too late to mature as the voice of the dissident movement's next generation. But it was ready. Many people involved with *Urlait* did not particularly care for the music, according to its editor, Ilya Smirnov. They joined *Urlait* for the independent social structures it had built away from the state.

During perestroika, more and more youth groups gathered in staircases, underpasses, parks, student dorms, basements, and "squatted" houses for impromptu concerts, dance parties, and even exhibitions of unofficial art. The *tusovki*, the informal youth groups, linked people to a certain meeting place, based on their preference of a certain type of music, leisure activity, or a style of dressing, for example, punk. The *tusovki* developed their own slang, sometimes specific to a city district or a particular activity, as seasoned *tusovka* members explained to me. *Tusovka* became the term for a network of young friends. Accordingly, many *tusovki* were to later serve as infrastructures for informal trading networks.

The state-sanctioned rock laboratory had its own magazine, published by a state publishing house, the monthly *Sidvig*. In its March 1990 issue, while *Urlait* fought for the opening of the society, *Sidvig*'s lead article called for the "de-Satanization of culture." The author, drummer Sergey Sharikov, termed democracy the "favorite dream of the Jews" and pushed for the swastika to become a symbol of the hardworking Russian peasantry.[16] Thus Soviet rock, subverted by some obscure state organization, most likely the KGB, had become part of the Communist-nationalist apparatus. Paradoxically, this happened at the moment when the apparatus began to crumble.

In 1986, Riga, the Latvian capital and one of the centers of Soviet rock music, experienced riots related to a concert. Coincidentally, the film author Yuris Podnieks attended the rock concert of five thousand in Ogre south of Riga to shoot a documentary, *Is It Easy to Be Young?*[17] On their return trip from the concert, some 150 teenagers vandalized a railway car. One person recorded the riot with a video camera. Podnieks included this material in his film, making for an explosive document. He portrayed a doomed generation with no future. "Today nothing is worth living for, dying for," one interviewee said, expressing a mood widespread in his generation.

Four years later, the sentiment had changed radically. On May 5 and 6, 1990, the weekend after Latvia's Supreme Soviet passed its (tentative) declaration of independence, the festival "Rock for Independence" was held. Despite the title, in dozens of interviews the Latvian musicians stressed that, contrary to their Russian colleagues, they were not political.

In the Baltics, they claimed, rock music was not as repressed as it was in Russia. By claiming not to be political, they meant that their lyrics did not have any explicit political message. Unaware of the political significance of his statement, Ainars Mielavs, the New Moon's lead singer, told me, "Rock does not need lyrics about freedom, because rock is the music of freedom."[18] Nevertheless, at the end of the festival, all of the musicians joined on stage to perform a song for liberty.

Music—first jazz and later rock and roll—unambiguous in its implication, fun, and yet not dangerously explicit, was the medium of choice for the people who wanted to be different. More often, what mattered was not primarily the music. Jazz and rock served as nonverbal languages to challenge the state's monopoly of aesthetics. However, the politically motivated music did not survive the collapse of the Soviet Union. Russia's popular culture has mostly become integrated into the world pop culture, in the same way that Norwegian or Greek popular cultures are—with their own stars and lyrics, but nonetheless fashioned after international models. Although Russian rock to this day is heavily influenced by Russian folk music—the lyrics are still more important than those of its English-language counterpart—it has willingly parted with politics and the moral values it once stood for and has embraced formalization and commercialization. On various occasions, such as the fiftieth anniversary of the end of World War II and Moscow City Day, rock and roll, the music genre that some artists had gone to jail for playing only a decade earlier, was performed on Red Square, next to the Lenin Mausoleum, the very heart of Communist Russia. Rock has become, as anywhere else, a branch of the entertainment industry, with its stars and its scandals, its gossip magazines and celebrity cult. DDT is still around; Akvarium, which had disbanded in 1991, later resurfaced. In 1997, it "celebrated" the "official funeral" of "*otechestvenny rock*," the "fatherland's rock."[19] Alla Pugachova, the superstar of Russian pop culture, sings, "Life cannot be turned backward and it is impossible to stop time."[20] *Estrada* (Russian light pop), traditional rock and roll, punk, rap, hip-hop, and the various kinds of jazz all coexist.

Russia might be slow to integrate into the world market, yet it was very quick to absorb market mechanisms for its entertainment business. When it comes to popular music, Russia has become just like most other countries. Within a few years, the previously banned musicians became TV celebrities, some with their own shows.

Classical music is in a slightly different situation. It was the music of the regime, pampered, though regulated, by the Communist state. Religious and contemporary classical music suffered restrictions, but ballets, opera ensembles, and classical orchestras were exported by the Soviets. They helped the country earn hard currency, so they enjoyed generous funding. Consequently, the fall of Soviet power worsened conditions for these musicians.

They have to cope with the harsh reality of the market. Some do that well by playing abroad or for newly rich Russians. I was once invited to a private birthday party with professionals from a top orchestra playing chamber music for a dozen chatting guests. Others have trouble adjusting. The latter think that the quality of the performances has decreased enormously. More interesting, however, are the changes that the audiences of concerts, opera, and traditional theater have undergone. Here, it is fair to say that the quality has deteriorated, as the old regulars frequenting the concert halls, the Maly or the Mariinsky Theater in St. Petersburg, willingly confirm. The Soviet audiences consisted of professional musicians, devoted music lovers, and foreign and domestic tourists; for everybody else, it was difficult to obtain tickets. The end of the Soviet Union saw the collapse of the specific concert culture, dominated by insiders. Many chance visitors now go to cultural events; the New Russians consider it prestigious to be seen at the symphony. In the opera, people nowadays chat, play with their cell phones, or munch on food or gum. Others search through their loudly rustling plastic bags. The cloakroom attendants, once respected, have lost their hold. They cannot bar people from bringing their belongings into the hall anymore. The tourists use their flashlights; after the second act, they are bussed away for dinner. These people do not know any better, a music teacher explained to me in the Mariinsky. Earlier, she would have reprimanded them, she said, but this could no longer be done: they might yell at her. Thus, classical music, stripped of its semisacred status, has turned into another branch of the entertainment industry, almost on par with rock and roll.

It is common knowledge that background music influences human behavior. Department stores increase their customers' readiness to shop by playing soft melodies. The constant roar of traffic noise stresses people, even if they barely notice it. Russia's cities have grown louder since the end of the Soviet Union, even inside the houses. More people stay up late, blaring their music; they do not care if they disturb their neighbors. The cities' noises have grown more diverse, if not more aggressive. More than ever, the cities resemble world metropolises in this respect.

In stores, restaurants, and the streets, and on the local radio stations, foreign languages can be heard. True, many educated Soviets had studied foreign languages, and often they knew them quite well, but they spoke with phony accents and, in the case of English, with a deliberate British pronunciation. They had learned their German, French, or Japanese from textbooks, but they had few opportunities to use these languages. Nowadays, American slang is more common in Russia than the English taught in schools.

If the Russians' acoustic environment has changed, one can safely conclude that their attitude has, too. Music and the white noise of the big city stimulate expectations of further changing attitudes.

SCENTS

"Dust and heat, curious smells, a dug-up cobblestone road and houses being rebuilt"—thus Dostoevsky began his 1873 sketch on St. Petersburg's architecture.[21] An olfactory experience can be more powerful than a visual one. One distinguishes good smells from bad ones; the smells to which one is accustomed seem neutral. Therefore, over time, incremental changes in smell pass unnoticed. Boarding a train in which people have been traveling for hours encourages one to hold one's breath; the passengers who have been sitting in the car are oblivious to their own stench. However, despite a person's unawareness of the foul air, it might affect his or her perception of the environment. Pleasant odors make the world seem more agreeable. Some of the strongest olfactory experiences involve smells that remind one of childhood. During such experiences, the Soviet Union appealed to me more than otherwise.

The scents of hard soap, bleach, chlorine, and floor polish have all but disappeared from Western households and given way to more elegant odors. In the Soviet Union, they prevailed. Thus, time and again I encountered scents that had not touched my nostrils since childhood. Soviet apartments welcomed their visitors with a putrid smell, to which more often than not some feline contributed, especially in the shabby residences of the intelligentsia. They smelled like my grandparents' house: slightly stuffy, of wet wool, with a strong addition of what I identified, rightly or wrongly, as mothballs. The bookshelves were dusty, emitting the scent of old newspapers and never-opened books, for most of the Soviets I met at their homes hoarded objects, even if they did not use them. They were collectors. A person's belongings are often perceived as an extension of his or her personality, as the remarkable geographer Yi-Fu Tuan noted in *Topophilia*, echoing Walter Benjamin.[22] The Soviets felt attached to the relatively few things they owned, and they kept them for years. Their affection for objects also reflected their troubles, the sweat and emotions—a rite of passage—they had endured to acquire things. Replacing an item would be difficult, should they, a friend, or an acquaintance find a need for it or should they use it for barter. People kept their grown children's toys and first books, just as my grandmother did (she had a closetful of memorabilia of my father). That's one reason why the Soviet apartments smelled soggy. Another was the fact that people rarely acquired new furniture. Over time, the tenants adopted the odor of their homes.

Foreigners were not supposed to visit Soviet citizens at their homes. If they did, the hosts had to report the foreigners to the KGB. Gorbachev eased these restrictions and some Russians began to invite foreigners to their places. Housework, however, did not rank high on their list of priorities. Kitchen stoves were greasy and tinted brown. The oven, once turned on, reeked. I was surprised at how private bathrooms stank, reminding me of public urinals, especially in some of the homes of the Soviet intelligentsia, people who were proud of their *kulturnost* (high-culture mindedness). The dirt did not seem to bother them; neither did the stink. Presumably, they were oblivious to it. On the outskirts of big cities, some people raised chickens on their balconies, an activity that was not odor free.

The bed linen in hotels bore the scent of unperfumed detergent and starch, the bathrooms the smell of a strong disinfectant. I assume the first few Western-owned hotels in Moscow owed their success partly to the fact that their bedclothes and bathrooms carried the scents characteristic of hotels the world over; the Western guests' noses recognized this as "clean." Their restrooms emitted a smell of bitter almond or cherry. After weeks in the Russian provinces, when visiting one of those washrooms I had a sensation of freshness and hygiene. My nostrils had forgotten how pleasing and intense these artificial odors are.

Soviet men's perspiration reminded me of my father. When he returned from a long hike on a hot summer day, he reeked of sweat, untouched by deodorant. As a child, I relished that because it conveyed strength, adventure, and accomplishment. Hence, despite its being mostly unpleasant for the five senses, living in the Soviet Union ultimately felt like going back in time to my own childhood. In the West these days, everything is deodorized and reodorized: human beings fashion their olfactory appearance with the same consideration with which they dress. The Western nose has become a delicate instrument, always ready to crinkle.

Soviet streets smelled of diesel and dust, Soviet houses of cabbage and chlorine. The staircases were musty and reeked of garbage and cat urine. Often, one encountered the stench of dogs and dead rodents. And the stairs looked as bad as they smelled. Therefore, even on a cold winter day, when it was freezing inside the house entrance in St. Petersburg and thus impossible for the nostrils to detect anything, one still believed that one could smell the dirt, since one could see it. The place was littered with items that would have emitted a bad stench, were it not for the frost. Soviet cars had small pine-scented air fresheners hanging from the rearview mirrors. Many years earlier, in postwar Germany, these had been popular and Russia in fact imported them from East Germany. These days, even in Russia, new cars are prepared with the "smell of a new car." They do not require deodorant anymore.

The air of some cities, Sverdlovsk, for example, was choked with yellow and red smoke. In Magnitogorsk, within a few days after a snowfall, the snow turned black. Since the collapse of the Soviet economy, the air quality has improved vastly all over the country. Many plants have closed down. Other companies, some with the support of Western governments, have begun to reduce their emissions. When I visited Magnitogorsk in

December 1999, many people were happy about the almost white—or grayish—color of the snow.

An early achievement of the opening up of the Soviet Union was the emergence of Western soap, shampoo, deodorant, conditioners, cosmetics, and perfumes, both the well-known brands and counterfeits. Many Soviet men did not care; many barely brushed their teeth. Women, however, pursued these grooming accessories. Before perestroika, imported cosmetics were scarce and the domestic products were of inferior quality. Some women applied their own combinations of egg, oat, honey, vinegar, milk or cream, and vegetables to preserve their skin. The Soviet ideology opposed cosmetics; being natural was the order of the day. In schools, girls were indoctrinated with the beauty ideal of short hair or braids and no makeup. This, however, made cosmetics all the more enticing. The ultimate trophies were ointments, makeup, and perfume from the West or, easier to obtain, from Eastern Europe. Soviet-made cosmetics tended to dry out, crack, and flake off. This is one explanation of why many women applied far too much. Other reasons I heard for their abundant use of cosmetics were to show off one's bounty and, most important, that heavy makeup represented an ideal of female beauty that differed from the Western ideal. Makeup in the Soviet Union was applied to be noticed, it was not—as it is in the West—to emulate natural or "baby" skin, as though no makeup had been applied. Although of better quality than the rare Soviet products, Eastern European—mostly Polish—cosmetics did not meet Western standards. Their fragrance was too strong.

Beauty salons have always existed in the Soviet Union. Obviously, so have hairstylists, even nail studios. Their importance transcended the beautification of their clientele. Hairstylists acted as confidantes and advisers; they loaned money and helped to track down scarce goods. They had connections to good gynecologists and could obtain medication, Nadezhda Azhgikhina and Helen Goscilo observed.[23] The hair salons were hubs of the informal networks. The hairstylists offered cosmetics and counseling. They served as "neighborhood black market's godmothers" and as psychiatrists. Their customers depended on them, because the customers' self-perception depended on their appearance. Goscilo quotes the Moscow psychologist-cosmetician Galina Selivanova, who sees Russian women's self-confidence being, at least temporarily, revived by a transformation of their looks. "The visible reconstitutes their sense of the invisible." This was more relevant for Soviet women than for Westerners, Selivanova maintains, since many of them differed from Western women in "their exaggerated readiness for self-abnegation" and a general "indifference to their physical appearance." That's why, before special occasions, they visited the cosmetologist. Their concern with physical appearance, the authors believe, fulfilled a "largely compensatory function."[24] Other women purposefully neglected their looks.

The end of Communism has changed this, especially for younger women, thus widening the gap between the generations. Today, no longer is there a basic "indifference to the physical appearance." As in most cultures, women are constantly concerned with their appearance. Azhgikhina and Goscilo lament the frank sexualization of post-Soviet Russian women's lives, but they acknowledge that pluralism "has ushered in multiple images as varied and random as all of current Russian life."[25] A single standard for the beautiful, *soignée* young woman no longer exists. Ironically, many and possibly most young women seem content with what Azhgikhina and Goscilo rightly describe as "commodification of the female body."

Russian women smell different from how they smelled ten years ago; they smell milder and more pleasant, not like Soviet women anymore, but merely like women. Perfume stores emerged in the big cities and even the provinces and remote former union republics. As early as 1993, in Ashgabat, the sleepy capital of Turkmenistan, an Yves Rocher branch opened. St. Petersburg and Moscow witnessed the arrival of countless stores. On the street in front of them, women sold black-market imports, gifts or pirated replicas of the very same perfumes available inside, but at discounted prices.

However, Russian men, or the huge majority, have not changed their grooming habits (yet). One of my women friends once declared that she could not believe in the irreversibility of the social transitions in Russia as long as Russian men did not wash daily. Indeed, in the early 1990s, on Mondays, Valeri, our twenty-two-year-old secretary, smelled of soap and laundry, the embodiment of my grandparents' way of cleanliness. On Tuesdays, he was odorless. On Wednesday, one wondered if he had had to run to catch the bus or if he were sick. On Thursdays, his scent remained with us long after he had left the office at the end of the day. By Friday, we avoided close proximity to him. After having been with us for almost two years, Valeri purchased a men's fragrance in one of the new stores. This changed not his grooming habits, but his smell: it added a strong smell of perfume to his already strong aroma.

A ride on the Moscow or St. Petersburg metro overstimulates all senses, including scent. The public transport system provides the visitor with an olfactory adventure. In the Soviet days, the metro smelled of garlic and sweat, cabbage and indigestion, heartburn and alcohol, old meat and dirty feet, and of engine grease, blood, and hair. Often, one felt as if one were entering the locker room of a high-school gym. In winter, the stench of drenched shoes and wet wool dominated everything. During the summer it was sweat and, on Sunday evenings, the smell of mushrooms, fresh strawberries, apples, and vegetables from the *dacha* gardens that surprised the nostrils. Sun cream is a very recent, post-Soviet addition to the potpourri of summer scents in the metro. Garlic is on the retreat. Some of the "Soviet" smells have survived the end of Communism; others have faded. In winter, the metro smells much less of earthy wool than before.

It is been a long time since running water was considered a luxury in the developed world. In the countryside, however, many Russian houses still lack plumbing, not to mention hot water. To this day, some hospitals are without water. In the city, people suffer regular water outages. In summer, the authorities shut off the hot water for a month, usually without notice—for maintenance, they claim. The heating plants and the tubes have to be serviced. Rumor has it, however, that this is a cost-cutting exercise. Until a few years ago, one district after another by turn awoke on a Monday morning to no hot water. As of late, the population is at least notified in advance, a fact people register with gratitude. At least they let us know, they say.

Post-Soviet Russia suffers serious epidemics; for example, tuberculosis is on the rise; cholera, diphtheria, and typhus break out regularly. Infections thought to be rare reappear. Yellow fever is back; for decades it was only sporadically seen. Sexually transmitted diseases, such as gonorrhea, syphilis, and AIDS, are spreading rapidly. Many epidemics have their focus in Russia's overcrowded prisons, with their poor sanitary conditions.

These problems can be generally explained by the collapse of the Soviet health-care system. However, the Soviet press had never covered health matters and, presumably, the statistics were flawed. That is why objectively assessing the deterioration of the health situation is difficult. Today, people are frightened because the press reports widely on medical shortcomings and epidemics. Magazines are flooded with health tips. President Yeltsin's detailed medical diagnosis regularly made headlines and he was often criticized for his unhealthy—yet typical—Russian lifestyle.

What does the above have to do with changing smells? Post-Soviet sanitation smells different. The Soviet health-care and disease-prevention system was—as almost everything else—conducted as if fighting a war. Disinfection measures and decontaminations were overdone. Soviet institutions smelled of chlorine, hydrochloric acid, or acetic acid. Schools, kitchens, kindergartens, restrooms, hotels, and hospitals were hardly dirt free, but they were thoroughly disinfected. Before the end of the Soviet Union, one could see cleaning brigades everywhere—in the streets, airports, office buildings, schools, and hotels. That did not mean that these facilities were clean, although they were constantly being cleaned. The brigades roamed the hospitals and kitchens; they may not have worked much, but they poured disinfectant everywhere. However, although the detergents used were aggressive, they were inefficient. This only added to their excessive use. The end of the Soviet regime ended these paramilitary cleaning brigades. Some were dissolved; others are still cleaning, though even more sloppily. There is no incentive to work properly; the salaries are miserable and often workers are not paid. There is no reprisal if the cleaners do not do their job: no one cares. Therefore, Russia looks dirtier than the Soviet Union did. The country is certainly less thoroughly poisoned with cleansing agents than it once was. It does not stink of chlorine anymore. And since the society is growing richer, there is more waste, some of which reeks.

But is there a deterioration of hygiene to speak of? And, if so, did it cause the increase in epidemics? Or were these diseases simply suppressed by a disinfecting overkill, but not eliminated, as the Soviet authorities liked to claim? If so, the general carelessness in disinfecting during the post-Soviet period would only allow that truth to come out.

Peasants tolerate more dirt. It is directly connected to their work; manure is even useful for them. Farmers certainly tolerate stronger stenches. Before the October Revolution, the Russian aristocracy had close connections to the peasantry. Most city dwellers, especially the poor—the former serfs—had newly migrated. They were used to strong aromas. But soon, handbooks were published to tutor women on physical cleanliness, for both their bodies and their houses. Prerevolutionary Russia was on the verge of developing an urban-bourgeois society. The visible manifestation of cleanliness has been read as a sign of this. The division between the clean private and the dirty public realms is characteristic of the existence of an urban middle class, like the one emerging before the October Revolution—and then driven into (inner) exile or murdered.[26] The cleanliness values of the urban middle class were subsequently adopted by the Stalinist elite. However, the process of cleaning and the olfactory evidence that a place had been cleaned seemed more important for the Soviets than the absence of dirt, as if it were the ritual, not the result, that mattered. It probably was.

As Svetlana Boym indicates, the Russian intelligentsia rejected cleanliness as petty bourgeois banality, or *poshlost*.[27] Since many post-Stalinist urban dwellers liked to consider themselves part of that intelligentsia, they quickly adopted its habits, especially those implicitly opposed to the government's rules and values. Thus, urban Russians toward the end of Communism defied the imperative of cleanliness for an ideological reason: it was banal to worry about dirt. Could this be read as evidence that at its core, Soviet society remained a peasant society, although most lived a semirural life in city-like landscapes?

In 1989, coal miners rallied for an 800 gram bar of soap per month. That was their primary demand when they went on strike that year. The shortages were so dramatic that soap hardly ever reached the remote coal mining areas. Initially, the miners did not ask for democracy, for free elections, or for the government's resignation. That came later. In the beginning, they wanted a piece of soap, since a person deprived of the possibility of washing is also deprived of self-respect. Without self-respect, there can be no freedom whatsoever and, thus, no democracy and no future to speak of.

The bar of soap for which the miners went on strike was a piece of human dignity, a precondition for freedom.

Capitalism originated in the spirit of extravagance and the desire for luxury, the German sociologist Werner Sombart wrote.[28] In an open society, he believed, luxury would indicate freedom and, thus, the chance for democracy. Is there a more fundamental luxury than expensive fragrances, money evaporating into the air?

However, freedom cannot be achieved overnight. As with anything new, some Russian men use perfumes as masks. They try to cover up their unwashed bodies with luxury perfumes, thus adding to an olfactory carnival. With the emergence of a middle class, physical cleanliness will become the intrinsic norm that it is in Western societies. The process is well under way; some of the prerevolutionary handbooks on cleanliness and health have been reprinted. Western detergents and cleansers are pursued, as are Western shampoos, toothpastes, cosmetics, and perfumes. Eating habits are changing as well, indicating a new awareness of health and hygiene.

The Soviet Union smelled different. Toward its end, a foul odor was an expression of the deficit economy, as well as a silent protest. The society's high tolerance of dirt was inherited from its not-so-distant peasant past. With a gradual gentrification of the cities, with the society refining its tastes and preferences, the noses have become more delicate. Simultaneously, the threshold of embarrassment for causing foul smell is gradually lowering.

One might say that if smells are more pleasant, then people are more accepting of their daily burdens. Even if they are oblivious to the changes in society, they can still smell them, and their outlooks respond to those smells. The availability of Western soap, cosmetics, and perfume can be read as signs of Russia's becoming more urban and more bourgeois—using Norbert Elias's term, one might say more civilized[29]—and, most importantly, more pleasant for the Russians themselves.

TASTE

Eating appeals to all senses, or should. Gathering with friends at a nicely set table, with the food carefully prepared—smelling, looking, and tasting delicious, and with a nice texture—makes the participants feel good and appreciated. Such a setting was rare in the Soviet Union, especially if one ate in a restaurant. In Soviet *stolovayas*, the no-frill eateries, ill-tempered women plopped the food onto Bakelite plates. Spoons and forks were aluminum and knives were not provided. The food was of low quality, poorly cleaned and prepared. Even in boarding schools the students did not get knives with which to eat their meals. Soviet restaurants mirrored people's reactions to the deficit economy, placing more emphasis on the quantity of food than on quality. Soviet menus listed the weight of meat and vegetables, while the service was similar to that of the *stolovayas:* careless, tacky, and rude.

In restaurants, what one ordered usually did not matter much. The names on the menu sounded fancy, yet either *kotlet* or *filet* stood for a slice of fried *gaviadina* (beef) accompanied by peas, potatoes, or rice. And despite a long list of dishes on the menu, the choice was usually reduced to fish or meat, or to chicken, pork, or beef. Dishes with different names often looked identical and many dishes were unavailable.

Although the Soviet Union could hardly be considered a nation, despite the party's attempts to turn it into one, there was a Soviet national cuisine that could be found all over the country. This cuisine blended an impoverished version of Russian cooking with Georgian, Armenian, and Central Asian influences. *Basturma,* the Armenian dried beef, and *plov,* the Central Asian rice dish, were integral to it.

A festive Soviet meal in a restaurant differed from a Western dinner in more than what was served and how it was served. For most of the evening, the dinner did not follow an order of courses, as has been common in Western societies since the seventeenth century. For a long period, the table remained full of *zakuski,* all sorts of hot and cold snacks, such as salad, pickled vegetables, dried meat, cold cuts, smoked fish, and caviar—more than enough for a full meal. Vodka, Soviet champagne, wine, beer, and soft drinks were served simultaneously. The eaters did not observe any temporal order, neither with the drinks nor with the *zakuski.* Only late in the evening, in what looked almost like a grudging concession to European customs, the *gariachi,* or "hots," followed, usually the above-mentioned slice of meat and potatoes. The insignificance of the *gariachi* is clearly illustrated by the fact that it was perfectly fine to skip them. A Soviet dinner concluded with dessert, which was normally ice cream. Historically, the Russian aristocracy ate their *zakuski* in a room separate from the dining room, where they proceeded afterward. This allowed people to eat while waiting for late guests to arrive, a necessity considering Russian transportation.

Russian lunches to this day often consist of a soup, a *borscht,* or a *solyanka,* which are full meals with meat or fish and vegetables. Lunch at a *stolovaya* is eaten quickly, with little or no conversation. The *zakuski* table, by contrast, is supposed to facilitate socializing.

Interestingly, in their homes, Soviet families followed the chronological order observed by bourgeois Europe. The three courses normally consisted of soup or salad, a main course, and a dessert.

Preparing a meal requires work; it has to if the cooks have a high regard for whom they cook for. This is a way to express respect. The amount of work and the quality of the ingredients are relative to the importance a host ascribes to his or her guests. Thus, the meal reflects the guests' status.[30] In private Soviet households, preparing food was a lavish process, especially for a festive occasion. It required additional effort, since it began with the hunt for the ingredients. Soviet families expressed high appreciation for their guests by cooking elaborate meals. Soviet restaurants, however, as well as school and work canteens—in short, the state—simplified the process of preparing food in every imaginable way. This, too, conveyed the degree of appreciation for the eaters, that is, the lack of it.

One can interpret the reduced or lack of temporal order within a Soviet restaurant dinner in several ways. It can be attributed to the rural background of the Soviet party leaders; Russian peasants were not used to serving meals in courses. In addition, by adopting the *zakuski*, they might have been trying to borrow from the aristocracy's habits. But why the *zakuski*? Were the Communists confining themselves to the anteroom of the nobility, secretly acknowledging that they did not belong any further inside, that this was the best they could hope for? Or was there a more pragmatic reason? When eating *zakuski*, one could devour huge amounts of food almost unnoticed, as some leading party members indeed were rumored to do.

Not all cultures observe a temporal order in eating; for example, the Japanese do not and the Chinese hardly do. In Japan, restaurants serve each guest a tray containing all the dishes; the customers decide upon their own order.

Soon after the fall of the state's economic monopoly, new bars and restaurants emerged, their names conveying themes, some invoking the exotic and some more ironic. "Manhattan Express," "Santa Fe," and "Monte Carlo" are examples of the former, while "Yolki-Polki" (a Russian curse) and "Parizhskaya Zhisn" (Parisian Life) represent the latter. "Titanic" reflects both. These restaurants have Western-style menus with a clear order: appetizers, salads, soups, main courses, and desserts. No commercial restaurant owner could be interested in a group sitting around a table of *zakuski* for the whole evening.

Under the pretext of providing healthful alimentation to the population, the early Communists tried to develop large-scale public food distribution. This had a great impact on culinary practices and consciousness about food and nutrition, as Halina and Robert Rothstein show.[31] As everything else in the Soviet Union, preparing food became scientific and mechanized, and was to be taken away from ordinary people. How could a woman consider herself a cook if she did not have a diploma? In reality, however, the hidden agenda behind collective feeding was the party's attempt to bring more women into the workforce.

The Rothsteins perceive the Soviet culinary revolution as another step in the process of eliminating the cultural differences between the city and the countryside, a process that culminated in the 1950s.[32] The process was a success of sorts. The authorities managed to level the two lifestyles. However, as with housing, they did not improve people's lives, but brought the shortcomings of the cities to the countryside and vice versa. In many villages, only processed food, if any, was available in the stores. For vegetables, both city dwellers and country people had to rely on their *dacha* gardens. The grocery stores were sparsely stocked and often empty. Only a few items—certain instant or canned foods—were available in abundance. And people refused to buy them because they tasted terrible. At the same time, fresh vegetables could rarely be found in the stores. Soviet milk, it was alleged, was reprocessed milk powder. People in the villages lived mostly on potatoes, cabbage, and vodka—with the cabbage at times being rotten. Home-grown and pickled cucumbers and tomatoes, along with dried mushrooms, rounded out the diet.

For certain Westerners, as with some scents, eating the villagers' simple, unprocessed and lightly spiced food was a trip back in time. Oriental spices, garlic, and processed food reached the northwestern European countryside only after World War II. Soviet food was therefore a reminder of the food that Germans and Scandinavians once ate, the food I encountered as a student on a farm in Norway, for example.

Except for the occasional Georgian restaurant, ethnic food was rarely seen in Soviet-Russian cities. Some Moscow restaurants got their names for the state's "friendship" with the "socialist" brother countries, but that did not mean that they served the food their names suggested. There was no Czech food in the Praga, no German dishes in the Berlin. The Peking served mostly Soviet food and only a few pseudo-Chinese dishes and had a vaguely Chinese décor.

The Soviet people enhanced their basic diet, and they still do—some more than ever—with what they grow in their summer gardens (tomatoes and cucumbers) and what they collect in the woods (berries and mushrooms), plus fish from the rivers. Ninety percent of the potatoes consumed in Russia are grown on private plots, although these *dacha* plots account for only 3 percent of the agricultural land. More than two-thirds of Russians never buy potatoes; they eat what their families grow. Furthermore, 76 percent of the vegetables, 55 percent of the meat, and amazingly, 47 percent of the milk is produced on the private *dacha* plots.[33] Stalin had mandated the creation of private plots to overcome the food shortages after World War II. However, he meant them to be provisional, but as with so many other Soviet temporary measures, the *dachas* were there to stay. The Communist government never succeeded in feeding its entire population. Today, 27 million private plots of land supply two-thirds of the population.[34] Until the end of the Soviet Union, the law prevented open trade in privately grown agriculture produce; it had to be exchanged or bartered. For many people, this has become an additional source of income.

Breakfast is the most important meal of the day, Russian mothers and wives believe. Therefore, in the morning, they feed their families full meals of potatoes and meat or *kasha*, the Russian buckwheat mash. Despite Tolstoy, a vocal proponent of a vegetarian diet,[35] a healthy breakfast never took root in Russia—until the end of the Soviet Union. In the United States and in Western Europe, it was the moral reform movement that brought about the breakfast that consists of cereal and milk. Representing a typical American breakfast, cornflakes have reached post-Soviet Russia and, as anything American, are seen as highly desirable. Thus, some people began to eat more healthful breakfasts.

Oddly enough, Kellogg's cornflakes unintentionally brought another change. For the first time, the languages of the newly independent Baltic nations have made it into Russian homes. Kellogg's manufactures its cornflakes in Latvia and its packages are marked in the languages of its markets: Latvian, Estonian, Lithuanian, and Russian. While I lived in St. Petersburg in 1996–1997, my breakfast was quite international: the milk was either marked *piim* (Estonian for milk) or *maito* (Finnish). Estonian milk was *kõrgpastöriseeritud*, or superpasteurized. The orange juice was either *appelsiini mehu* (Estonian) or it was packed in St. Petersburg and then labeled in Russian and English. The cereals, however, implied equality of the Baltic nations' languages with Russia. No doubt the cornflakes company expects people to read what it prints on the packages. Otherwise, it would not reproduce cutouts on the back. Thus, together with introducing a new style of breakfast, Kellogg's taught Russia's children that other languages existed in the world that were equal to Russian (and English). That was more than the Baltic countries could have achieved with diplomacy.

The first Western foodstuffs to reach a wider public in the Soviet Union were probably the colas—Pepsi during the Olympic Games in 1980, soon followed by Coca Cola. The latter became ubiquitous. The opening of the first McDonald's restaurant in January 1990 brought the Big Mac to Russia, although chopped beef in a roll was available long before, at the Cafe Diasto on Nevski Prospect in St. Petersburg, for example. Other non-Russian foods existed even earlier, such as the pierogi, sold on the markets, and the Georgian *khachapuria*, hot turnovers filled with melted cheese. And in its way, a Soviet *stolovaya* was a fast-food outlet; the service was immediate, from a buffet, and one could eat standing at a high table. There was no incentive to remain in the *stolovaya* after eating.

When McDonald's opened its first restaurant on Pushkin Square in Moscow, people supposedly wanted a piece of America. But many Russians said they liked McDonald's because it was the only place where they knew what they would get, where everything on the menu was available, and where the service was efficient and friendly. This was probably true in 1990. At that time, the stores were empty and the Soviet restaurant offered Potemkin-style menus. The waiter usually recommended a dish; then by asking for a different item, then one after another, one eventually found out that what had been recommended was the only dish available.

McDonald's was new and it was American; for many people, this was a good reason to queue for an hour. However, I would question that these Russians thought they would swallow modernity or Americanness by eating imported foodstuffs, as has been proposed (and disputed) in the case of McDonald's Chinese customers in Southeast Asia.[36] Unlike many Americans, neither the Chinese nor the Russians would consider a hamburger menu as offering a viable meal. The Russians consider themselves as belonging to the European food culture and, for them, a Big Mac is not real food, but entertainment for the palate, like ice cream. "Real food" is what they eat from a plate, normally at home, at work, in a *stolovaya*, or on special occasions in a restaurant. The idea that by eating another culture's food they would internalize its values might not have been completely alien to McDonald's Russian customers, but the craze for the Big Mac should be read as a curiosity: a kind of virtual tourism at a time when, for most people, traveling to America was still inconceivable.

The Russian diet has gained enormously in variety since the end of the Soviet Union. By eating foreign food, Russians learned to accept and even like the diversity of the world, something to which many Russians, and certainly the Communist Party, were once averse. They now eat Italian, French, Chinese, Japanese, and of course, American food. Implicitly, by eating Latvian-produced cornflakes, they have accepted another food culture as equal, as early in the day as breakfast time. Even the food cooked at home has become more international, now including previously unknown vegetables (broccoli, asparagus, and zucchini) and exotic fruit (bananas, kiwis, and mangoes) as well as Heinz ketchup, Campbell's soup, and Hellman's mayonnaise. German bouillon cubes and Italian spaghetti from Barilla are regular ingredients, the latter made in Poland and labeled in Polish, Czech, Hungarian, and Russian. And there are few places in the world where one can find beer and wine from more countries than one can in Moscow.

Many Russians quickly learned to distinguish between quality cuisine and fast food. They are eager to acquire knowledge about Western food for the newly discovered health reasons, as well as for taste and prestige. Numerous newspaper articles and books teach their readers how to refine their eating and drinking habits. The weekly magazine *Kapital* runs an advice column on which wines to drink with which foods.[37] Cookbooks have been published in waves, with some printing translations of foreign recipes and others reprints of old Russian collections, including the *Domostroi*, a sixteenth-century household manual. New volumes have also been written, both for the affluent and for the less well off: one book showing a thousand ways to prepare potatoes and mushrooms, for example.[38]

The Okhotny Ryad shopping mall, under the Manezhnaya Square in Moscow, includes Asian, French, and Russian fast-food outlets and, despite the collapse of the Russian currency in 1998, many of the pricier restaurants serving French, Korean, Japanese, Indian, Irish, and Mexican cuisine remain in business. Some Western fast-food chains, on the other hand, have closed their Moscow branches, succumbing to the newly created Russian fast-food eateries such as Bistro, Moscow's own chain. The lines at McDonald's have long disappeared. Russia has developed confidence concerning its own cuisine. The Moscow press runs stories about Russian restaurants abroad, for example, in New York.

Not only have eating habits changed and grown closer to the West's, eating disorders have reached Russia. Not eating has become a trend. Women fast to lose weight.

With the Orthodox Church regaining a broader following, its eating rules have also become more widely accepted, including those concerning Lent—not eating as a form of worship.

The collapse of the ruble in August 1998 may have adversely affected eating habits. People passed over milk and meat for cheaper food, especially potatoes; for many, imported fruits were again out of their reach. Yet, even in the winter of 1998–1999, bananas were sold on many street corners in Moscow and St. Petersburg, and they found their buyers—although certainly not among the newly rich, who would not deign to buy their bananas on the street. Only ten years earlier, bananas belonged to the ultimate icons of Western affluence. Now, a newly emerging middle class regularly consumes this most healthful and practical fast food. People have developed an awareness for what they eat and drink and many eat according to what they want to be, which is worldly, urban, and bourgeois.

Food from all over the world has made it to Russia (again), but table manners have not. Many New Russians in the decent, often very expensive, restaurants devour food with their hands. They will eventually learn etiquette from the how-to books and manners will become part of their self-stylization, as have their material achievements. Eventually, they will try to impress each other with an elaborate etiquette. Gradually, new table manners will ascend and new everyday rituals and new imperatives will be formed. These are, according to Elias, typical signs of an emerging middle class.[39]

Russia has become more open, more diverse, more refined, and even more hedonistic than she has ever been. This is reflected by the changes in Russian food and Russian tastes.

TOUCH

What would caviar taste like if it were a homogeneous paste? The texture is what makes it special. The haptic sense provides humans with a vast amount of information, though often it is supplemental. One sees a mug and, by touching it, discovers its material properties. It does not require any special skill to distinguish different, though similar, materials, such as glass versus plastic or, to go further, glass versus china. One need only feel the surface with the tip of a finger. One is always "in touch," as Yi-Fu Tuan notes.[40] However, people are often unaware of the degree to which the sense of touch shapes their perception of the world, all the more so since it does not matter if one's mug is made of Bakelite or china, as long as the coffee tastes good.

There were many typical Soviet tactile experiences. A Soviet man's handshake differed from what I was used to. It was firm, sometimes almost a squeeze, as if to convey commitment, even conspiracy—a "real man's" grip. During my first year in the Soviet Union, I was regularly reprimanded for having a woman's handshake, instead of a "real" one. Shaking hands with women was considered bad form, and most women were puzzled when I held out my hand—after having clasped hands with their husbands.

Shaking hands over a threshold was illicit; it meant bad luck. This belief was observed by almost everyone, even by those friends who hoped to be mistaken for foreigners. And while some handshakes have become more gentle recently, the unwritten rule on shaking hands over a threshold is still observed. Even abroad, no Russian will do it. It is a sign of a looming quarrel, as my friends patiently explained, every time I automatically stretched out my hand.

Only an outsider is able to note the particularities of a society's habits. In Europe, much is made of the fact that in some societies, in greeting one another, people kiss. Further, in some societies, it is one kiss on the cheek, while in others people kiss twice and in France they kiss three times. And men? An awkward pause follows when the greeting parties' assumptions differ, when one person's face moves into the void while the other withdraws.

However, some of Soviet society's most important haptic experiences had been perceived only visually. The Soviet leaders kissed each other and the leaders of the brotherly Communist parties in public, especially at airports, and they kissed each other on the lips; for example, Leonid Brezhnev and the East German leader Erich Honecker. What a paradox: a political leadership that went at lengths to ban any sexual, especially homoerotic, reference turned a kiss exchanged by old men into one of its most publicized touches.

Even when he already was at odds with Honecker, Gorbachev kissed the East German on his lips. The brotherly kiss has been explained as a Russian tradition, but this implies that the bosses of the party that sought to abolish nationality and religion deferred to Christian tradition. In addition, Erich Honecker was neither Orthodox nor Slavic. East Germans read the kiss as a sign of their country's looming russification. Other interpretations are possible: were the top Communists Russian nationalists in disguise or were they refashioning the rituals of the Orthodox Church for their own purposes? They clearly did that for Lenin's funeral and the subsequent Lenin cult.[41] Sometimes a kiss tells all, but what was Gorbachev trying to say, perhaps subconsciously, when he attempted to kiss other, including Western, leaders?

Russia's visual changes, such as clothing, newspapers, furniture, homes, and transportation, have a tactile dimension also. Clothes, our most personal belongings, both extend personalities and affect them, perhaps more than anything else. People dress the way they want to be perceived and they are judged by what they wear. This is true not only in regard to visual appearance. Russian clothes were different to the touch from imported ones; they were rougher. One could easily tell Soviet jeans from those of Western origins. The fabric of the short-sleeved Soviet polyester shirts men wore in summer felt like a shower curtain. Soviet shoes pinched and, in winter, they inevitably got soaked. How could this not affect a person's behavior or perception of reality? Imported shoes were hardly available. It was difficult enough to find a Soviet-made pair. Can there be human dignity if one's feet are wet because one's shoes are soaked?

Textiles may provide us with our most common haptic experience, since we always wear clothes. With the Soviet Union opening its borders to imports, the range of possible tactile sensations was broadened dramatically. A variety of previously unheard of textiles appeared: light, warm fabrics for the winter, Western underwear. Real blue jeans became available, replacing the Eastern European replicas. Waterproof shoes made it to Russia—and they did not even pinch.

Sometimes, however, people fooled themselves. In 1993, a Soviet company put American labels on some of its lingerie, while attaching Soviet labels to the imported American apparel. The Soviet underwear with the U.S. labels sold much faster than the Western product that was branded Russian.[42] Thus, the visual appearance defeated the tactile experience.

Apparel has come a long way. Since 1996, the department store GUM has promoted "Soviet lingerie" on the "first Soviet glamour wear website" for online shopping. A model, "tempting Tatyana," sports a "slinky bra," implying that Soviet apparel has lost its negative connotation.[43] At the same time, bras have become a method of payment. For some time, a Vladivostok factory producing women's underwear paid its employees— male and female—seven to nine bras a month, since it was short of cash.[44]

In the West, a bra might connote beauty, femininity, sexiness, and youth. For Russian women, however, its significance extends beyond that and, more important, has been changing constantly in recent years. Before, a Soviet bra was a piece of underwear that supplanted the object of desire—a real, sexy bra from the West. Then, along with Western perfumes, imported lingerie suddenly became available. Some women began to don Western underwear for special occasions, while sticking to their Russian undergarments for everyday use. At the same time, with the progressing sexualization of the young, urban Russian woman's life, it became fashionable not to wear bras at all. Therefore, at a certain moment, bras were either Russian bras and out of favor or highly charged, imported objects that happened to serve as bras, too, but which denoted much more.

Like garments, Soviet paper felt different; the newspapers reminded one of pre-World War II Western newspapers, particularly in the way they felt. Antiquated methods were used to produce the paper. Soviet stationery was easy to distinguish from Western stationery, by sight as well as by touch. Newspapers, clipped into pieces, were also used for the toilet.

Toilet paper, like soap, was in short supply in the Soviet days and was sought after, hoarded, and often replaced by newspaper when not available. Tampons did not exist in the USSR and neither did menstrual pads, or they were at least very hard to come by. Mothers just taught their daughters how to fold a piece of cloth. With the opening of the market, these products for women's personal care became available and, despite their relatively high prices, they were soon widely used.

Soviet furniture felt cheap and outdated; the Formica tables and plastic taborets evoked the memory of my grandparents' house in Switzerland, which had been furnished in the 1940s and 1950s. The sofas were covered with numerous pillows and upholstered in dark, earthy colors; the fabric felt cold. Most sofas could be converted into beds. Having slept on such a sofa bed, one will never forget that single spring that shoves into one's back, nor the creaking of the bed when one turns over. I have often wondered how Soviet people could accomplish anything after sleeping on these beds. It was simply not relaxing, at least for me. I wondered also if the Soviet people would still accept sleeping on such a bed after getting used to simple, comfortable beds, for example from Ikea, the Swedish company now selling thrifty furniture in Moscow. Indeed, there is now a high demand for plain, cozy furniture. Even movie theaters have installed new seats, as have restaurants.

As mentioned earlier, after their first trips to the West, many of my friends stopped inviting me to their homes. Nothing had changed; they had merely become aware of the differences. A standard of living they had accepted as "normal" suddenly seemed shabby to them and also must have affected their self-perception. All of a sudden able to make the comparison, one friend felt as though she and her family were being housed like cattle. What was one to make of the way the leaders treated the people when the picture the party painted diverged as widely from reality as it did in the Soviet Union? my friend asked after she had visited Western countries.

Other factors contributed to making Soviet homes unpleasant. Russian cities are centrally heated by district heating stations, which work according to the calendar, not the outside temperature. When it turns cold in September, people freeze in their homes; the heating period starts at a certain date in October. In spring, however, the heating stations keep working, even if it is already warm outside. Many buildings are so badly insulated that, during the coldest period—December through February—the flats never get warm, only to become overheated during the mild weeks at the end of the winter. And since most radiators do not have valves, one has to open all the windows to keep the home at moderate temperatures. Of course, it is not uncommon for the heating system to break down for days or even weeks in midwinter. In that respect, not much has changed since the collapse of the USSR, and neither have the expectations. Thus, when, in the chilly September of 1995, Moscow's city authorities announced that they would start heating several weeks earlier than usual, this was met with great surprise and appreciation.

Soviet roads were full of potholes. In Nizhni Novgorod, Russia's third largest city, a driver joked that the city did not have roads, only directions. One of the first highways in Moscow to be paved according to Western standards was the one to Domodedovo Airport, built in 1990 by a German construction company. When I traveled to that airport, my driver almost always commented on the smooth ride and asked me if the roads in Western Europe were as good. Some drivers could hardly believe that they were. Subsequently, they concluded that anything in the West must be much better than in Russia. They were not satisfied that Moscow finally had a highway of such superior quality; they were upset about the conditions of all the other roads. They cursed the inability and disinterest of the government in improving them. The well-paved roads made them realize that it was possible to build smooth roads, even in Russia.

From the smooth roads, the conversation regularly turned to Western cars. It was with awe that many drivers spoke of their first ride in an imported vehicle, and they spoke contemptuously of domestically built automobiles. Until the ruble crisis in August 1998, no one wanted to buy Russian-made automobiles, despite some obvious quality improvements that the industry had introduced with their new models. A used foreign car was considered a better bargain; a decade-old German or Japanese vehicle was taken as more reliable than a new Russian one, although some finer Western cars could hardly handle the bumpy Russian roads.

Today, the ride on many roads is as smooth and orderly as on the highway to Domodedovo, especially on Moscow's ring freeway. So people would trust the impression that this was no longer the Soviet ring road, but a new Russian one, it was lined with gas stations—some Western companies, others Russian but parroting the colors used by Western companies, such as the BP green and yellow and the Esso/Exxon red. Electronically controlled road signs and glass-covered pedestrian bridges add to the ring's breach with its past, and people notice it. For a while, there was rarely a driver who did not comment on the smooth ride and ascribe the achievement to Moscow mayor Yuri Luzhkov's can-do politics. This perception helped the mayor get reelected with an overwhelming majority; people *felt* that he got things done.

The pavement matters, and not just for cars. Pedestrians read the surface of a street with their feet; then they compare with what they have memorized from other streets. They register the differences subconsciously. In downtown Moscow, the ramp leading from Manezhnaya Square to Red Square has been newly paved with cobblestones, as have other pedestrian areas. These walkways provide the walking public with the sensation of strolling through a historic site, however fake Moscow's newly created "historic" center is. Westerners generally "understand" the message; so do Muscovites, it seems. A Yakut friend, however, recently settled in Moscow, complained about how stupid it was to replace a perfectly flat asphalt surface with cobblestones. She found it difficult to walk on them with her high heels. On her, the city authority's message was lost.

A ride on the Moscow subway entertains all senses, especially during rush hour. People push, elbow, and punch. During Soviet times, in a mixture of aggression and obliviousness, the passengers kept an almost complete silence. They shoved, ignoring each other all the while. Although the mood has somewhat brightened, to this day a lot of wrestling continues. Has this become a behavioral pattern? Did they so often have to resort to pushing that it has become second nature? No one seems to mind, since it is the crowd that pushes—not an individual, but the collective, a superior being, as David Rancour-Laferriere argued in his controversial yet profound book, *The Slave Soul of Russia*.[45] Thus, there is no one person to be angry at. Occasionally, someone about to get off the train will ask a person who is standing in their way if he or she will be getting off at the next station. I read this not as propriety, but as an attempt to form a collective that will fight its way together through the crowd. There is a certain reassurance that one—as part of the instantly formed collective—will manage to get out in time at the right station.

Many Russians do not have access to a car or the money for a taxi, and so move their belongings on the subway. Officially, the subway bans large pieces of luggage. They have to be smuggled past the monitor controlling the gates. Somehow, the peddlers manage to lug their huge bags of merchandise through the barriers, often in the infamous three-color (blue and rose on white) bags,[46] which are slung against other passengers' legs and balanced on their feet. Passengers have to climb over piles of luggage to exit the train. In other industrialized countries, this might still happen on public transportation to an airport, but not downtown during the rush hour. It conveys, of course, a lack of means.

Even when they board an airplane with assigned seats, many Russians push and shove as if there will not be room enough for everyone. Unlike with Western passengers, the race to board first cannot be explained by the limited space for luggage. On older Russian planes, the overhead bin is only for coats and hats. The passengers squeeze their bags under the seats; some newer planes do provide spacious storage space for luggage that is accessible upon boarding.[47] However, for some time, on flights to Armenia, people had good reason to wrangle: the flights were oversold. I have flown from Moscow to Erivan on a Tupolev 154, a plane that carries about 180 passengers, with some fifty people standing in the aisle, just as they would on a bus or subway.

These days, many airlines operate Western-built aircraft, even on domestic flights; others use Soviet systems refurbished with a Western standard cabin. Many Russian passengers appreciate the difference, yet they react the same way as they once did to the Western-built road to Domodedovo Airport—not with satisfaction over the improvement, but with disgust for the Russian product they had been used to. Sometimes, their fury spirals into a kind of Russian self-hatred.

Transaero was the first private Russian airline to compete with Aeroflot.[48] From its beginning, Transaero has operated Western aircraft. Prices were higher, but people claimed that they received better treatment. On some routes, this might have been true; on others Aeroflot matched Transaero's service, certainly on flights between Moscow and St. Petersburg. Most of the harassment one has to endure when flying in Russia originates from fellow passengers, anyway. Yet many customers believe they are served better on Transaero—with more dignity, as fellow travelers told me. This alleged dignity, I suspect, has not been provided by the cabin crew, or not entirely. Instead, the more luxurious interior of the cabin makes the passengers feel appreciated and, thus, they are better behaved. This renders flights more agreeable.

To further explore the Russians' specific relation toward touch, one is well-advised to visit the *bania*, the traditional Russian steam bath, the realm of Russian masochism, as Rancour-Laferriere called it.[49] According to Nancy Condee, the *bania*, in the imagination of the city dwellers, is an amalgam of recollections and fantasies—of a village *bania*, a family *bania*, and the peasants' black, unvented *bania*.[50] The *bania* presumably has its roots in the necessity to wash; for the peasant in the countryside it was much easier to heat air than water, and the sweat served to help lather. Today, most city dwellers have a bathroom of their own, though people living in a communal apartment may still rely on the public bath. The majority, especially men, go to the *bania* to relax and to meet friends.[51] The *bania* provides them with a space for camaraderie.

The *bania* also produces a sense of well-being, though this entails a dash of masochism. The Russians suffer in the *bania*. They sigh and moan; pain is written all over their faces. They heat the *bania* to a temperature they can barely stand and steam until the skin burns, as though the *bania* were a damp purgatory—obviously a kind of self-punishment. The cleansing bath is usually followed by rewards for one's endurance in sustaining the pain: food and beer or other drinks.

The *bania* serves all senses: sight, sound—with the people groaning when beaten with the *venik*, the birch switch—scent, touch, and taste. There are many references in Russian sayings to "eating" punishment from the *venik*, such as "to eat birch *kasha*," as Rancour-Laferriere noted in his book on the Slavic soul.[52] Of course, the *veniki* were not eaten; the idiom for punishment stood for swallowing the pain inflicted by flagellation.

The *bania* cleans the body and soul, popular belief has it. It removes guilt: "Bania vse grekhi smoet" (the *bania* washes away all sins).[53] The *venik* serves as the main instrument for cleansing and (symbolic) punishment in the *bania*: "Venik v bane vsekh (I tsaria) starshe" (the *venik* is superior to everybody [including the czar]). The *bania* rinses away chronic, low-level guilt. Peasants would typically take a steam bath once a week, usually on Saturdays. Ritual cleaning and prenuptial parties were held in the *bania*; in some regions, the bride had to undergo flagellation by her girlfriends. Historically, Russian husbands were free to discipline their wives with beatings and many Russian men still claim this "right." Even if the bride participated in choosing her husband and even if she happened to love him, Rancour-Laferriere wrote, that did not mean he would later refrain from exercising his tacit right to abuse her.[54] A quiet fire during the prenuptial *bania* therefore symbolized a home life free of beatings for the bride. Water wrung out of the towel to wash the bride during the prenuptial *bania* was used to make dumplings, which the groom would later eat.[55] In rural Russia, women used the *bania* to give birth. It was probably the most hygienic place.

The dash of masochism is still present; the *bania* guests beat each other up with the *veniki* and pour so much water on the stove that they can barely endure the hot steam. Some do not, especially the New Russians. Often, I encountered them leaving the *bania*, evading the "punishment" they were provoking, leaving it to the others to stand the hot steam. Does this reflect real life? Post-Soviet society has created all sorts of strategies in the striving for fun, but also in the avoidance of the "punishment" or the hardships it has inflicted on itself.

It was only after the collapse of the Soviet Union that, along with other Russian traditions, the *bania* culture was revived. Some bathhouses have been expensively renovated; the Sandunovskaya in Moscow has become fashionable. In the world of organized crime, it is said, tricky meetings are often held in a luxury *bania*, since one can be sure that the business partner is not armed there. In rural, historical Russia, the *bania* was a sphere where the sexes and generations mixed. In the Soviet Union, it became a damp and often greasy place to wash, with the sexes strictly separated. Though, as the 1988 film *Ch.P. Rayonnogo Mashstaba*[56] had it, the *banias* also hosted illegal orgies of alcohol and sex, not least for the party bosses or, as in the film, the leadership of the local Komsomol.

Arguably the ultimate experience of touch is sex. During a 1988 TV bridge, a live connection between two television audiences, one in the Soviet Union, the other in the United States, a Russian participant called the Soviet Union "a country without sex"[57]—or was it a country "with no love: only sex," as a teenager in the documentary *To Die for Love* says?[58] Public life was desexualized and, in Soviet cinema, sexual references were rare. Writing about sex in literature was an act of dissidence worse than celebrating drunkenness. The main purpose of sex in literature was to break a taboo.[59] Statements such as the one about the Soviet Union being "a country without sex" imply the conclusion that, in general, the Soviets experienced little pleasure in touching each other. Soviet sex was often quick and crude, primarily due to lack of privacy. If sex was all but banned from life, its representation was even more so. The censors reacted as sharply to erotic art and literature and pornographic magazines as they did to criticism of Communism, as if references to sexuality would have undermined the Soviet state. So-called men's magazines were smuggled into the country and secretly traded for substantial prices. With the easing of the repression, they began to appear at the newsstands; some copies were more than thirty years old.

Soviet psychology, entrusted with the creation of a New Soviet Man, was encouraged to find ways to reduce people's libidos, so as not

to waste citizens' energies on trivialities. The New Soviet Man's psyche
was to be molded; the Soviet science of *psykhotekhnika* was supposed to
enable him to believe in the incredible, to endure the unbearable and
to love things people normally hated, the Russian scholar Alexander
Etkind wrote.[60] "Interpersonal feelings were supposed to give way to
'collectivist' identifications."

To this day, many Russian men comply with the perverse Soviet ideals
and deny themselves any human needs or weaknesses. To them, whatever hurts is heroic; whatever depersonalizes is superior and serves the
collective, the party, and the eternal state—Soviet or Russian—thence,
humankind.

A friend who studied psychology at Moscow State University (MGU)
in the late 1960s recalls how he and his fellow students were aroused by
the few classes they had on venereal diseases. Another friend, an en-
docrinologist who in 1992 instructed physicians from the provinces in re-
fresher coursers, noted that many doctors, even females, lacked the basic
medical knowledge of sexuality. Igor Kon, the most eminent Soviet sex-
ologist, thinks that, by banning all erotic art, the bureaucracy opened the
way to vulgarity and abuse. Soviet "barracks eroticism" was much
cruder and more primitive than the most sordid foreign pornography,
Kon maintains.[61]

The opening up of the society brought about a radical change in the
society's attitude toward sexuality. In the spring of 1989, I visited a
semiofficial art exhibition in St. Petersburg; on display were female
nudes, innocent-looking young girls, realistically painted in oil. The
Soviet friends—sociologists and members of the democracy-minded
intelligentsia—who took me there were shocked. To my Western eyes,
the paintings seemed timid and boring.

As everywhere, eroticism is now used in advertisements. Within only
a few years, Russia and the other former Soviet republics have made
the transition from a society seemingly with no sex to an oversexed one.
Yet, sex is still crude, quick, and often cruel. There is obviously a lot of
promiscuity, as an explosive increase in sexually transmitted diseases
confirms. But strangely, the threat of an AIDS epidemic accelerated the
sexualization of the society. Since 1988, Russia has discussed AIDS,
though it was not taken seriously by the health-care system. However,
it served as a pretext for the publication of the first magazine that
openly dealt with sex. *Spid-Info* (AIDS info) featured information about
sex and published erotica, but contained little about AIDS.[62] Soon how-
to booklets appeared, providing the reader with basic sex education.
Openly pornographic publications printed in Russia followed. Bordello
and happy hooker stories now glorify the prostitute as a free-and-easy
businesswoman. They tell their readers what to do, how to do it, and

how often (and to do it more often), thus exerting a completely new kind of pressure. These days, classified personals for sex can be found everywhere. As mentioned earlier, some secretarial job openings even hint at the sexual services required.

Toward the end of the Soviet Union, the Communists eased their ban of homosexuality. In 1993, the Russian parliament decriminalized same-sex relations, though they are still openly despised by the society at large.

In the Soviet Union, abortion was the primary method of contraception. The Soviet Union had the highest abortion rate in the world; some women have had more than a dozen. In 1990 in the USSR, 98 abortions were performed per 1,000 women between fifteen and forty-nine, compared with 8.7 in the United States. Ignorance and a shortage of other contraceptives may have been the main reasons, but the general Soviet attitude toward the individual was responsible, too. It conveyed society's disrespect for a woman's body, and for the human body in general. The ever-increasing rates of rape and sexual assault only confirm this; the annual number of rapes has been estimated at 4 to 5 million a year, with only a fraction ever reported, and one-third of the police-registered rape cases involve children.[63] Post-Soviet sexuality is torn between freedom and rape, Sergey Menzheritsky wrote in *Literaturnaya Gazeta*. He characterizes Russians' sex lives as "rude, humiliating, hasty."[64]

The disrespect for the more vulnerable individuals, inherent to all Communist systems, and the increased commodification of life led to an almost complete disappearance of any protection of the weak. The daughter of my housekeeper in Moscow was gang raped in 1996; she knew the names of her aggressors but refused to report them to the police. They would not do anything anyway, she said, just harass her. And if the police acted against her expectations, her molesters would come back to take revenge, she feared.[65]

Thus, in post-Soviet Russia, the senses are subjected to new and very different sensations, pleasant ones and horrible experiences. Their range has grown; the Russians enjoy and suffer more diversity than ever. In the Soviet Union, people's everyday experiences were rough. They often felt as though they were being treated like cattle, herded around and deprived of basic necessities. Barely a decade later, people can experience refined and agreeable sights, sounds, scents, tastes, and textures.

In 1997, 6 million Russians have traveled abroad to see, smell, hear, taste, and touch other societies. At home, Russians and foreigners mix as never before; there are relationships and marriages between Westerners and Russians. Thus, many people immerse themselves in a world of different values and ethics and they do it very intimately. It is not necessarily a better world; but unlike the one they were used to, this one requires decisions and responsibility, and it offers choices and plurality.

Some people vote with their heart, others with their brains. However, having to chose between, on the one hand, a system that is incapable of providing coal miners with soap, women with adequate menstrual products, and anyone with toilet paper and, on the other hand, a disorganized state in which these items are abundant, people will not base their choice upon political arguments or sympathies.

The well-being of Russians, as advertised everywhere, has become important. This is a fundamental change that affects their everyday lives, their self-image, their dignity, and, thus their behavior, even if they cannot afford to benefit from these changes—yet.

NOTES

1. Yi-Fu Tuan, *Topophilia: A Study of Environmental Perceptions, Attitudes, and Values* (Englewood Cliffs, N.J.: Prentice-Hall, 1974), 6.

2. Jacques Lacan, *Ecrit* (Paris: Editions du Seuil, 1966).

3. S. Frederick Starr, *Red and Hot: The Fate of Jazz in the Soviet Union, 1917–1991, with a New Chapter on the Final Years* (New York: Limelight, 1994).

4. Dmitry Shostakovich, *Jazz Suites Nos. 1 and 2*, Royal Concertgebouw Orchestra of Amsterdam, Riccardo Chailly, London Decca 433702 CD, 1995.

5. Laurel E. Fay, *Shostakovich: A Life* (New York: Oxford University Press, 2000), 113.

6. Starr, *Red and Hot*, 241–243.

7. Hilary Pilkington, "The Future Is Ours: Youth Culture in Russia, 1953 to the Present," in *Russian Cultural Studies*, ed. Catriona Kelly and David Shepherd (New York: Oxford University Press, 1998).

8. Starr, *Red and Hot*, 324. The author, obviously biased in favor of jazz, differentiates between "rock 'n' roll," the medium of disagreement for the masses, and free jazz, an elitist, more cultured mode of expression. This distinction has little social and political relevance.

9. Starr, *Red and Hot*, 333.

10. Artemy Troitsky, *Back in the USSR: The True Story of Rock in Russia* (Boston: Faber and Faber, 1987), 40.

11. J. Frederick Bailyn, *Territory*, http://www.planetaquarium.com/eng/pub/doc_jfb1.html (accessed September 2000).

12. Ilya Smirnov, editor of *Urlait*, in an interview with author, "Rock unterm Hakenkreuz," for *Weltwoche*, June, 28, 1990, 9.

13. Troitsky, *Back in the USSR*, 125.

14. Troitsky, *Back in the USSR*, 137.

15. *Urlait*—the name itself—was an absurdist statement, combining the English word "light" and the German prefix "*ur*" or "prehistoric"; one possible reading of the term is "light of the big bang."

16. Sergey Sharikov, *Sidvig*, March 1990. On June 7, thanks to a copyright violation, a judge in Moscow's Bauman district recalled 3,500 unsold copies. The magazine's anti-Semitic insults were not even mentioned in the verdict.

17. Yuris Podnieks, *Legko li byto molodym?* (Is it easy to be young?) (Riga: Latfilma, 1986), film.
18. Ainars Mielavs, interview with the author, May 6, 1990, in Riga.
19. Arkady Sosnov, "Vykhodit is Akvariume," *Ogonyok*, no. 48 (1997).
20. "Zhisn nevasmozhno povernut nazad i vremia ni na mig ne ostanovit."
21. Fyodor Dostoevksy, *Dnevnik pisatelia za 1873* (Diary of a writer for 1873) (1883).
22. Tuan, *Topophilia*, 99.
23. Nadezhda Azhgikhina and Helen Goscilo, "Getting under the Skin," in *Russia, Women, Culture*, ed. Helena Goscilo and Beth Holmgren (Bloomington: Indiana University Press, 1996), 94–121.
24. Azhgikhina and Goscilo, "Getting under the Skin," 111.
25. Azhgikhina and Goscilo, "Getting under the Skin," 112.
26. Nadya L. Peterson, "Dirty Women," in *Russia, Women, Culture*, ed. Helena Goscilo and Beth Holmgren (Bloomington: Indiana University Press, 1996), 177–205. For her statement that cleanliness is characteristic of middleclass society, she quotes Georges Vigarello, *Concepts of Cleanliness: Changing Attitudes in France since the Middle Ages* (Cambridge: Cambridge University Press, 1988), 119.
27. Svetlana Boym, "The Poetics of Banality," in *Fruits of Her Plum: Essays on Contemporary Russian Women's Culture*, ed. Helena Goscilo (Armonk, N.Y.: Sharpe, 1993), 61.
28. Werner Sombart, *Liebe, Luxus und Kapitalismus: Über die Entstehung der modernen Welt aus dem Geist der Verschwendung* (1922; reprint ed., Berlin: Wagenbach, 1983).
29. Norbert Elias, *The Civilizing Process: The History of Manners and State Formation and Civilization*, trans. Edmund Jephcott (Cambridge, Mass.: Blackwell, 1994).
30. Mary Douglas, "The Genuine Article," in *The Socialness of Things: Essays on the Socio-Semiotics of Objects*, ed. Stephen Harald Riggins (New York: de Gruyter, 1994), 20–21.
31. Halina Rothstein and Robert A. Rothstein, "The Beginnings of Soviet Culinary Art," in *Food in Russian History and Culture*, ed. Musya Glants and Joyce Toomre (Bloomington: Indiana University Press, 1997), 177.
32. Rothstein and Rothstein, "Soviet Culinary Art," 192.
33. *Obshaya Gazeta*, no. 5, February 4, 1999, 6.
34. Andreas Schwander, a correspondent in St. Petersburg and my housemate there, in 1997, obtained these numbers from the Ministry of Agriculture.
35. Ronald D. Leblanc, "Tolstoy's Way of No Flesh," in *Food in Russian History and Culture*, ed. Musya Glants and Joyce Toomre (Bloomington: Indiana University Press, 1997), 93.
36. See James L. Watson, ed. *Golden Arches East* (Stanford, Calif.: Stanford University Press, 1997). Watson laments the burger company's triggering Westernization in Asia. He reads the fact that, although the entire family goes to McDonald's in Beijing, only a single child will eat a hamburger as an attempt to allow the child to devour American culture, because the family cannot afford burgers for every member. Chinese people dispute this forcefully as condescending: they counter that Chinese adults do not eat at McDonald's because they do not like the food and because they consider McDonald's fare as food for children.

37. "Konsultant, kotori snaet, shto i kak pit" (The adviser who knows what to drink and how), *Kapital*, July 8, 1998. For another example, see "French Chef Opens Moscow's Newest Wine Bar," *Moscow Times*, May 29, 1997.

38. L. B. Ivanchenko, *Kartofel i Griby, 1000 Kulinarnikh Retseptov*, vol. 1 of *Entsyklopedia Domashnego Khosiastvo* (Moscow: Pisatel, 1993), and *The Domostroi: Rules for Russian Households in the Time of Ivan the Terrible*, ed. and trans. Carolyn Johnston Pouncy (Ithaca, N.Y.: Cornell University Press, 1964).

39. Elias, *Civilizing Process*, 424–436.

40. Tuan, *Topophilia*, 8.

41. Nina Tumarkin, *Lenin Lives: The Lenin Cult in Soviet Russia* (Cambridge, Mass.: Harvard University Press, 1997).

42. See also Ludmila Maksimova, "The Women's Apparel Market in Russia" (Moscow: American Embassy, July 1994). The majority of Russian women (up to 70 percent, according to some opinion polls) prefer to buy foreign-made goods. However, there are big differences in preferences, depending on the age and geographical location of the consumer. For example, elderly people, especially in provincial Russian cities and towns like Saratov, Samara, Volgograd, Kazan, Ulyanovsk, and Perm, generally prefer domestic products. The rural population maintains a strong loyalty to domestic goods. Generally, many Russians want simple and reliable products made of pure cotton or wool and silk. But this does not automatically preclude Western products. German products are highly regarded, their acquaintance having been made during and after World War II. Scandinavian products benefit, too, from this general admiration of northern European reliability. American apparel is in big demand because it is considered in general to be reliable, convenient, and practical.

43. GUM online, http://www.ukloansuk.co.uk/gum/body.htm (accessed December 2000). In full, the text reads: "Tempting Tatyana wears a slinky bra in lightweight canvas, with wide straps to avoid marks on those sexy shoulders of hers. Tatyana is only 18 but her ample charms and uncommon linguistic abilities have already secured her a high-powered job as personal assistant to the production director of Workers Tractor Plant No. 47 Omsk District."

44. Penny Morvant, "Far Eastern Factory Workers Paid in Bras," *RFE/RL Daily Report*, January 21, 1997. "Workers at a factory producing women's apparel in Vladivostok have been receiving bras in lieu of their wages, *Izvestiya* reported on 21 January. Short on cash, the factory has handed out seven to nine bras a month to both male and female employees. Owing to the problem of inter-enterprise debt and delays in the payment of state subsidies, workers at many enterprises receive wages in kind."

45. Daniel Rancour-Laferriere, *The Slave Soul of Russia: Moral Masochism and the Cult of Suffering* (New York: New York University Press, 1995), 205. The author is quoting Miller Wright, *Russians as People* (New York, 1961).

46. I was puzzled one Sunday morning on the subway, the "T," in Boston; something was different and reminded me of Russia. But what? It was a group of elderly people, each with three or four bags; some were in those old Soviet colors. When they got off, I heard them speaking Russian.

47. The Yak-40 and the Yak-42 at the back of the plane, the Il-86 on its lower deck.

48. Aeroflot was not a monolithic company, but a brand name encompassing many different local air transport administrations.

49. Rancour-Laferriere, *Slave Soul*, 182.

50. Nancy Condee, "The Second Fantasy Mother, or All Baths Are Women's Baths," in *Russia, Women, Culture*, ed. Helena Goscilo and Beth Holmgren (Bloomington: Indiana University Press, 1996), 3.

51. Condee, "Second Fantasy Mother," 3–11. The author stresses the differences between the male and female *bania* and a *bania*'s reflection of the communal apartment, where everyone washes "unobserved" for all to see.

52. Rancour-Laferriere, *Slave Soul*, 184.

53. Vladimir I. Dal, *Poslovitsy russkago naroda, sbornik* (Proverbs of the Russian people: a collection) (St. Petersburg: Wolf, 1855), as quoted by Rancour-Laferriere, *Slave Soul*, 182–184.

54. Rancour-Laferriere, *Slave Soul*, 195.

55. Rancour-Laferriere, *Slave Soul*, 199.

56. Sergei Snezhkin, *Ch.P. Rayonnogo Mashstaba* (Leningrad: Lenfilm, 1988), film.

57. Most notably during one of the TV bridges, "we have no sex" was a woman's reply when host Vladimir Pozner asked the audience to compare the availability of sexually explicit material in the United States and the USSR.

58. Tofik Shakhverdiev, *Umeryet ot Liubvi* (To die for love) (Moscow, 1990), documentary film.

59. Gassan Gussejnow, "Facetten neuer Identität in der Mitte des Jahrzehnts: ein Literaturbericht," in *Das neue Russland in Politik und Kultur: Forschungsstelle Osteuropa* (Bremen, Germany: Temmen, 1998), 123.

60. Alexander Etkind, "Psychological Culture," in *Russian Culture at the Crossroads: Paradoxes of Postcommunist Consciousness*, ed. Dmitri Shalin (Boulder, Colo.: Westview, 1996), 109.

61. Igor Kon, *Sex and Russian Society* (Bloomington: Indiana University Press, 1993), 26.

62. SPID is the Russian acronym for AIDS. The magazine has been published monthly in Moscow since 1990.

63. Sergey Menzheritsky, "Nyelyubov," in *Literaturnaya Gazeta*, no. 44 (October 29, 1997). The author writes that, in 1996, the Russian Interior Ministry registered fourteen thousand cases of rape. Estimates put the figure three hundred times higher, at approximating 4 to 5 million, with 34 percent of the registered cases involving children between two and fifteen years.

64. "Grubo, unizitelno, naspekh."

65. This is by no means a singular incident. Other people knew similar stories. Menzheritsky, in "Nyelyubov" mentions a police reaction much like that feared by my housekeeper's daughter.

6

+

Space: The Sixth Sense

The Soviet Union felt narrow and crowded. Wide areas of the vast country were off limits and people's movements were severely restricted. Wherever one went—sooner rather than later—one bumped into a wall, a fence, or some other barrier, or was stopped by guards. Access to almost any building required a *propusk*, a special permit.

The country's external border was sealed for almost all of its citizens, as were wide areas inside the country. Most provincial towns were closed to foreigners. For some areas, even Soviet visitors needed a *propusk*. Secret cities existed that did not appear on any map. Domestic travel was regulated, if not restricted; the police guarded the cities' entry points and the main intersections. Officers stopped cars and checked the drivers' personal documents and the contents of the trunks. The people living on *sovkhozes* and *kolkhozes*, the state and collective farms, did not keep their own internal passports, the most essential items for them to move around the country. The passports were deposited in the director's office. To resettle, especially in one of the big cities, one had to get a *propisk*, a residence permit. For Moscow, such a paper was unattainable for anyone who did not have influential contacts. Young people from the provinces could apply for a time-limited residency if they had a job. Streetcar drivers in Moscow typically worked in the capital as *limitchki*, holders of this type of residency. The authorities could rescind their permits at any time and for no reason. Thus, even within the Soviet Union, there was no freedom of movement. Most people were confined to a very limited space.

The chronic shortages were another reason why the Soviet Union felt narrow. Wherever scarce goods were available, the place was packed and people pushed and shoved. Despite their being declared priorities, transport and housing capacity were never adequate. No Soviet city managed to supply its public transportation system with enough vehicles. In 1990, more than one-third of the Soviet population had less than nine square meters of living space, the minimum required by Soviet law.

Boundaries, fences, and other landmarks structure the land over time and become parts of the landscape. In England, hedges have separated the properties for centuries. Elsewhere, partitions are formed by the piling of stones cleared from the field. These demarcations have molded the landscape. In the Soviet Union, hardly any such structures existed. On the *kolkhoz,* nobody cleared the fields of stones. Imperial Russia, with her endless forests and steppes, was a vast empire with very few delimited borders, either inside the country or along its frontiers. Only recently, some freshly erected stone walls have partitioned the fields of privatized farms. The lack of clearly marked borders granted Russia some spatial elasticity, both for offensive and defensive purposes. An accidental border violation did not necessarily trigger a hysterical reaction by the czarist government. The capital was at the fringe, in the swamplands shared with the Karelians, the Inkis, and the Finns. (When St. Petersburg was founded in 1703, the city was located on enemy territory, claimed by the then Nordic superpower Sweden.) The rich and powerful of the Russian empire avoided living inside the country that they called their own. Among themselves, they did not even use the Russian language. As elsewhere in Europe, the aristocracy fenced themselves off from the people, not literally, but by speaking French, as we have learned from Yuri Lotman.[1]

For economic reasons (to expand the fur industry) and allegedly for strategic purposes or—perhaps out of fear—to serve the emerging nationalism, the czar and later the Communists expanded their territory over eleven time zones. The Soviets colonized the mostly uninhabitable north with people who were unfit for a life in the Arctic. They rewrote history and remapped their country. They created an ethnic and political mosaic with units that had not distinguished themselves from their neighbors before. But their creation was chiefly cosmetic and they helped to further divide the country.[2]

Imperial Russia was weakened by its expansion. Since the empire could not uphold its spatial extension peacefully, it paid dearly for its megalomania, with the defeat against Japan in 1905 and its collapse during World War I. Similarly, the Soviet Union bankrupted itself with the permanent battle to maintain its hegemony, namely in Afghanistan. In 1991, the cost of keeping the Soviet Union together clearly surpassed the Kremlin's means.

Today, paradoxically, Russia's size—the increase of which was of prime concern to the country's leaders and a goal for several centuries—is used as an excuse for Russia's inability to reform its economy more quickly.

Russians often boast of their country's size and wealth in resources, only to lament that its size is a burden.

Contrary to the Russian empire, the Soviet Union lacked any spatial flexibility. It sealed its boundaries and the border troops reacted hysterically to any assumed violation of the state frontier—in addition, the Soviet military reacted similarly to violations of its sphere of influence beyond the state border, such as in East Berlin in 1953, Hungary in 1956, and Czechoslovakia in 1968. The Soviet Union imposed its politicoeconomic system on its so-called satellite states, including a supranational division of labor, and it guarded their borders. This might have been meant to strengthen the Soviet state, but it can be read as a sign of weakness. Inside the USSR, the regions and republics were administratively isolated from one another. People in neighboring provinces or republics knew little of each other and the traffic between the regions was light. Their attention was focused on Moscow, the center. While Aeroflot operated several flights a day between Moscow and the republics' capitals, such as Tbilisi, Baku, Kiev, Tallinn, and Vilnius, service between those cities was sparse—two or three times a week—and by small plane.

Soviet space was fragmented. This was the only safe way to control the "containers of social power," as Foucault has termed it. The authorities explained the fragmentation as being part of their drive to modernization; they created separate spaces for different activities or particular social projects. They maintained that fragmentation was necessary to minimize interference in their reengineering of society—a task they performed much in the same manner in which those who breed cattle perform theirs. Even the quest for hygiene, that grand project of modernization, has been used to justify such separations.[3]

The spatial composition of the living environment affects people's manners. The Soviet power crammed people into certain spaces, narrow communal apartments, tiny *Khrushchevka* flats, villages, and cities. The gulag and the packed trains going there were the most dramatic example of a pattern. Ironically, the people who were packed together in public transport and constantly treated as "the masses" were prohibited to assemble freely in public places.

Soviets citizens had no access to open, yet structured space. The hobby mountaineers may have been an exception. This might in part explain the popularity of mountain climbing among the Soviet intelligentsia. Mostly, Soviet people were confined to restricted areas. What was beyond was off limits to almost everyone and fenced off and secured by guards. Nobody knew what was behind the walls. Therefore, to most people the biggest part of the country seemed to be a huge void—undistinguished, far away, and inaccessible. They knew little more than the place where they lived, the way to their *dacha* by car or commuter rail, and possibly, the way to a resort on the Black Sea or the Baltics, where they would go for their vacations. Many Muscovites were not even familiar with their own city and did not care to be. They just knew their daily itinerary, which was unvarying.

Delimitations of space also constitute signposts, both in reality and on people's cognitive maps.[4] Assigned meaning, memory, or a purpose turn space into a place, as Edward Hall emphasized. His book, *The Silent Language,* helped me to see the changes in the Russians' attitudes toward space.[5] In the absence of landmarks, there is little that is distinctive on cognitive maps. One is more likely to lose one's way in the desert than in a city. The Soviet cities were stripped of landmarks. Initially, to me, they looked the same everywhere. Huge areas, such as squares and boulevards, after being cleared of everyday life and, thus, of the cities' urban quality, were reduced to serving as traffic arteries.

One way to learn about the locals' cognitive maps is to regularly ask for directions. In Soviet cities, such questions were either met with ignorance or long, complicated explanations. In the beginning, the responses were unintelligible to me. For example, once, while being given directions, I was told to turn left at the red light, which was actually the second red light because the first was not really a red light, so it did not count as one. Then I was to pass a fish store called Ocean. (I never saw any fish store; it was somewhere off the street, hard to identify as a store, as I later found out.) I was then supposed to take the second doorway to the right, no . . . to the left when coming from the street, but not the little side entrance, that one did not count . . . and so on. People did not seem used to giving directions, at least not in a way that Westerners would easily understand. Often, I could not find the signs they considered to be landmarks, such as the fish store. And I could not see the difference between a red light that counted and one that did not. Some Russians made it even more complicated by explaining the obvious or telling stories I could not relate to my request for directions. And they did not comprehend what it was I could not grasp. Of course, it was difficult to tell if the failure was mine in not understanding them or if theirs were weakly developed cognitive maps. When asked for directions myself, I understood how few landmarks a Soviet city had. As a Westerner who was used to much more obvious street signs, I was prone to overlooking what the Muscovites considered to be remarkable: a fish store on a street with hardly any shops or a street corner with a peculiar shape. No other landmarks could be used as a reference. For people who drove a car, things were even more complicated because it could be impossible to take a left turn for miles.

Soviet addresses, it seems, were not meant for people who were not familiar with the locale. A street number applied to several houses, the *corpuses.* These *corpuses* bore subnumbers and each had several numbered entrances, accessible only with a number code. Finally, since there were no name plates in the hallway, one had to remember the floor and the apartment number. Thus, hundreds of people live at the same address, for example, Prospect Vernadskogo 95. Different *corpuses* under a single address can be far from each other. I would easily find *corpuses* 1, 2, and 4, but *corpus* 3 was nowhere to be seen. Not that the Soviet authorities had done this purposefully to confuse the visitor, but it forced a stranger—Russian or foreign—to act conspicuous by asking for directions. Perhaps it had not occurred to anyone that addresses are not only for postal delivery.

The way a society structures its space, it is said, reflects the architecture of that society. Western Europe's cities grew slowly, shaped by the needs of their urban economies and a relatively open society.[6] However, Manuel Castells maintained that space is not "a reflection of society but one of society's fundamental material dimensions." Matter and consciousness are interrelated, he argued.[7] St. Petersburg was drafted on the drawing boards of eighteenth- and nineteenth-century city planners; Moscow was remolded by Stalin's architects. During the nineteenth century, hundreds of thousands of poor migrants flocked into the cities. Thus, these cities must have shaped the people.

Soviet cities were not patterned into affluent and less affluent quarters (with the exception of the party bosses who spatially isolated themselves from the rest of the nation and who also had their own *dacha* villages), nor was there a clear distinction between residential and industrial districts. There were no blue-collar quarters, nor were there areas for the rich—officially, there were no "rich people," anyway. To this day, large factories are located in downtown Moscow. During the Soviet period, new residential areas were developed at the fringes of the city, often for years detached from the public transportation system. In a developed city, since the introduction of streetcars, subways, buses, and private cars, the planners could disconnect workplaces from the homes; the Soviet cities, however, failed to fulfill the requirements of a modern city.

Soviet state companies—conglomerates that included everything from the engineering offices and assembly lines to a construction branch, special stores, kindergartens, polyclinics, and leisure facilities, for example, a movie theater—often had their own residential housing. People of different backgrounds who worked for the same (state) company—engineers, workers, kindergarten teachers, janitors, and dishwashers—lived in the same building; pilots lived next to other pilots, flight attendants, and ground staff, and artists lived in houses that belonged to their union.

Professional unions, such as the writers' union or the composers' union, were specific to the Soviet system. Membership was compulsory in order for a writer to publish, a painter to exhibit, or an actor to perform. In many ways, these unions acted as employers. They, too, owned apartment buildings. Thus, some houses accommodated mostly musicians, academics, or writers. In the appearance of the city, this segregation was not visible. However, the *dacha* villages, some with up to fifteen thousand plots, repeated it. Just as with housing, these private plots of land were provided by the employers. Railway workers had their *dachas* next to other railway workers, writers lived next door to other writers, and workers at an automobile factory shared their *dacha* neighborhoods with other employees of their factory. The privileged enterprises, typically the plants belonging to the military-industrial complex, were in the *dacha* areas with better soil, that were closer to the cities, and that had the best traffic connections.

Most buildings served only one purpose—residential, administrative, or manufacturing. Even the functions of the buildings had to be segregated, although premises for different purposes would adjoin each other. To this day in Russian cities, some factories are situated in residential quarters and in city centers.

Physically, the segregation or pulverization of space was accomplished with fences, walls, barriers, stop signs, and guards, or simply by insurmountable distances. "Secret" cities were surrounded by forests. The inmates of the Arctic gulag coal-mining town of Vorkuta knew they would never be able to make it through five hundred miles of taiga to the next settlement and that the few people who lived closer to the gulag would inform on them. Thus, there was no need to install barbed wire around the Vorkuta camps.

The difficulty in crossing borders and barriers rendered the place of residency both fateful and permanent. The hometown determined access to jobs, leisure facilities, and consumption; for most people, it was beyond their dreams to move to a more desirable place. The Soviet regime observed a strict hierarchy of places: *sovkhoz, kolkhoz,* village, small town, regional center, republic capital, St. Petersburg, Moscow.[8]

Barriers were everywhere and they all looked the same; the society was spatially atomized. When traveling to Samarkand, the poet Joseph Brodsky encountered the standard Soviet fence of the type he had seen every day in the yard of the Arsenal factory in Leningrad, where he once worked. That turned the Central Asian city into Soviet home territory for him; its orientalism vanished.[9] Even more ubiquitous than the fence was the standard concrete wall, normally seven feet high.

The atomization of space deprived the Soviet people of geography. Despite their broad knowledge of the names of cities and countries, the people lacked spatial imagination. They were not used to putting the geographical information they had into a spatial context and they had trouble with the concept of overlapping spaces. Distance did not seem to matter, and neither did proximity. "Abroad," even if it meant being just across the border, was truly abroad, since the borders were sealed. Traveling inside the Soviet Union, however, felt like staying in the home region. I had friends, owners of a joint venture, who in the last years before the collapse of the Soviet Union traveled to Kamchatka for a few days of skiing, but they could not go to neighboring Finland, only a couple of hours drive from where they lived in St. Petersburg. They did not understand when Aeroflot began to increase the ticket prices to Kamchatka. "But this is a domestic route," they argued.

Geographical curiosity was rarely rewarded. Few people traveled on their own, except to visit relatives. The backpacking youth, the children of the intelligentsia, were a small minority. The traveler, such as the geologist exploring the outposts of Siberia played by Vladimir Vysotsky in the film *Brief Encounters*, became an icon of rare freedom, but was also a social outcast.[10] The price the traveler paid for an iota of independence was spatial detachment from society.

Compared with people of other societies, the Soviets' cognitive maps representing their everyday world seemed simple. The space of activity that the individual enjoyed was restricted. "Adultery and movie going are the only forms of free enterprise. Plus Art," Brodsky famously said of the Soviet Union.[11] People did not have much freedom over what to do or where to go. They were presented with a limited number of options. The authorities decided on their behalf, but a few areas for consumer and leisure activities existed. People did not eat out, except for special occasions. Few sports facilities were open to the general public and there were no coffee shops, bars, shopping malls, or pedestrian districts. It was hard to obtain tickets for the opera and the theater and, for an average citizen, these tickets were expensive. Even the number of movie theaters, despite their alleged value for propaganda, was relatively low.[12] Masha Lipman called the Soviet Union a "consumer society without consumer goods."[13] Thus, people had little to do and to consume and nowhere to go. Their trips around the city were few, long, complicated, monotonous, and had high degrees of repetition. On the way to and from work, many had to take the children to day care or school and to go shopping. Once at home, one rarely ventured out again in the evening.

Many Soviets' cognitive maps of imaginary environments, such as literature, may have been superior in complexity. Many Russians lived in an imaginary world. They were dreamers: if only they could, they often said, they would. Even now, after the collapse of the system that deprived them of their access to an uncensored reality, some of the learned, the intelligentsia, continue to live in virtual spaces—in the eternal Russian culture, as they tend to call it.

In the Soviet Union, the term "geography" implied some unreality. Overseas geography was knowledge of the world beyond. Its names stood for daydreams: Paris, Rome, New York. No realistic Soviet citizen would have expected to ever see those places, but this did not make these cities less distinct. Their names were filled with anecdotal facts—some cultural, some mystical—about luxury, frenzied nightlife, exotic food, or the size of the cockroaches. A young Muscovite once spoke in awe of the New York cockroaches as being bigger than any other cockroach; hence, even America's pets were superior, she half-seriously joked. Other anecdotal geographical facts were related to the world of sports. Many Soviet men would list European soccer teams, complete with rankings and the names of the players. Anywhere in the Soviet Union, such as Tajikistan or Sakhalin, I met fans of Italian soccer clubs who might have AC Milan's pennants hanging from the rearview mirrors in their cars. Other people could name a country's "national" writers; many knew geographical crossword puzzle facts, such as the names of capitals, cities, rivers, lakes, and mountains and the numbers of inhabitants. If geography is the science of labeling the world, the Soviets were good geographers. But theirs was a virtual world, a list of names with no spatial architecture.

The Soviet republics displayed little local color and Russia's regions displayed even less. There were hardly any contemporary local particularities—neither regional architectures nor regional cuisines. The Soviet buildings looked the same everywhere and so did the monuments, although a few different casts of Lenin were acceptable. Despite the dramatically different climate, residential areas in Vladivostok, Tashkent, or the far north looked like a Moscow suburb. Only with the opening up of the borders did the stores begin to acquire local color. In border areas, the stores began to mirror the neighboring countries; in the south, the range of goods finally began to reflect the wealth of the regions. In the Far East, used Japanese cars began to dominate the streets, with many small trucks and buses still showing Japanese characters or the logo of the previous owner's business. In western Russia, some cities acquired used German, Norwegian, and Swedish buses, still advertising in German for Sparkasse (a German savings bank) or for a local Scandinavian bank.

As mentioned above, many people's cognitive maps tended to be simple, full of blank spots. The same was true for the country; it had hardly any actual maps and the few that were available were oversimplified and flawed. Soviet school atlases and road maps were sketchy and, naturally, they omitted the secret cities. The lack of maps was a paradox: both imperial Russia and the Soviet army possessed good maps and the czar's military maintained a well developed mapmaking industry. As with many other politically sensitive items, some pseudomaps could be found. But the rare town plans for tourists were intentionally inaccurate. Atlas, a little Moscow map store previously called Slavyanka, has existed for a long time.[14] There, one could find a map, not detailed and probably not the specific map one was looking for, but at least a map. If I passed by the map store often enough and bought whatever was available, I could eventually assemble a substantial collection covering most of the Soviet territory. The map store was always crowded with men who indulged in virtual wanderlust. Today, it sells tourist maps, travel guides, and phrase books for trips all over the world.

Address lists, guide books, and phone directories constitute the abstract part of a map; they are essential for the mapping of a city. But neither address lists nor phone directories existed in the Soviet Union, although they did exist before 1917.[15] For a city map to be readable, buildings have to convey their purposes, either through signs, the facades, or at least their addresses, as listed in the directory. In the Soviet Union, most premises did not indicate their purpose; some stores were difficult to detect from the outside. Yellow pages only emerged after the introduction of private businesses, while a decade after the end of Communism, private phone numbers remained unlisted.[16] To find a person, one had to call or visit a special office, the Mosgorspravka,[17] in Moscow or the corresponding office elsewhere. But this agency was perhaps more interested in knowing who was looking for whom than in providing people with the requested information.

In prerevolutionary St. Petersburg, a city well-equipped with phones, the yellow pages included the seating plans of the theaters and concert halls and a complete plan of the markets, with the name of each stall owner. For the year 2000, Moscow's yellow pages reintroduced this unique service; it includes maps of the airports and railway stations. Thus Russia is becoming a carefully mapped space again and the maps are available to its citizens. Today, the Atlas store has a full set of maps in stock covering the whole of Russia—detailed, well-printed maps—even of the most remote parts of the country, such as Magadan, Chukotka, or the Kuril Islands. In addition, it sells specialized maps, road atlases, reprints of historical maps, the town plans of many Russian cities, satellite photos of the Moscow area and the Caucasus Mountains, and specialty maps, such as meteorological and ecological ones. Russia has begun to map herself. This includes some curious maps, such as one dividing Moscow according to the prices of a prostitute's services and one displaying the different criminal gangs' zones of influence in the capital.[18]

The Soviet state denied spatiality to its citizens; geography did not go beyond high-school knowledge of naming places. Worse, however, in its economical decisions the Soviet government often ignored geography.

Many factories' sites were determined by political considerations, out of sheer nepotism, favoritism, or cronyism, or haphazardly. After World War II, huge industrial complexes were built in the formerly independent Baltic states, in places where neither the required resources nor an adequate workforce was available. These complexes had to be supplied at huge cost. The plants' main purpose was not to produce goods, but to change the ethnic balance and thus help to wedge these countries into the Soviet structure. Hundreds of thousands of Slavic workers were compelled to move to the areas, causing ethnic tensions; these workers' close ties to Moscow subverted the Baltic republics' determination in opposing Soviet rule. The mobility of the workers does not contradict my assessment that the USSR was highly partitioned and that its internal borders were hard to overcome. The migrant workers did not settle and they rarely mixed with the locals. The regime used them like an army, temporarily dispatching them to areas where they were "needed." In addition, the people in the Baltic states, Ukraine, and the Caucasus alleged that Moscow would move a potentially hazardous industry to the fringes, that is, to the non-Russian republics. Obviously, politics prevailed over any economic rationale, including geography.[19]

Soviet politicians' decisions ignored obvious realities. When, in 1959, Khrushchev ordered corn to be grown in Kazakhstan, he ignored climatic considerations. Impressed by the production of the corn farms in the United States, he initiated the "Virgin Lands campaign," under which corn was planted unsuccessfully on newly arable lands, with devastating losses of crops.

The bleakest examples of disregard of geography were the plans to redirect the Siberian rivers and the construction of useless canals, such as the Belomor Canal. The river project ignored the potential costs and ecological damage and lacked any economic rationale; the channel was exclusively constructed by prisoners, with the purpose being to reeducate and punish the prisoners who built it.[20]

The Soviets' disregard for geography—or nature and climate—was especially obvious in Moscow's quest for the north. The Siberian Arctic was conquered for its resources and to demonstrate that Communism could defy nature. This endeavor left stranded on the fringes of the Arctic nine million people—freed gulag prisoners and people lured there with high salaries, long holidays, almost free flights to the Black Sea, the chance to visit relatives, and the promise of early retirement. Going north was the only way of legally earning more money. Also, being unable to travel abroad, many Soviets romanticized the north as the mysterious unknown, a kind of abroad inside the country. Ironically, the word *sever* (north), refers to anything cold and far away, even parts of Siberia and the Far East, which lie south of Moscow's parallel. Thus, a cardinal compass point became a climatic condition. Accordingly, the south was not primarily a cardinal point, but the home of unruly non-Russians.

Going to the *sever* was a way of escaping one's previous life. To this day, one finds migrant Russians, Ukrainians, and Estonians in such remote places as Vorkuta, Chukotka, or the Kuril Islands. They praise their lives as hard but rewarding and the relations with their fellow "northerners" as much better than *na materiki* (on the motherland), as the Russian homeland is referred to, as though the north consisted of overseas island colonies. However, if the conversation continues, one hears heartbreaking stories of lost loves, children who died, broken promises, and other sufferings.

Post-Communist Russia does not have the will or the resources to follow through on the Communists' promises. That has turned the pioneers in the north into prisoners (again); they are trapped. For example, many mines have shut down, salaries have not been paid for months, even years, and the airlines have significantly increased the fares and reduced the number of flights, from once a day to once a week, for example. Suddenly, geography matters.

As shown previously, the city of Magnitogorsk on the Ural River, the border between Europe and Asia, was another Communist project realized against the odds of geography. The model steel mill was constructed fifteen hundred miles from the coal it needed for its furnaces, and almost the same distance from the factories that were to use its steel. But the costs of transportation did not matter. Officially, transportation did not cost much. In any case, the companies had no incentive to be profitable. Although this was a site where iron ore had been found, its stock was soon to be exhausted. But time has improved the steel mill's geographical location as western Siberia has industrialized. "Magnitka," as the locals call the steel plant, has replaced its coal furnaces with foundries running on electricity. Most importantly, situated in Russia, with its low wages, Magnitka can now competitively sell in the world marketplace. Thus geography rescued an endeavor that had been built against geography.

The Soviet Union was the caricature of a Fordist society, mass producing goods, primarily for the military, although it also produced some consumer goods that did not necessarily find niches. The Soviet industry did not produce what was demanded, but what the central planning authority ordered. Most production sites were arbitrarily located and badly placed, which complicated distribution. Thus even many sought-after goods did not reach consumers. In fact many items, such as spark plugs, were produced by a single manufacturer for the whole country, further jeopardizing the allocation of goods.

Not only the external borders were sealed. By erecting internal fences and barriers, the Communists made the vast country feel narrow. Stalin ripped out many of the society's layers, leveling the social differentiations. By homogenizing the society, he made the country appear smaller. Nevertheless, he also enlarged the Soviet Union to the north, onto the steppes, and underground. He added a secret interior empire to the Soviet state, the gulag, with its capital at Magadan, a newly founded anticenter at the fringe of the empire—a negative St. Petersburg.[21] The subway systems, with their depictions of utopian Communist lives—first in Moscow and later in other cities—extended the cities into the underground. With its exaggeratedly clear signs—directing the passengers where to walk and keeping the masses moving—its reliability, its route maps, and its frescoes of Soviet heroes and the happy collective life, the Moscow subway represents a shining future, the Communist dream come true. Indeed, the subway systems—reliable, fast, efficient, and with a high capacity (a train every forty-five seconds during peak hours in Moscow)—are among the few huge Communist projects that succeeded. The subway reversed the burdensome reality above ground, but this happy life existed only in the underground, in images far from reality, showing a virtual paradise lit only by artificial light.

The Soviet regime did not just erect fences and close off parts of cities; it created new single-purpose cities as ghettos, for scientific, military, production-related, and punishment purposes. Akademgorodok was built as the Siberian capital for science and research; Obninsk, near Moscow, was turned into a special town for the development of nuclear technology for arms, power generation, and medicine. Many Soviet cities were run like (state) companies, as were the gulag cities.

Subconsciously, with the sense of spatiality, one constantly assesses one's environment. One experiences the spatiality of an apartment, a building, a city square, or a street and, as with the other senses, one extrapolates and generalizes. Thus the perception of a city such as St. Petersburg changes, depending on where one stands—in a muddy backyard behind Sennaya Ploshad, on the vast Palace Square in the wind, or at the winter palace, glancing through a window overlooking Neva River. Both imperial Russia and the Soviet state created urban environments that were meant to impress the individual. Wide streets and enormous squares made the passersby feel small and powerless—no taller than a matchstick, as the Austrian writer Joseph Roth noted.[22] Streets like Tverskaya in Moscow (reconstructed under Stalin) or Nevsky Prospect in St. Petersburg (constructed in the eighteenth and nineteenth centuries) were built to show off and to present the capital of a great power to its visitors as well as to the inhabitants. Accordingly, it was prohibited to stop a car on Gorky Street, as Tverskaya was called during the Soviet period. There were very few aboveground pedestrian crossings; people had to use underpasses. Flowing traffic implies power and order; cars slowing down or idling imply the opposite. Not surprisingly, then, the use of bicycles and motorcycles was, though not strictly prohibited, clearly discouraged.

"Previously," Foucault said, "architecture was concerned only with the necessity to make visible power, dignity, and might," but since the end of the eighteenth century it has addressed questions of population, health, and residential construction.[23] Indeed, at least in theory, the new Soviet suburbs were an attempt to mechanize and sanitize housing, as were similar green cities in other countries. In the city centers, however, the Soviet authorities opted for the display of power. The facades looking onto Tverskaya are built of granite, the rest of the houses of shabby brick. "First we shape our buildings and then they shape us," Winston Churchill observed.[24] For imperial Russia, as well as Soviet Russia, more than for other cultures, one is tempted to say that the regime built phony facades that in turn shaped the society. On Nevsky Prospect in St. Petersburg, walking through the gates of many of the impressive palaces, one enters a different world, a small-town Russia, the opposite of the world the facades seem to represent. Yet the address is still Nevsky Prospect. Even the courtyard of the general staff building between Nevsky Prospect and Palace Square seems provincial and remote.

Stalin's pet construction project, the Palace of the Soviets and its statue of Lenin on top—the building with which, above all others, Stalin hoped to impress the world—was never realized. It was projected for twenty years to replace the Christ-the-Savior cathedral in central Moscow, west of the Kremlin. The church was demolished in 1931, but construction of the palace never got underway. After Stalin's death, the time for grand projects was gone, as if the Communists did not believe in their own grand statements anymore. Khrushchev finally transferred the project to the Kremlin; his modest Palace of the Soviets is hardly visible from the outside. On the site of the demolished nineteenth-century cathedral, which had been the tallest of its kind, a swimming pool was eventually built, a negative monument, or a "minus cathedral," as Mikhail Yampolsky called it.[25] In 1995, the pool gave way for the reconstruction of the cathedral.

Ironically, the last Soviets to extend the spatial scope of the Soviet Union (if in an imaginary way) were the conceptualists, a group of artists that emerged in the 1980s. They claimed to take seriously the Soviet aesthetics, such as the depiction of a bright future under Communism as the savior of humankind, but parodied its icons. Igor Stepin and Igor Martynchik extended the bright Soviet world into their imagined empire of the Kho. This new world was populated by weird animals, strange plants, and six different ethnicities: the Kho themselves, the dominating nation, plus the Shombo, the Bunaba, the Ashtuasafta, the Kugue, and the Ulla. Each nation had its own history and original territory; under the leadership of the Kho, they lived peacefully together, each on its assigned territory. The artists modeled their Kho country in plasticine, accompanied by detailed ethnographic descriptions, mocking the Soviet encyclopedia.[26] For works of art like this, the conceptualists, during the short tenures of Andropov and Chernenko, were constantly harassed and threatened by the KGB.[27]

Cultures develop specific proximity patterns. Even between closely related societies, such as the German, French, and American societies, these patterns differ greatly, as Edward Hall in his comparative studies has convincingly shown.[28] Different cultures perceive a person poking his or her head in a door differently, Hall wrote. In an American office, the person is considered to still be outside the office; thus he or she is not intruding. In Germany, however, the person has already entered the office and the sphere of the office occupant. Different societies organize their space differently: Europeans and Americans name streets and number houses; the Japanese name intersections, but not the streets, and number quarters. Japanese addresses do not in any way facilitate the finding of a place. Westerners organize their rooms along the walls, while Japanese do so from the center, with sliding doors indicating the separation of space. When staying in a "Japanese-style" hotel, many Westerners miss their privacy. The Japanese vocabulary does not even include a word for privacy.[29]

Most Soviets did not have a sense for a Westerner's territorial needs. In restaurants—even in the hotel restaurants, which basically catered to foreigners—complete strangers were often seated together at a table, not because no other table was available, but to spare the waiters some effort. In the provinces, Soviet hotels would put strangers in one room, despite having vacancies. In my experience, no Russians seemed to object; some seemed to even enjoy my company. But as a Westerner, I perceived this practice as an intrusion into my private sphere.

In Estonia, through the years of Soviet occupation, almost all Estonians were anxious to distinguish themselves from the local Russians. They were Europeans, they claimed, stressing that wherever there was a line they could detect a Russian from an Estonian. The former stood much closer to the person in front of him or her, even touching that person, disregarding an (Estonian) person's need for space.

Spatial behavior begins at home. In Western houses, before the advent of the bourgeoisie, the notion of privacy among family members did not exist. There were no specialized spaces or spaces prohibited to some—such as children or visitors—no parents' bedroom and no children's room. A home was open to strangers; there were no private rooms or private times, such as eating hours, during which it was considered inappropriate to visit. When dining, affluent Russian households used to keep a place setting ready, in case an unexpected guest showed up. In Western houses, rooms with particular, fixed functions first emerged in the eighteenth century, as did the quest for privacy.[30] Rooms began to be arranged with doors opening into a hallway. At the same time, the home became a refuge with a higher moral value than the public realm, as Hall has said.[31] This concept did not reach Russia before the revolution, or it reached only the thin layer of urban bourgeoisie that was subsequently eradicated, and there was certainly no space for privacy during Stalinism. Even in the West, it is a recent phenomenon that the people—even members of the same family—desire to get away from each other's olfactory boundary zones. Never before have humans been as fastidious about each other's smells. Only an increasing amount of space available to the individual allows one to become so meticulous.

The Soviets did not discover private life until the 1970s,[32] long after the Communists had rooted out everything they perceived to be bourgeois, including the notion of privacy. Thus, the fight against privacy preempted the concept itself. The early Soviet authorities attempted to systematically communalize living; in the 1920s, they tried to establish huge residential collectives with only one central kitchen.[33] Since the 1970s, the urge for privacy has steadily grown, despite the fact that many Russian families are incomplete; mothers and grandmothers raise the children and the fathers are mostly absent. Some Russian men refuse to be in touch with their children; others have simply disappeared.[34]

With no fixed functions designated to any room or part of a room, visitors who showed up at almost any time felt free to enter all of the rooms. When they visited me, a Westerner in an apartment with a clearly distinguished bedroom, they did not hesitate to open the closed doors and enter them on their own.

People whose spatial behavior differs from what others are accustomed to, whether as individuals or as a nation, are perceived as strange. The conventions of spatial behavior are deeply rooted in a society, wrote Edward Hall. Is it thus safe to assume that if proximity patterns differ, then the cultures do also? If so, and if I can show that the Russians' proximity patterns have changed fundamentally since the fall of Communism, then I can conclude that Russian society has become an essentially different society.

Soviet people—city dwellers as well as farm workers—barely structured their apartments or their living spaces. The main reason for this may have been the lack of available space, especially in communal apartments, but those who had enough space did not seem to care.

The control over the spatial organization and the authority over the use of space mirrors power relations, not the least inside an apartment.[35] In the Soviet Union, women dominated the domestic sphere. With the household barely organized spatially, if at all, there was no space left for the men to control; men did not have rooms of their own—neither workshops nor studies. Thus, in their homes, with three generations living together, Soviet men usually felt powerless and unwanted, Elsa Håstad, a Swedish journalist who grew up in Moscow, noted.[36]

The kitchen was the place to meet. Here, one received friends and traded ideas, stories, and possibly goods more or less freely. Political opinions were expressed at the kitchen table, intellectuals exchanged manuscripts, singers sang their critical songs, theories were aired, and political changes were imagined. The kitchen provided the space for any hidden economic activity and other kinds of networking; here deals were struck. The ensemble of all the kitchen tables in the country could be seen as the Soviet Union's (only) civic space. However, as a foreigner, I was sometimes received for dinner in a bedroom. Despite the availability of a nice kitchen with a table, I balanced my plate on my knees on a sofa bed. They could not possibly make me eat in the kitchen, my hosts told me. However, I was granted interviews while sitting next to children doing their homework in the kitchen, despite the next room being unoccupied. The interviewees did not seem to consider the possibility that we would disturb the children, who seemed unbothered by our presence. Many people had a couch in the kitchen; a child or the grandmother slept there. Even bathrooms served several functions, often including storage. They might be stuffed with books, skis, and many other belongings, as well as dozens of rolls of toilet paper. The Soviet habit of hoarding added to the impression that the apartments were cramped and spatially disorganized.

For those living in a communal apartment *(kommunalka)*, where each family or party lived in one room and the kitchen and bathroom were shared, it was impossible to bring structure into the living space. In 1997, St. Petersburg still counted more than 200,000 *kommunalkas* occupied by 1 million people, or 20 percent of the city's inhabitants. *Kommunalka* dwellers did not, and still do not, live together; they ignore each other as best they can, as Brodsky insisted. They have separate doorbells. Each party has its own light bulb in the kitchen and in the bathroom, with the switches in the respective rooms; the switching on of a bulb, for example, signals who's intending to use the toilet. The dwellers' rhythms in communal apartments are such that they hardly ever meet; they use the same stove but at different times. In some kitchens, they even have several stoves. Nothing is communal in a communal apartment; people try to separate themselves from each other as best they can. Their private spheres, as minimal as they are, are constantly being threatened. Hence, they defend them by building walls—mostly false walls (a bookshelf in Brodsky's case)—and fencing off the neighbors with piles of garbage, which is also a way to rail against social control, an inevitable response in the cramped *kommunalkas*. Spaces overlap, but residents do whatever they can to separate them. Thus the people themselves add to the atomization of the society and its space—even within one apartment. This was very much in the interest of the Soviet power.

Communist societies were divided into *my* ("we" or "ourselves") and *oni* ("them" or the "others"). Basically, *my* referred to the people versus the authorities, while *oni* was the privileged, the party *nomenklatura*, those for whom the rules and laws did not apply. But *my* was also used to mean the Soviet people versus *oni* outside, the allegedly threatening capitalist world, or to mean the people standing in a line, as opposed to *oni* who already had what the *my* were queuing for. By enjoying access to special stores or to direct supply channels, many Soviet citizens belonged to some group of *oni*. Thus *oni* was applied differently depending on the person and the situation. A city was invisibly divided into very many *mys* and *onis*. The regime tried as much as it could to keep those spaces discrete and to not let them overlap or even connect.

Discrimination in providing access to information creates special spaces of privileges. Closed distribution systems are exclusive in terms of both general information and news concerning the availability of scarce goods. Those with access to more information were always *oni*; the population at large was cut off from any real news.

The hallway of a communal apartment was a shared space; therefore, it was treated as the anonymous *oni*'s territory, more alien than common. The intrusive gaze through an open door—whether the bathroom, the kitchen, the hall, the stairs, the backyards, or the streets—was that of *oni*, the other dwellers. Thus, while a visitor, once inside someone's living space, felt free to move around, another party's visitor in a *kommunalka* was treated as a complete stranger and an unwanted intruder. Together, however, the occupants of a *kommunalka* formed a *my* against the neighboring *kommunalka*, the *dvornitsa* (janitor), and the rest of the world.

Yuri Lotman called the communal apartment a "false home" or an "anti-home," the "center of an abnormal world."[37] He contrasted "home" with "living space," concluding that materiality needs space, while spirituality can do without space but needs a home. Accordingly, Brodsky celebrates his own generation as living in spirituality only, since its homes were castles in the air. His own St. Petersburg was one of those castles; the longer he was gone from the country, the more ethereal it became. Thus the ultimate home of the Soviet Russian intelligentsia was a virtual space.[38] By contrast, there was the communal apartment, where you can tell by the volume of the fart who occupies the toilet, Brodsky wrote, "what he or she had for supper as well as for breakfast. You know the sounds they make in bed and when the women have their periods." Those experiences stripped him of any illusion about human nature, Brodsky recalled in "In a Room and a Half."[39] He might also have read them as evidence for a human being's need for a certain territory. Can one turn Lotman upside down: is the deprivation of a home the root of the New Russians' materialism?

The communal apartment was introduced for two different reasons: ideology and need. As with so many other features of Soviet life, it was originally meant to be a transitional measure.[40] After taking power, the Bolshevik authorities expropriated the luxurious apartments in downtown Moscow and St. Petersburg to "socialize the households."[41] They moved in poor people, the "model proletarians," from the outskirts and the provinces. Thus, the periphery was brought to the center, changing the urban geography forever.[42] The affluent were either evicted or confined to some allotted space, usually one room. Bigger chambers were divided with newly inserted walls.[43] In many *kommunalkas*, these "provisional" partitions prevail to this day. People who have privatized their apartments usually tear them down.

Generally, "our space" stands for order and safety, while "other people's space" connotes danger, hostility, and chaos, as Lotman emphasized.[44] Soviet apartments, however, looked disorganized and not spatially structured, while *oni*, the state, maintained order in its realm, although it was the order of the army barracks.

Between "our space" and the alien space out there is another space: the neighborhood. From fear of subversion, however, the Soviet regime prevented neighborhoods; it obstructed their development and, thus, the development of "local knowledge."[45] Neighborhoods both constitute and require context,[46] which is what an authoritarian or totalitarian regime dreads, since context is hard to control and tends to create sources for independent decisions.

A neighborhood is a tentative attempt to (semi)privatize some public space. It bridges the intimate sphere, the home with the unknown, the city, or the world. It is the area of passage—neither private nor anonymous—and the neighbors are neither friends nor strangers. The neighborhood is a place for children—but not only for them—to practice life in a public, yet sheltered sphere. Within the limits of the socially acceptable, one can do what one wants. Yet, one is supposed to be polite. There is a degree of social control, since people know each other and will meet again. Michel de Certeau considers the neighborhood to be "a place to teach propriety."[47] Here, the different ages and sexes meet; it is literally a playground to practice social skills. It thus facilitates personal development.

Soviet Russia lacked neighborhoods; apart from some parked cars, most backyards were empty. A *babushka* might sit on a bench, but children rarely played outside, and then only when guarded by their grandmothers. In the dark of the evening, a couple of men might share a bottle of vodka before going home. Nevertheless, the streets and the backyards, that is, the space for a potential neighborhood, were not part of the living space. The doors were kept closed; everyone was suspicious. The society lacked a field where social skills could be practiced. There was no living space between the private sphere and the state sphere. Indeed, everything outside the apartment actually belonged to the state, though the state did not claim its space, at least not the potential neighborhoods. It spied on its citizens, eavesdropped on their phone conversations, and recruited informers in the communal apartments, but neglected the space in between.

It intruded in the potential neighborhood, but did not take care of it. It left the staircases, courtyards, and backstreets alone, but these spaces were also ignored by the residents. They considered these places to be enemy territory, infiltrated with informers and envious persons. Even in the city centers, the backyards therefore had no value and were of no use to anyone. Marc Augé calls a space with no historical or relational identity, with no relevant extension, a space that is passed through, a "non-place."[48]

Anywhere in Soviet Russia, most backyards were always open to the public. People walked through them; they even slipped between the planks of fences. There were trails over the lawns, through the dirt or snow, and often through three and four courtyards; thus people routinely trespassed on cloistered, if not private, land. With the Soviet regime coming to its close, no one cleaned these backyards anymore, nor did they clean the vestibules, staircases, and hallways. No one mended the broken windows in the corridors or the cracked doors. No one, not even the *dvornitsa*, felt responsible for the communally used spaces. As nonplaces, these spaces left no mark on the cognitive maps; it was almost as if they did not exist.

My backyard in downtown Moscow, on Bolshaya Yakimanka, was always littered, as was the entrance; additionally, the latter was adorned with graffiti: love hearts, anti-Semitic slogans, and swastikas. The paint was chipping; the wall looked like and smelled like a public restroom's. The entry door could not be closed, so there was a constant draft, especially in winter. But no one cared. The elevator was dirty, once splattered with vomit and occasionally with human feces, but again no one seemed to care. People simply took the stairs instead of the elevator. In the house where I used to live in St. Petersburg, I once stumbled over false teeth on the stairs, where they remained for several days; the staircase cats sniffed at them, the rats ran by, but nobody removed them for a time.

Only now, among the newly published how-to advisories, will people find some guidance to create neighborhoods.[49] There is more life in the yards; new workshops and kiosks have opened for business; in some backyards, especially in the cities' centers, additional buildings have been erected, adding at least density to the city. At the same time, more cars need parking space; one can see luxury sedans behind shabby apartment blocks. Also, the streets have become much more alive: people are trading, playing, reveling, eating, drinking, and hanging out. Dozens of street cafes have opened. In the evenings, gangs of youths roam the city, doing all the things teenagers do. Fifteen years ago, the police might have arrested them.

The Communist Party's main instrument for maintaining control was physical segregation: apartheid. The party tried to stop the society from breeding uncontrolled ideas and from exchanging prohibited goods—the way farmers separate their cattle to control breeding. The Soviet regime blocked the citizens' spaces from overlapping, yet the regime itself meddled with spaces. By keeping some borders obscure, by blurring the limits and definitions, the regime deprived its citizens of any safe landmarks and thus exerted power. People never knew how far they could go, to what extent it was possible to trespass on the state's space. This blurring was done strictly among the hierarchy; any superior person kept his or her subordinates uninformed.

The Soviet society was thoroughly militarized, "a peasant's dream of order," as Brodsky called the army. Spatial separation was the tool for achieving that order. There was a space specially designated for every activity, including leisure.

Soviet factories, administrative premises, universities, and other buildings were sealed off by guards: in politically sensitive places, the watchmen were KGB officers; everywhere else, access was controlled by *babushkas*. One needed a permit, a *propusk*, to enter. Often, one guard sat at the main entrance and another at the entry to each department. They checked documents, possibly collecting and holding them as long as one was on the premises. Access to the few hotels for foreigners required a special permit. Soviet people had to hand in their domestic passports to the guards. To this day, many hotels have a *dezhurnaya* on each floor to hand out the keys and, presumably, register all the movements of the guests.

The state tried to keep its citizens confined to narrow areas; it managed their workday and tried to control them during their free time. Anything not sanctioned by the regime had to be hidden away. The average citizen's vicinity was small, and "abroad" was beyond reach.

People's cognitive maps were shaped by their *propuska* and *propiska*, their passes and permits, the tickets they could get to enter certain walls. This certainly affected their self-images; the more access one had, the more important he or she seemed to be, and people behaved accordingly. Thus the walls and fences, guarded by anonymous gray faces, reinforced the partition of the society into *my* and *oni*. The Soviet regime aspired to fix its citizens in space and time; metaphorically, every little group of *my* lived confined to an invisible bubble. "The family was the lowest level of society that the state was able to regulate and everything that happened outside the boundaries of the family was regarded as suspicious," a commentator for the *Moscow Times* noted.[50] The majority seemed to comply with that. The *tusovki* (the youth groups), some work collectives, and any other *my* were such bubbles. Inside the bubbles, however, there was little or no spatial structure. The *tusovki* and the kitchen-table circles of the intelligentsia were even proud of their disorganization; people read it as a sign of disapproval with the regime's order.

Boundaries separate, but they also unite. They are a part of the two sides they are to separate; hence, they constitute a zone of interaction. The guards who protect a border deal with both sides. They control the flow of goods and people across the border, be it the frontier of a country or the entrance to a building. For a bribe, they turn a blind eye to smuggling.

Adjacent units influence each other mutually. For relations between the two sides to remain stable, some borders require rituals of sorts, including the countries' particular ways of performing passport control and customs clearance. This was not what the totalitarian authorities aimed to achieve by erecting separations. To stop interaction from happening, the Soviet regime reverted to boundaries with a significant extension. Its state border comprised a special zone, in some cases, five to fifty miles wide, even encompassing whole islands or provinces. It was enclosed by two barbed-wire fences—some equipped with automatic shooting machines—half a mile apart. Adjacent to the outer fence, a gravel strip of about one hundred yards in width was kept free of brushes.

To this day, Russia's border has not been fully demarcated (as with boundary stones, landmarks, fences, or other physical indicators) and there is not even an agreement on its delineation in some areas, most notably on borders with Norway, Mongolia, and less surprisingly, the former Soviet republics of Lithuania, Georgia, Belarus, and Ukraine.[51] With China, a treaty has been signed defining the 2,647-mile-long border, but leaving a few portions still undetermined.[52] The then governor of Primorski Krai, the region that includes Vladivostok, Evgeny Nazdratenko initially objected to the treaty, thus refusing to recognize his own state's border. He mobilized local Cossacks to physically obstruct the frontier's demarcation.[53] To this day, the Russian government is not fully in control of its own territory.

The Soviet Union's heavily fortified outer border, as well as its fences and guards inside the country, were to protect the system against the capitalist threat and Western spies, as propaganda would have it. Indeed, in one way or another, most industrial plants were involved in the production of military hardware or other defense-related material. Thus, it might have been reasonable to seal these factories and maybe the research institutes with watchmen. But why did the hospitals and the humanities' departments of the universities have to be "protected"? For the sheer sake of the principle, as it has been stated? Because the Soviets did not know any better? Or as a means of controlling the population, for the sake of segregation? To maintain a paramilitary discipline, as Brodsky thought?[54] Or to hide its industry's backwardness?

There was a practical reason to keep out the unauthorized. Almost every institution provided its workers, members, or students with some minute privileges: a *stolovaya* (canteen), as well as a place to buy cheap food and maybe medication. The bigger factories maintained stores and often a pharmacy. In the halls of scientific or educational facilities, rare, new books were on sale. The army had its own special department store, the Voyentorg, in the center of Moscow, opposite the Lenin library. Since everyone was interested in protecting his or her own privileges, the restriction of access was widely accepted. The otherwise useless trade unions offered their members inexpensive holidays in union homes and sanatoriums. For the party bosses, literally everything was provided through separate channels, including health care in special clinics. Only by keeping the city atomized into particular spaces could these privileges, however small, be maintained.

In a democratic market economy, the government is relatively powerless to shape geography. Money structures the space, dividing it into zones of classes that function as economic differentiators.[55] Today, companies choose their sites for manufacturing carefully. Countries and regions compete with each other to draw industries to their territories. In the centrally planned economy of the Soviet Union, things worked differently. The country presented itself as a highly urbanized, technologically advanced state. However, as I have shown above, the Soviets' was a Potemkin-style industrialization. The vast agglomerations in the industrial regions looked urbanized. In the countryside, the population was moved from their traditional wooden houses into concrete apartment blocks; suburbs were built all over the open land and all looked the same. A truly urbanized society, in which goods and ideas were to be exchanged freely, with free speech and the freedom of assembly and movement, would have implied the opening up of the society. Urbanity requires pluralism; the process of urbanization renders a city speculative, innovative, and unpredictable, contrary to what the Soviet authorities had in mind.

In spite of the regime's fervor in seeking to become a modern industrialized state and its pride in its technological achievements, it obstructed the urbanization of the society. For example, it was very slow in providing ordinary citizens with phone lines, yet it boasted of its command of the technology necessary to build and maintain railways, airplanes, highways, and communication networks, including satellite telephony (to the Soviet Far East). Nevertheless, it did not allow the population to take full advantage through the removal of the spatial barriers—quite the opposite. The authorities replaced spatial barriers with police barriers or simply kept the means of free movement unavailable. A highway is useless if one does not have access to a car and gasoline. Transparency through technology existed only in one direction: through the bugging of apartments and the monitoring of the telephones. Long-distance calls generally had to be ordered through the operator, and they were registered. Travel to vast areas of the country was restricted and air and train travelers had to identify themselves when they checked in. Thus, the modern means of transportation and communication to facilitate the free movement of people, goods, news, and ideas across the country's space existed, but their use was obstructed by the secret police. The Soviet regime seemed to observe a hierarchy of places; landmarks such as Palace Square in St. Petersburg or Moscow's Pushkin Square were kept under strict order. This was especially true for Red Square, once a lively marketplace. The Soviets emptied the square and kept it "pure"; even smoking was prohibited, since cigarette butts would have stained the sacred center of the Communist world. The police immediately dispersed any gathering of even small groups of people. Tourist groups in front of the mausoleum were ordered to move on. Ironically, the people visiting Lenin's mausoleum had to assemble in a long line. It was one of great ironies of the Soviet regime that it prohibited uncontrolled gatherings of people but forced people into long queues.

On the boulevards, the police enforced this less strictly. There, it was possible to stroll in small groups. Secondary streets in residential districts and the parks were rarely monitored, and the outskirts were watched even less. A similar pattern could be observed in the provincial towns. Order and cleanliness were kept for the eyes of the party bosses or a chance visitor. Not surprisingly, the cleaning regimen of the cities reflected the policing pattern. While the landmarks were swept daily, the fringes looked like garbage dumps. Abandoned cars, wreckage, and spare parts lined the streets and littered the backyards. For years, half a dozen partly dismantled cargo ships were moored on the Leitnanta Shmidta Embankment in St. Petersburg. The Soviet Union was a mosaic of garbage dumps and carefully cleaned landmarks, often adjacent to each other, but primly kept apart.

Snow plowing followed a similar pattern. In St. Petersburg, the snow was first cleared from the main arteries. Soon after that, the main squares were plowed, primarily Palace Square, despite its not being used for traffic. Then, the snowplows cleared the streets in front of the big hotels and other areas frequented by tourists. The snow was piled up and carted away before the side streets on Vassili Island saw any plow. Busy yet less presentable places, such as the Haymarket or the square in front of the Vassili Island subway station, were left alone for weeks. There, the people stumbled over the snow and trampled it into ice, so that the squares became slippery and walking became dangerous. This snow clearing order or precedence gave the impression that it was snowing much more on Vassili Island than in the city center.

Why did the Soviet state not strive to effectively police such areas as the back streets and courtyards? Why did it not guard the more backward places of its own state territory? In a state that was otherwise so secretive, many official buildings let people trespass on the property surrounding the building. Why did the state not take care of its space, especially its out of the way spaces? Peripheral space is of no use to display power. Preoccupied with its appearance, the regime focused on landmarks, turning their spaces into places, imposing meaning onto them, however fake, while it made sure no one else would do anything to add significance to any other location.

A modern marketplace consists of elastic, permeable spaces. They organize themselves and thus develop a spatial hierarchy, with the financial realm and the sphere of consumption on top, as we learn from David Harvey.[56] Money, with its "time-and-space-defying qualities,"[57] brackets them. Able to move more quickly across space, liquid capital in the market economy moves toward the workforce and the resources more than vice versa. In the Soviet Union, however, independent investment capital did not exist. The central planning office was the only investor; it allocated the means for construction. But it acted very slowly; in 1989, the construction of a new factory on average took twelve years.[58] That's why part of the workforce, that slow and usually immobile factor, had to be mobilized. The Soviet economy's spaces lacked both elasticity and permeability and they were kept closed against each other. Perhaps the most telling example of how the state obstructed any kind of exchange, even a basic retail transaction, was the typical Soviet counter, whether at a savings bank, a money exchange, a theater box office, or any other ticket counter: the window of the counter was not much bigger than a postcard and it was set very low, so that one only saw the hands of the clerk behind it. To purchase a ticket, one had to bow and practically crawl before the window. Not only did this obstruct any exchange, it humiliated the buyer, turning him or her into a petitioner, asking for the state's grace.

Only in emergencies, when people were forced to improvise, did the walls between the different spaces become permeable. When people were mobilized with a rhetoric of catastrophe, for example, during a war, things were accomplished. Every summer, the battle for the harvest required a "planned heroism," as Stephen Hanson showed.[59] On construction sites, after years of lost time, emergency workers had to rush buildings to completion. New economic initiatives, such as the meat and milk campaign and the chemicals campaign, were launched like battles.[60] While mimicking a modern industrialist society, the Soviet Union lacked the basic spatial architecture of such a society, including the means to connect the spaces far apart: that is, a currency. Elasticity and permeability had to be forced onto the seemingly integrated, though spatially atomized, petrified economy.

Since 1991, the fences and walls have become permeable; the old apartheid has vanished. All of a sudden, that year it became easy to enter almost any premises; either the guards were gone or they were easy to persuade. A well-thought-out explanation opened most doors; a bribe added persuasion. Everyone understood that the old categories had been voided. The post-Communist state stopped reinforcing the segregation imposed by the Communists. The country opened itself up, most closed zones were abolished, and traveling became much easier. For Russians, for the first time, the outside border became permeable. Today, millions of Russians travel abroad for leisure, business, or emigration.

As a state, post-Soviet Russia tore down the Communists' walls and fences or simply abolished them. However, private citizens, private companies, and (semi)criminal organizations began to erect barriers, fences, grids, and walls—for the first time since 1917. Even before 1991, squatters occupied state-owned fallow land, including some with abandoned houses. In 1990, along the Leningradsky Chaussee on Moscow's northern fringe, people began to grow potatoes. To protect their crops, they organized a group of armed watchmen. Backyards and empty houses were unofficially taken over. Soon, private security services began to emerge to guard legally and illegally privatized property.

In 1993, the Russian parliament passed a law to transfer state housing to its tenants, free of charge. Despite stopping short of allowing private ownership of land, this law made millions of citizens property owners. For the first time in their lives, Russians could own space; they became a nation of proprietors. Implicitly, residential space—though not yet land—was turned into a commodity. A legal market for real estate emerged and with it a class of petit bourgeois landlords. Some people privatized their apartments but moved to their *dachas* and rented out their places, mostly to foreigners or to newly well-off Russians. Or they renovated and legally sold the apartments at high prices. Agencies emerged; some of them hired criminal groups to oust people from their apartments. In the absence of any legislation regarding residential space, the most savvy were quick to play the market, becoming grand *rentiers*, (semi)legally or underhandedly. Apartments were already being traded under the Communists, but not for money and not officially.[61] The deals were complicated, slow, and labyrinthine; they often involved dozens of parties exchanging diverse goods for payments. After 1993, money allowed a quick and efficient market to evolve. Communal apartments were converted into single-family homes and flats were turned into offices. People began to run businesses out of their homes. The separation of the buildings' uses became blurred. The newly rich Russians built pretentious estates protected by high steel fences, security staff, and video cameras.

The fence, one of the most important devices to keep the Communists in power, has been privatized. However, where the Soviet barriers were all erected and controlled by one single institution, they now secure hundreds of thousands of different, diverging interests. Thus, the newly erected fences impose a degree of plurality; they protect competing interests against each other. This is fundamentally different from the segregation imposed by the Soviet power.

In the public realm, money has replaced the fence. Expensive restaurants and stores initially required U.S. dollars or credit cards, means of payment most Russians had no legal access to. Now high prices keep the less affluent away.

For a brief period, the Russian state was "fenceless." It was only after the standoff between the Yeltsin government and the Communists and nationalists in 1993 that the Russian state began to refortify itself and erect new fences. However, it does not impose divisions on the population anymore, but limits itself to the protection of the state itself and the property of some of its favorite clients—the average citizen's assets remain largely unprotected.

The nonspace between the homes and the streets, meanwhile, is gradually being conquered. From 1992 to 1995, Bolshaya Yakimanka, the street where I lived in downtown Moscow and the main artery from the Kremlin to the city's southwest, was regularly cleaned; the side streets, however, were cleaned much less often. In the stairwell, an ashtray appeared on a window sill in one mezzanine and most of the time was filled with cigarette butts. A young couple used it; they were forbidden to smoke in the communal apartment where they lived. Some doorways in the neighborhood became known as drinking and partying venues, while again and again some men mistook my entrance for a public restroom. The backyard was used for garbage collection. The people rushing through the backyard ignored the trash, the dirt, the old newspapers swirling in the wind, and the tramps rummaging through the trash containers for leftovers. But even this sort of activity in this place can be read as a sign of revival, as this no-man's land began to show some signs of rudimentary life again.

One afternoon in the fall of 1992, in the backyard lay a high pile of potatoes—many tons of humanitarian aid from the European Union. The potatoes were ready to be taken by whoever was first. Some pensioners showed up and timidly filled their bags. Then cars arrived and men with shovels grabbed as much as they could. Within a few hours, the potatoes were gone. For the first time in years, the backyard had served a purpose—the distribution of food. Soon after, a kiosk was erected. Then construction teams arrived. The adjacent house was generously renovated and surrounded by a newly erected wall. A bank moved in. Although there was still no law for private ownership of the land, and it was therefore illegal for the bank to occupy part of the backyard, the wall made the bank's appropriation of the space a *fait accompli*. Other backyards in the neighborhood saw the erection of fences for obvious commercial reasons. Some young men next door began to hire out parking spaces in a backyard; they guaranteed that they would watch the cars around the clock. Thus they made money out of a lot of land that previously had not existed on the mental maps.

To leave a Western car with a foreigner's license plates in the backyard overnight seemed risky. The security guards of the President Hotel across the street, the former lodge for high-ranking party officials, were happy to watch it. One simply had to park it on the street in front of their cabin, to notify the watchman, and to ensure his attention with a tip of approximately one U.S. dollar. By extending their area of surveillance onto the public street, the security guards profited from a lot of land over which they had no legal control whatsoever.

In Soviet cities, parking was free, though street parking on the main arteries was prohibited. In post-Soviet Moscow, the scheme of the President Hotel guards soon became prevalent. Parking guards in questionable uniforms began to collect fees. Regardless of whether they were officially working for the city or masquerading as officials to extort money, one paid what they requested. They physically controlled the lot of state territory they worked, although most likely they had no right to do so. A car that was not paid for would have been damaged. Eventually, the city established its own parking brigade, then parking meters were installed, thus rendering the parking fees official and automating their collection.

With the breakup of the Soviet economy looming, liquid capital began to flow, however slowly. A capital market emerged and the ruble became a real currency. Yet financial transactions were mostly done in cash, often in U.S. dollars. Therefore, capital could not travel faster than persons or goods; the transactions had to be executed physically. Investors who bought stock in a company had to travel to the company's headquarters to ensure that they were registered as shareholders. Traders began to take advantage of the early permeability of the formerly closed barriers, both the external border and the internal walls. Shuttle dealers began to travel to China, Vietnam, India, and to some Eastern European countries. *Babushkas* flew from the Siberian cities to Moscow to buy imported goods. Wholesale markets emerged. For the first time since the New Economic Policy of the 1920s, the market, and not some bureaucrat, set the prices—through supply and demand. The first independent merchants, whether legal or illegal, disrupted the apartheid that had been imposed on the society. They crossed borders and, by doing so, monetized the society.

At the same time, the first private (or cooperative) coffee shops opened. They began to provide the society with an unpoliceable space, a civic space for the exchange of ideas. Soon, the cafes began to put tables on the sidewalks. Abandoned buildings and parks were turned into bars or restaurants. Music blared from loudspeakers, claiming an invisible space of entertainment far into the street's space. Advertisements—not

the leftover Sparkasse banners, but advertisements for local markets—
turned buses, houses, and subway stations into sites of communication.

People became accustomed to overlapping spaces: a street overlapped
with a café, which was a place to exchange ideas and to sell goods. There
was nothing to hide about doing business there. However, the dismantling of the Soviet apartheid had to be followed by a reorganization of the
space. People began to erect private barriers and close doors. Their demand for privacy increased. In apartment buildings, neighbors got together to install metal grates or iron doors at the entrances to their corridors, barring the unwanted from even reaching their apartment doors.
Thus, for the first time, people shared control over space. They were willing to communally protect their respective properties and their privacy. In
newly built houses, functions such as dining were ascribed to particular
rooms. Not surprisingly, many of the newly rich exaggerated. One joke
has a New Russian telling his architect to build three outdoor swimming
pools. The architect hesitates: "Would not one pool suffice?"

"No," says the New Russian, "I have friends who like to swim in warm
water and other friends who prefer icy water."

"Okay, then we'll plan two swimming pools, not three," argues the architect.

"Three," insists the man. "I have friends who do not swim at all."

Spatial order (temporarily) abandoned, the authorities not in full control, and a multifunctionality of spaces are all characteristics of a carnival.
The fringes of Russia's cities reached the centers, including the garbage
that had always littered the outskirts. More and more abandoned cars
lined side streets and were slowly scavenged. The fringes of human society, the beggars and gypsies, the disabled and disgruntled, made it to the
downtown areas. Not that they did not exist before, but they had not been
visible; the police had always chased them away or arrested them. Streets,
squares, railway stations, and subway entrances were turned into
bazaars; people peddling, begging, and playing music revived the cities,
reflecting prerevolutionary Russia, where there was "life everywhere."[62]
In 1910, Russia's then capital saw 150,000 registered street traders, more
than the number of factory workers. When reading accounts of the trading, haggling, and peddling in prerevolutionary St. Petersburg, one feels
as though the past has returned.[63] And, in fact, the old names have returned to the streets and squares—though for a while, people used both
the old and the new, since they could not agree on which was the "right"
one and which one was the carnivalesque mask.

Beggars populate the Moscow subways, along with homeless children
and an Afghanistan veteran with no legs who moves about sluggishly on
a skateboard. Priests or fake priests collect money, while vendors sell
newspapers, videos, T-shirts, sunglasses, lottery tickets, flowers, and

seeds. In the long pedestrian tunnels of the subway, street musicians bring a buzz to this (re)vitalized underworld. Some play only to advertise their services; one man, Volodya, hands out his business card: "Volodya, Tamada, Accordionist, Santa Claus, Weddings, Jubilees, New Year Celebrations." Playing in public is not prohibited, only accepting money for doing so is.

Some of the small businesses in the subway are licensed; others work illegally. Rival gangs of racketeers claim the bazaars and subway stations as their own spaces, and the police are usually part of it. Officers patrol the grounds to check permits or faces. The units collect bribes, not from individual vendors, but from their protectors. Eventually, the police reinforce their authority with arrests (to increase the price). When a police officer appears, the *babushkas* holding their merchandise in their hands stuff the goods into their bags and pretend to be subway passengers. For many people, therefore, the subway has been turned into their *Lebensraum*, an underworld of sorts.

While the fringes made it to the city centers, the centers reached for open space on the fringes. The rich are building their villas there, while some Western companies and newly privatized Russian corporations are building their new headquarters. RAO UES, Russia's electric utility company, moved into an estate situated in a deserted land in Moscow's southwest; the building conveys the atmosphere of a bordello, with an arcade-like conservatory resembling a swimming pool and an auditorium in light blue plush. Is this a Soviet bureaucrat's dream of the Western good life? To me it looked like a nightmare of bad taste.

The drivers and guards who work for RAO UES seem to understand the message. As long as they stay outside the premises, chatting, smoking, and hanging out in the parking lot, they exhibit Soviet (bad) manners. As soon as they get inside, however, the same men turn into courteous employees, zealously performing their duties. The phony interior of the building alters their behavior and, possibly, their self-image.

People's cognitive maps have changed fundamentally. Their complexity has increased and different shades of gray have begun to appear on them. The blank areas—backyards, the parts of the country that were sealed, buildings housing mysterious and unknown institutions, the "abroad"—have been filled in. The maps—the cognitive and the printed ones—not only have gained in complexity, but also these days they indicate how space can be used. People have begun to explore their environment for opportunities to make money. During Soviet times, ordinary people did not claim any share of a city's open space, for example, streets, squares, and parks. They did not think of those spaces as theirs. They belonged to *oni*, or "them." To get into Gorky Park in Moscow, one had to pay an entrance fee and was informed about the rules governing this zone "of culture and leisure." In Aleksandr Garden at the Kremlin Walls, the police chased people off the grass.

Some of the first to successfully violate the ban to assemble were not protesters, but brokers. In 1989, when it was still prohibited to sell goods or services privately and the ban was still enforced, on Leningrad's Ploshad Mira (Peace Square)—today the St. Petersburg Haymarket—hundreds of people stood in rows, each holding a number of cardboard cards on a string. On the cards, they noted their offerings. Strictly speaking, they were not trading and certainly not selling anything, they were just mediating exchanges. As soon as the police showed up, they hid the cards under their coats.

The political demonstrations in public were soon to follow. Already, in 1987, some Crimean Tatars who had been deported (relocated from their homes) in 1944 had staged a rally. They sought permission to move back to the Crimea. Their demonstrations never lasted for more than a few minutes; the KGB would seize their banners and detain them. At the same time, Erivan saw its first tolerated mass rally; the Baltics followed in the spring of 1988. During the party conference in June 1988, small groups with flags, some of the participants true supporters of Gorbachev, assembled on Moscow's Pushkin Square. Plain-clothes police encircled them, while the uniformed police chased onlookers off the grass. As soon as a flag—the then-illegal Russian tricolor—was raised, the police stepped in and confiscated it. A larger manifestation later that year, commemorating the victims of the political terror, was allegedly co-organized by the KGB, as were the first mass rallies in Erivan, persistent rumors had it.

As early as August 1987, a *samizdat* newspaper, *Ekspress Khronika*, overcame the obstacles imposed on communication; it began reporting protest actions taking place all over the country. It thus connected the different centers of disaffection, effectively creating a civic space bracketing the whole of the USSR.[64]

By assembling in groups; discussing political developments, as they had since 1988; or trading goods and services in the vicinity of subway entrances, people began to use the public space in ways thus far unheard of. Implicitly, they claimed the open space for expressing their convictions, for doing business, or just for gathering. The state had lost its monopoly on the use of public space and even lost control over this space, since it was unable to enforce its own "rules"—it had to let the street regulate itself. The gangs and police units competing as racketeers might try to establish monopolies and, in some instances, they might succeed, though only on a local level. But they have broken the state's monopoly. Their existence guarantees a plurality of decision making, privatization, and competition, by all means and certainly including criminal ones. The spaces overlap and superimpose on one another. Thus, despite the racket fiefdoms, Russia has become an open society—perhaps too open—and indeed more open than most other states.

Buildings are "the prose of the world as opposed, or apposed, to the poetry of monuments," Henri Lefebvre wrote.[65] The Communists did not care much about the prose of everyday life, for theirs was a poetry of propaganda, and a distinctly modernist one. Their main "monuments" were the megaprojects like Magnitogorsk, the gulag, the Belomor Canal, the complete remodeling of Moscow, and the subway.[66] Their most pathetic monument, because it was never built, was the Palace of the Soviets: the Soviet Union failed even in its plan to create its own supreme monument.

Ever since the 1950s, seven monumental towers, the so-called wedding-cake high rises, have dominated Moscow's skyline.[67] They all face the city's center, the hub around which the buildings were constructed. In this hub is the reconstructed cathedral Christ-the-Savior, which was completed in 1997. The most prominent examples of Stalinist architecture connect with the tallest building of imperial Moscow, thus molding both into the city's history. The high rises as well as the cathedral represent the taste of the rulers of their respective periods and are not as alien to each other as one might think. Both were commissioned by authoritarian powers—Nikolai I and Stalin—and reflect their wishes to project visible grandeur, urbanity, and historicity. However, both the cathedral and the weeding-cake high rises exaggerate in their attempt to create monumental space; they thus seem fake or kitsch. The connection between the high rises and the cathedral at their hub is no accident: the wedding cakes were to be directed toward the Palace of the Soviets, which was to stand on the site of the original cathedral and which was never built. Instead, what was allegedly the world's largest swimming pool came to be placed on the site of the cathedral, so that, ironically, the hub was a void, making the grand plan to reshape Moscow as the capital of Communism into a bad joke.

Monuments offer to "each member of a society an image of that membership, an image of his or her social visage." A monument thus constitutes a "collective mirror more faithful than any personal one."[68] Monuments bring about consensus with an inherent momentum of exaltation or repression.

Historically, unlike Europe, Russia did not place her monuments in the center of squares, but at the edge of places or on river embankments, the scholar Blair Ruble showed.[69] The concept of stand-alone monuments was an idea imported from Europe by the Romanovs, another attempt at Westernization.[70] The Pushkin monument on Pushkin Square in Moscow, sculpted in 1880 by A. M. Opekushin, was moved to its present location in 1950 by Stalin "with a flick of his wrist from his limousine," Timothy Colton noted in his monograph on Moscow.[71] The stand-alone statues became widespread only during the Soviet time, with the erecting of thousands of Lenin monuments around the country and of statues of Dzerzhinsky on the Lubyanka and Mayakovsky at the intersection of Garden Ring and Tverskoy Boulevard in Moscow. For the main Lenin memorial of the country, in the middle of October Square in Moscow, the whole area was reconstructed; no historical building was left to challenge the eternity of Lenin.[72] Curiously, Lenin's mausoleum, despite being the most central Soviet monument, is located according to Russian tradition at the side of Red Square. It is not surprising, then, that Marshal Zhukov's statue in front of Moscow's historical museum and Tsereteli's gigantic statue of Peter the Great were placed according to the old Russian style.

Aside from a few historical landmarks, all Soviet cities looked very much the same. Their main streets were named the same: Lenin, Dzerzhinsky, Gogol, Pushkin, Red Army, Revolution, October, and Peace. Only a few variations of the major statues existed. The monotony, inertia, and gravity of the Soviet Union's monumental space reflected the state of mind of the Communists in power; the space tended to be big, bleak, coarse, dull, rigid, and menacing. The space was *oni*'s, as were the monuments. When people began to demonstrate on those distinctively Soviet squares, their rallies looked as though they were played out on the wrong stage. Alive, optimistic, and ready to take off, they seemed disconnected from the "monumental space" of stagnation; they seemed out of place, like they were in a carnival.

Once in power, the Yeltsin government, contrary to most new regimes, did not try to rewrite history or to create new maps, yet it helped to rectify the Soviets' falsifications. It did not erect new monuments nor indulge in iconoclasm. The toppled statues of Dzerzhinsky, Kalinin, and Sverdlov in Moscow were a few exceptions. Together with a bust of Khrushchev and the last remaining statue of Stalin, they found a final resting place in the park behind the Tsentralny Dom Isskustv (the main gallery for contemporary art). There, for a few years they were climbed upon by children, painted by youths, visited by dog walkers, and marked by their pets. Later, the park was turned into an open-air exhibit for socialist monuments.

The Yeltsin government did not erect any new monuments. The complex on Poklonnaya Gora was constructed in the early 1980s to celebrate the "victory of socialism"; it was not yet finished when socialism met its final defeat. Untouched for the better part of a decade, in 1992 it was recycled, renamed, and rededicated as a "museum of the great patriotic war," thus providing a link between the Communist and early post-Communist periods. Inaugurated on May 9, 1995, the anniversary of the Soviet victory over Nazi Germany, it became the venue of the first co-celebration of a holiday by the democrats and the Communists-nationalists since the collapse of the USSR.

Private groups or city governments erected the few other new monuments. Remarkable among them are the memorials for the victims of Stalin's repression—a simple black stone in granite—on Lubyanka Square in Moscow, the sculled sphinxes on St. Petersburg's Robespierre embankment, and Gogol's nose at the corner of Voznesensky Prospect and Rimski-Korsakova, also in St. Petersburg. Svetlana Boym particularly referred to the new—sitting—statue of Peter the Great.[73] Monuments as "social condensers"[74] create their own space. Memorials erected by nongovernmental organizations, therefore, produce a diversity of spaces in the public sphere that could not have existed in the Soviet era. Some of the first Western advertisements that appeared in Russian cities had an almost monumental quality. They were noticed as new landmarks, as standing for an idea, and as memorials of a distant future. They, too, created space independent of the monopoly of the Communist regime then in power.

The first Western supermarkets, the most obvious among the early signs that Soviet life was changing, became part of the monumental space. In contrast, the empty Soviet grocery store could be read as inverted monumental space; displaying a few carefully stapled packages of salt and some cans of inedible fish, they revealed the true face of the Soviet economy. Many people who could not afford to shop in the Western supermarkets visited them as a museum of Western life—a window into the future.[75] For the first time in seventy years, some space that was open to the public was privately owned and shaped by various nonstate agencies. Within a short period, more such "exhibitions" opened—fashion retailers, perfume stores, a Volvo outlet, other car dealerships. Advertisements for consumer goods began to replace the Communist slogans.[76]

The church got its old premises back, including the lots of land on which demolished houses of God used to stand. It subsequently renovated or reconstructed its own monuments and churches, first and foremost the Christ-the-Savior cathedral. As before 1931, the cathedral now dominates Moscow's cityscape, while many other churches have regained their prominent visibility.[77]

In the Soviet Union, one single institution with one set of values made all the decisions concerning the shaping of a city. Now, for the first time since 1917, space can be owned privately by almost anyone and, since what laws exist are flouted, every homeowner can do almost anything with his or her home. All of a sudden, thousands of different people with different tastes and different goals are shaping the city's space. A construction boom has begun, even the completion of unfinished Soviet style residential blocks has been accelerated, and new types of housing—single-family houses and "castles"—are being built. New city districts are emerging for the rich. The less affluent have left their apartments in the city centers to more affluent buyers.

The center of Moscow defies the newly found pluralism. Yuri Luzhkov, the mayor, runs the city like a Soviet conglomerate: single-handedly, secretively, and with an authoritarian style. The Okhotny Ryad mall, under the former Manezhnaya Square, just north of the Kremlin, betrays Luzhkov's propensity for kitsch. Once a quarter of petty shops, it was leveled by Stalin and turned into a dead zone. Circled by cars, the square was used for only one purpose. There, the May 1 and November 7 demonstrators, worker collectives, and army units readied themselves to march over Red Square, passing the old men on Lenin's mausoleum. Pedestrians were not allowed to cross the Manezhnaya. In 1990, the square became the main venue for anti-Communist demonstrations, some of them with several hundred thousand participants. This is where many Muscovites first formed some democratic convictions. On August 24, 1991, the square was the site of the memorial service, attended by more than a million people, for the three young men who had died during the putsch. Thus Manezhnaya Square became a monumental place, full of recent history and of memories threatening a government that feared becoming the third Russian revolution's Girondists. Hence, the new city authorities stripped the square of its recent memory by pretending to explore its more distant history; they commissioned archeologists for excavations. After the archaeologists left the dig, a huge underground mall, the Okhotny Ryad shopping center, was built, with a pseudohistorical park, fountains, and statues depicting folk tales.

Luzhkov thus turned a place where people were looking ahead and rallying for a better future into an area evoking cheap reminiscences of a fairy-tale past—in short, a Russia that never was. Members of the (post-)Soviet consumer society stroll about, indulging in doing nothing. Nearby, in front of the former Lenin museum, a small and noisy crowd of nostalgic Stalinists occasionally assemble. Instead of facing history, Russia once again tries to block her own gaze into the past, as she did when erecting the Christ-the-Savior cathedral and the wedding cakes.

For a brief period before the collapse of the Soviet Union, public squares turned into civic space. Each city had its meeting point where people gathered to discuss politics, often throughout the night. They exchanged views and information and tried to mobilize their fellow citizens and to learn. In a modern democratic society, civic space is provided by the media—at least it should be. At the time, the Soviet media were not yet ready for that step, although gradually they opened up to provide civic space. During the August coup, the pristine walls in the subways and all over the city turned into bulletin boards: leaflets, pamphlets, and appeals were posted. A group of newspapers defied the GKChP's censorship and created the *Obshaya Gazeta* (the common paper). The public had conquered a space as public space. To a certain extent, it has since lost it again.

Today, it is argued, the Russian media are neither free nor democratic; the independent television stations have been forced to close. The newspapers are owned and run by oligarchs with their own purposes. But in the big cities there are no longer monopolies. (The local press in many regions is still controlled by monopolies—old and new.). The wealthy have conflicting interests; thus, a pluralism of sorts is guaranteed. Local broadcasters retransmit Western radio networks, such as the BBC, the Deutsche Welle, and the U.S.-backed Radio Liberty. People use the Internet and most cities—even regional Siberian centers such as Magnitogorsk and Anadyr in Chukotka—have their own Web sites, with independently posted information and chat rooms. True, one has to assume these sites might be monitored by the FSB (Federalnaya Sluzhba Bezopasnosti, the Federal Security Service), the renamed KGB, as is e-mail traffic. Web sites can be manipulated and it is still a minority who use the Internet, but the cyberspace is there to stay and its users are the most active and vocal people in the New Russian society. It seems thus impossible to reerect the barriers and contain information as the Soviet government once did.

Without private ownership of land, the transformation toward a modern, civic society with its complex spatial architecture would not be completed. Nevertheless, within a few years Russia and the world have changed in the minds of her citizens. An obscure space, run like an army barracks, has turned into a structured place, however complex, and so have the cognitive maps.

Another area of change is post-Soviet Russian literature, which is exploring hitherto unknown realms. Contemporary Russian women's writings encompass a broader range of (territorial) possibilities than ever. Women are mobile and restless; they leave their conventional spaces: "they move out," as Helena Goscilo metaphorically noted.[78] The bubbles have burst. Another example of a writer charting a new territory is Victor Pelevin. His novel *Omon Ra* takes the reader to outer space.[79] A young pioneer is recruited to pilot a supposedly unmanned Soviet spacecraft to the moon. The craft is not to return and the protagonist will die as a suicide pilot, an anonymous hero of socialism. This rite of passage can be read as an escape into the great unknown. It ends, happily, in complete failure, as the sacrificed young pilot survives. The Soviet space program was, according to Pelevin's novel, a Potemkin-style endeavor. Recruited to make the world believe that the Soviet Union could construct unmanned crafts, the little hero himself is fooled by a make-believe.

NOTES

1. Yu. M. Lotman, *Besedy o Russkoi kulture: Byt i traditsy russkogo dvoryanstva (xviii–nachalo xix veka)* (Talks on Russian culture: Life and tradition of the Russian aristocracy [eighteenth–beginning of the nineteenth century]). (St. Petersburg: Isskustvo, 1994).

2. See the case of the Belarus villages in chapter 2.

3. Most Soviet and post-Soviet maternity clinics strictly prohibit the fathers from visiting their wives and newborn babies.

4. A cognitive map, according to Tommy Gärling, Anders Böök, and Erik Lindberg in "The Acquisition and Use of the Spatial Layout of the Environment during Locomotion," *Man-Environment Systems*, 9 (1979): 200–208, "stored information about the relative location of objects and phenomena in the everyday physical environment." Quoted in Reginald G. Golledge and J. Robert Stimson, *Spatial Behavior: A Geographic Perspective* (New York: Guilford, 1997), 234.

5. Edward T. Hall, *The Silent Language* (New York: Doubleday, 1959), 1–19, 164. Hall gives such idioms as "a place in her heart," to "have a place in the mountains," or to be "tired of a place" as evidence that it is easy to understand the difference between place and space.

6. Depending on their geographical location, some cities became commercial centers, while others became production sites. Capitalism seemed to work. The medieval European cities saw streets occupied by guilds, where all the carpenters, all the blacksmiths, or all the butchers worked in the same street. Since it was impossible to commute over longer distances from home to work, affluent businesses made their districts of the city more affluent, thus the differentiation of cities along social differences began very early.

7. Manuel Castells, *The City and the Grassroots: A Cross-cultural Theory of Urban Social Movements* (London: Edward Arnold, 1983), 311.

8. See Hilary Pilkington, "The Future Is Ours: Youth Culture in Russia, 1953 to the Present," in *Russian Cultural Studies*, ed. Catriona Kelly and David Shepherd (Oxford: Oxford University Press, 1998). The author shows that, similar to the *stiliagi*, the most daring and rebellious of the last generation of Soviet youth were children of the *nomenklatura*; only they and only those living in Moscow had access to a Western lifestyle, to Western visitors, and in some cases even to travel abroad.

9. Joseph Brodsky, *Less Than One* (New York: Farrar, Straus & Giroux, 1986), 25. Brodsky meticulously describes this typical Soviet fence: "a row of twenty-inch-high planks with two-inch spaces between them, held together by a transverse lath made of the same material, painted green."

10. Kira Muratova, *Korotkie vstrechi* (Brief encounters) (Moscow: Odessa-Studios, 1967), film.

11. Brodsky, *Less Than One*, 22.

12. In 1993, there were 102, including the film center and a children's movie theater, for approximately 10 million Muscovites.

13. Masha Lipman, "Fade to Red: Letter from Moscow," *New Yorker*, September 21, 1999, 107.

14. Atlas, Kusnetsky Most 9, Moscow.

15. Until 1917, a phone and address directory, *Vso Petrograd,* was published annually in St. Petersburg.

16. The only exception was a booklet that compiled the names and numbers of foreign businesses, airlines, embassies, and correspondents in English for the small expat community.

17. Mosgorsprav(ka) was an acronym for Moskovsky Gorodsky Spravka— Moscow City Enquiries.

18. "Nochnykh babochek" (Nightly girls), *Argumenty i Fakti* 24 (July 1997): 14.

19. The plants in the Baltics produced mostly for the military, not for export, thus lower shipping costs could not have played a role in the decision to establish heavy industry near the sea.

20. Cynthia A. Ruder, *Making History for Stalin: The Story of the Belomor Canal* (Gainesville: University Press of Florida, 1998).

21. David J. Nordlander, "Origins of a Gulag Capital: Magadan and Stalinist Control in the Early 1930s," *Slavic Review* 57, no. 4 (Winter 1998): 781–812.

22. Joseph Roth, "Leningrad," *Frankfurter Zeitung,* March 18, 1928. Roth saw the Palace Square as mirroring the vast empire of the Soviets and compared the humans crossing the square to dressed matchsticks.

23. Michel Foucault, *Power/Knowledge: Selected Interviews and Other Writings, 1972–77* (New York: Pantheon, 1980), 148.

24. The quote has been attributed to Thomas Merton, Ralph Waldo Emerson, Albert Schweitzer, and the Dutch architect J. B. Bakerna as well. See Jan Tanghe, *Living Cities: A Case for Urbanism and Guidelines for Re-urbanization* (Oxford: Pergamon, 1984), 61.

25. Mikhail Yampolsky, "In the Shadow of Monuments: Notes on Iconoclasm and Time," trans. John Kachur, in *Soviet Hieroglyphics: Visual Culture in Late Twentieth-Century Russia,* ed. Nancy Condee, 93–112 (Bloomington: Indiana University Press, 1995), 101.

26. *The World of the Kho* was repeatedly on display in Moscow and in summer 1993 was at the Gelman gallery.

27. Vladimir Sorokin, the most prominent writer of the group, interview with the author, *Vogue,* German edition, March 1993.

28. Edward T. Hall, *The Hidden Dimension.* (New York: Doubleday, 1966), 131–138.

29. Hall, *Hidden Dimension,* 131–163.

30. Hall, *Hidden Dimension,* 104.

31. Hall, *Hidden Dimension,* 80–90.

32. Svetlana Boym, *Common Places: Mythologies of Everyday Life in Russia* (Cambridge, Mass.: Harvard University Press, 1994), 138.

33. Timothy J. Colton, *Moscow* (Cambridge, Mass.: Belknap, 1995), 222. Similar attempts were made in Western European cities, such as Vienna and Zurich. See Günther Uhlig, *Kollektivmodell "Einküchenhaus"* (Giessen, Germany: Anabas, 1981).

34. Richard Sennett, *The Fall of Public Man* (New York, Knopf, 1977), 20, 177. Sennett sees the emergence of the core family as the main justification for the quest for privacy; thus, the Russian one-parent families would require less privacy.

35. David Harvey, *Justice, Nature and the Geography of Difference* (Cambridge, Mass.: Blackwell, 1996), 187.

36. Elsa Håstad, "Rysska rollspel, (Russian role-play)," *bang*, no. 3 (October 1995): 26. The Swedish journalist argues that a lack of space of their own might be the reason men are unable to cope with communism. "Mannen var den som sämst klarade kommunismen. När kvinnorna dominerade den privata sfären och staten den offentliga fanns ingen plats kvar för mannen." (The men coped most poorly with communism. The women dominated the private sphere and the state the public sphere, so that there was no space left for men.) Håstad grew up in Moscow and went to a Russian primary school.

37. Yuri M. Lotman, *Universe of the Mind* (Bloomington: Indiana University Press, 1990), 186.

38. Brodsky, "A Child of Civilization," in *Less Than One*, 123–144. Brodsky argues that art should be an alternative world, and that his was the only generation of Russians that had found such an alternative home for itself; for members of his generation, artists such as Giotto and Mandelstam were more important than their own personal destinies.

39. Brodsky, "In a Room and a Half," *Less Than One*, 29.

40. In Dostoevsky's *Poor People*, Makar Devushkin rents nothing but a corner in a room. In St. Petersburg, before 1917, the poor and the lumpen lived in the basements of rich people's city estates, while the landlords lived on the Bel-Etage. The society was stratified within one residential building. In the basement and in the back premises, the communal apartment existed before the revolution, though in the prerevolutionary communal apartments people seem to have lived together, following Dostoevsky. This could not be said of the self-policing Soviet *kommunalkas*.

41. Nikolay Bukharin, quoted in Colton, *Moscow*, 121.

42. Lotman, *Universe of the Mind*, 141.

43. Colton, *Moscow*, 121.

44. Lotman, *Universe of the Mind*, 131.

45. Clifford Geertz, *Local Knowledge: Further Essays in Interpretive Anthropology*, (New York: Basic, 1984).

46. Arjun Appadurai, *Modernity at Large: Cultural Dimensions of Globalization* (Minneapolis: University of Minnesota Press, 1996), 186.

47. Pierre Mayol, "Living," in *Living and Cooking: The Practice of Everyday Life*, Vol. 2., ed. Michel de Certeau, Luce Giard, and Pierre Mayol, trans. Timothy J. Tomasik (Minneapolis: University of Minnesota Press, 1998), 11.

48. Marc Augé, *Non-places: Introduction to an Anthropology of Supermodernity*, trans. John Howe (London: Verso, 1995), 77ff.

49. "Teaching Citizens How to Be Good Neighbors," *Moscow News*, May 29, 1997, 16.

50. Irina Glushenko, "AIDS Epidemic Was Russia's Sexual Revolution," *Moscow Times*, September 30, 1998.

51. *Izvestiya*, March 19, 1998.

52. "Russlands weiche Grenzen," *Bundesinstitut für ostwissenschaftliche und internationale Studien, Köln* 13 (1997).

53. In May 1991.

54. Brodsky, *Less than One*, 14.

55. John Goode, cited in David Harvey, *The Urban Experience* (Baltimore: Johns Hopkins University Press, 1989), 178.

56. Harvey, *The Urban Experience*.

57. Georg Simmel, *Philosophie des Geldes* (Leipzig: Drucker und Humbolt, 1900).

58. Yegor Gaidar, interview with author, "So wurde die Sowjetwirtschaft in den Kollaps geführt," *Weltwoche*, June 28, 1990, 3.

59. Stephen E. Hanson, *Time and Revolution: Marxism and the Soviet Institutions* (Chapel Hill: University of North Carolina Press, 1997), 143.

60. One of the campaigns aimed at overtaking the West, the meat and milk campaign led to the wholesale slaughter of Soviet livestock. See Stephen Hanson, *Time and Revolution*, 176.

61. It was legal to exchange apartments before the end of the Soviet Union, though no money could be paid. This led to complicated barter deals; money had to be replaced by goods.

62. Vasili Ivanovich Kuleshov, *Fiziologiia Peterburg* (Moscow: Nauka, 1991), 71–91.

63. See, for example, A. A. Bakhtiarov, *Bryukho Peterburga: Ocherki Stolichnoi zhisni* (1887: St. Petersburg: FERT, 1994).

64. *Ekspress Khronika*, a *samiszdat* weekly launched by Aleksander Podrabinek in August 1987.

65. Henri Lefebvre, *The Production of Space*, trans. Donald Nicholson-Smith (Cambridge, Mass.: Blackwell, 1991), 227.

66. Colton, *Moscow*. Colton writes, "Stalin looked on his adopted hometown as a Brobdingnagian sandbox in which he could sift, heap and bore at will."

67. The State University, the Foreign and the Transportation Ministry buildings, two hotels (Ukraina and Leningradskaya), and two apartment houses, on Kotelnicheskaya Naberezhnaya and Ploshad Vosstaniya.

68. Lefebvre, *Production of Space*, 220.

69. Blair Ruble, *Money Sings* (Washington, D.C.: Woodrow Wilson Center Press, 1995), 129. The author discusses the location of monuments in his recollection of the Yaroslav controversy, over where to reerect the statue of Yaroslav the Wise.

70. Falconet's Peter the Great stands on the embankment. In imperial St. Petersburg, only Catherine the Great, Nikolai I, and Aleksandr III were placed in the center of squares. The Pushkin statue on Ploshad Isskustvo in St. Petersburg was not erected until the 1950s; the Gogol statue at the head of Gogol Boulevard in Moscow is of the same period. Erected in 1952, the statue has often been called the false Gogol, since there is another monument in Suvorov Boulevard that was created in 1909 by Nikolai Andreyev in the courtyard of the building where Gogol died. See Kristian Gerner, *Svårt att vara Ryss* (Lund, Sweden: Signum, 1989).

71. Colton, *Moscow*, 324.

72. Yampolsky, "Shadow of Monuments," 96.

73. Svetlana Boym, "St. Petersburg" (paper presented at the Davis Center for Russian Studies, Harvard University, Cambridge, Massachusetts, November 1997).

74. The term is Lefebvre's, *Production of Space*, 225.

75. Access to the few existing stores selling Western goods before 1989 was restricted to foreigners; occasionally, this was still enforced by police during the first years of transition.

76. While photocopiers were still restricted to official use and every single copy had to be registered, there was already a huge advertisement for Minolta copiers on the rooftops of buildings in cities of the Soviet Union and its satellites, most obviously in Prague in 1989, portending change.

77. Walter Benjamin, *Moscow Diary* (Frankfurt: Suhrkamp, 1980), 77, 96. Benjamin noted that wherever one looks, one sees a church.

78. Helena Goscilo, *Dehexing Sex: Russian Womanhood during and after Glasnost* (Ann Arbor: University of Michigan Press, 1996), 132.

79. Viktor Pelevin, *Omon Ra*, trans. Andrew Bromfield. (New York: Farrar, Straus & Giroux, 1996); originally published in Russian under the same title (Moscow: Tekst, 1992).

7

A New Time for New Times

Time is money[1]—but in the Soviet Union, it was not. Soviet people did not save time, they did not lose time, and they certainly did not make up for lost time. Time never seemed to run out; there was always more time to come. To my Western eyes, the Soviets were constantly wasting, if not killing, time, although they of course did not perceive it that way. At almost any hour, they found time for me, both privately and professionally.

Since the collapse of the Soviet Union, as with space, the people's attitude toward time has changed fundamentally; time has been commodified. For the Western world, the historian Stephen Kern and the social theorist David Harvey have read this transition as a crucial step of modernization.[2] And as with space, time has been extended: the (active) day has become longer, the scope of historiography has widened, and the future is more open.

Whenever, as a journalist, I succeeded in getting as far as their reception areas, factory directors, mayors, deputies, regional party secretaries, and warlords in the Caucasus took time to grant me an interview, often immediately. They made other people—their subordinates, petitioners, or friends—wait, or they helped them at the same time, talking to them for brief moments while I took notes. Often, they had people hanging around their offices who seemed to stay for hours. I might have interrupted a conversation, but the interview kept getting interrupted, too. In the provinces, the door to many bosses' offices remained open. People walked in and out, shaking hands with everybody, introducing themselves into the boss's realm, while he obviously carried out other tasks, usually several at once.

For Soviet people, doing several things simultaneously was not unusual. Often, when one had to get a permit, stamp, ticket, or other services, the person in charge helped several people at a time and, although there was invariably a line, one was never sure who was next. Many people seemed to jump ahead in the line; they would suddenly show up to claim a previously obtained place in it or they shoved themselves ahead with no clear justification. Appearing with small children was a well-worn trick; people grudgingly conceded them a place in the line, since time was not a deterring factor. To keep people waiting was common; almost everyone did it. Guests made long phone calls from their hosts' apartments or hosts talked endlessly on the phone themselves, while the guests waited, unintentionally overhearing the conversation.

The Soviets, in general, barely quantified their time. Private lessons did not last for the hour (or fifty minutes) agreed upon, but longer, until one was done with the program of the day. The housekeeper stayed for more than the four hours she was paid for; she did not even negotiate about hours, only about how many days a week she would come. Aside from the beginning and the end of the workday, people's time was hardly scheduled. There was no such thing as a time slot.

In his book *The Dance of Life*,[3] the anthropologist Edward Hall distinguishes nine different kinds of time; among them are sacred, profane, metaphysical, physical, biological, and personal times. He distinguishes monochronic and polychronic cultures. The American tradition is monochronic, according to Hall. Its time is linear and segmented like a road on which one travels forward into the future. To look into the past is to look back. All the important activities in a monochronic culture are scheduled. The members of a monochronic society compartmentalize time, as if it were a range of empty containers to be filled with activities. They speak of "time saved, spent, wasted, lost, made up, accelerated, slowed down, crawling, and running out."[4] This enables Americans and other Westerners to concentrate on one task at a time, but it denies context. By scheduling, one selects what one will do at any given time. A scheduled time permits only a limited number of events within a given period. The schedule sets priorities for both people and functions.[5] There is little temporal space for the unexpected.

For the Protestant societies in Western Europe, wasting time is "the deadliest of sins," as Max Weber wrote in his book on the Protestant work ethic.[6] Most Russians to this day would not understand the phrase "wasting time" and, besides, many would not consider it a sin to waste something that is free. By ideology, however, the Soviet Union aimed to become monochronic—perhaps more monochronic than any other society. The Communists were heavily influenced by the notion of the Protestant work ethic. They imposed on their subjects a Taylorism-like work discipline, which according to accepted wisdom was how an industrialized society should deal with time. For the Communists Henry Ford was a hero. In 1929, Stalin introduced a Soviet-style Fordism, including the *nepereryvka*, the "uninterrupted work week," which lasted five days. Incidentally, this also abolished the Christian week and, thus, sacred time. Then in November 1931 every sixth day was declared a resting day. Only on June 27, 1940, with World War II imminent, when Stalin needed to reconcile with the church, did he reinstate the seven-day week.

Arjun Appadurai, an anthropologist, identifies Taylorism as a "regimentation of labor by the prior restructuring of time."[7] In the Soviet Union, the highly divided labor caused an enormous degree of interdependence, far greater than in any Western society. And the more interdependent an industrial society, the more vulnerable. Delays cause disruptions; a high degree of integration thus requires a minute temporal organization and discipline. Individuals and institutions have to observe tight schedules to meet the society's request at any given moment: *"Vsegda gatov"* ("always ready") was the slogan of the Pioneers, the Communist Party's children organization. Time had to be standardized; each individual had to be aware of what time it was and to impose temporal self-control and subordinate himself or herself to the schedule.

High interdependence necessitates a great number of exchanges, all of which have to happen on time. Therefore, a centrally planned economy requires a high degree of scheduling, much higher than in a free market. Both individuals and institutions are required to keep a fast pace of interaction, which results in a quick rhythm of events: thus life in a highly interdependent industrial society is perceived as having a fast tempo.[8] The Soviet economy was indeed highly interdependent. Even tourism was regimented by a plan. However, monochronic time was but a mask. A brief visit to the Soviet Union was enough for any foreigner to understand that the tight schedules did not mean much: time discipline and self-imposed control barely existed and work did not go at a fast tempo. People did not observe any standardized time; many did not even wear a watch. Despite its ideology, the Soviet Union was obviously not a monochronic society.

In a polychronic society, such as a peasant society, one cannot tightly schedule oneself. A farmer has to be prepared for the unexpected, such as the weather. Additionally, polychronic people often place the completion of a task below the importance of being together with family and friends, as Hall has said.[9] In many ways, Soviet society was a peasant society set up in a seemingly urban environment. Thus, people lived in several time frames at once and they accomplished different tasks simultaneously. Men's favorite pastimes, such as the *bania*, fishing, drinking, drinking while fishing, or drinking in the *bania*, suspended time altogether; that is, they suspended measured, linear time. In the perestroika years, it became quite common to hold several jobs; for example, a physicist would moonlight as a casual taxi driver, trader, and painter.

In polychronic and thus connected cultures, if people know each other, there is no need for an imposed order; they will not cheat the others in a line because they will have to deal with them again. A polychronic society's chains of action are built around human relations; interruptions occur frequently and they are tolerated or even welcomed. Priorities shift constantly. In the Soviet Union, this was a necessity; one had to be ready for the unexpected—not bad weather but, perhaps, the sudden availability of normally scarce supplies. The need to rely on connections and networks to get the necessary goods or simply to survive, according to Hall, characterizes any polychronic society. Polychronic people, he wrote, "are apt to be involved in a lot of different activities with several different people at any given time."[10]

But polychronic systems require greater centralization than monochronic ones. Thence, a polychronic bureaucracy is more inward looking. Without gifted men, Hall noted, it can turn into a disaster[11]—the CPSU, however, favored loyalty over competence.

The monochronic and polychronic time systems are like oil and water, Hall stressed. They do not mix.[12] Thus, despite its monochronic, industrialized mask, the Soviet Union at large was an almost purely polychronic society. People hardly accepted the state's schedule as their own, not even the state's representatives themselves. Thus nobody lived up to the monochronic dogma. Negotiations with (foreign) business partners began with a huge breakfast, with toasts to the future cooperation and the friendship of nations; they continued, after a tour of the factory, with a lunch with the directors, who invited people with no direct connections to the deal in question (people to whom they owed favors, paid in the form of this free lunch). These meals included imbibing great amounts of alcohol. In the afternoon, either the discussions or the sightseeing continued, until in the evening the deal was concluded. If not, it was celebrated anyway. An extended dinner, with drinking and frolicking that might include prostitutes, sealed the "negotiations." Time did not matter—not for the finalization of a contract or for the directors. Soviet (state-owned) companies were often run like peasant communities.

Boris Berezovsky, the tycoon in control of Aeroflot and Logovaz, the Moscow auto plant, was known for going to the Kremlin and spending long hours chatting with President Yeltsin's daughter, Tatyana Dyachenko, or with the president's chief of staff, Valentin Yumashev. For a Western political administrator or a top business executive, this would be unimaginable—a "waste" of time.

A peasant's time is cyclical; it follows the four seasons or, in animal husbandry, the birth cycles. Yet, when agriculture was turned into a state-run industry, cyclical time remained in people's minds. The media reported on the harvests and many people were involved in small-scale gardening. Indeed, the five-year plans reflected a peasant's attitude toward technology. Except for the rhythm of the seven-day week, the cycles widely observed by humanity—the day, the year—correspond to a cycle of nature. Thus, the Communists "improved" nature by introducing a nature-like supercycle of their own.

One of the central temporal cycles Western societies observe, however, the political cycle of elections, obviously did not exist in the USSR. Soviet politics were timeless: top politicians moved upward until they reached positions they then kept for the rest of their lives. Khrushchev was the only party leader to leave office alive, and he did not do so voluntarily. When lower ranks lost their positions, they were often disgraced; some ended up in prison or were killed. To stage a political comeback was inconceivable. Boris Yeltsin was the first Soviet politician to succeed in coming back and, as Russia's president, to step down voluntarily. He understood that his time was up.

The introduction of linear time into the Western European society was part of the Enlightenment project. Measured monochronicity was perceived as a prerequisite for industrialization or modernization. The Communists—these self-promoted modernizers—had learned this lesson. As though preparing the country for industrialization, they attempted to organize labor scientifically and to quantify time and rationalize its use, even for leisure. They believed that, in doing so, they would ensure a high level of productivity, both at work and during the citizens' free time, according to Hanson. (They believed people should not waste their energy on irrational pursuits, such as drinking, idling, searching for entertainment, or performing mindless household chores.)[13]

As in so many instances, the Soviets overshot the mark: like in an army, some of their institutions, for example, domestic air traffic, ignored biological time. Flights were scheduled at odd times—often in the middle of the night. The quest for linear time led to a denial of any other time system—first of all biological time, in the shifting of day and night. Human beings were supposed to function like machines. Soviet propaganda made people believe that, in order for the technological revolution to succeed, people had to subordinate themselves to the machines. But how can social life be rationally planned and controlled, without the help of the abstractions of space and time, maps, clocks, and calendars? Yet, as shown earlier, maps hardly existed. Few people wore watches and public clocks were rare, contrary to prerevolutionary St. Petersburg.[14] After the collapse of Communism, they gradually reappeared.

Soviet factories imposed a Tayloristic time discipline—tellingly, many Soviet institutions preferred digital clocks. They monitored the start and end of the workday with clocks. The workers had to do overtime; eventually, they were compelled to sacrifice a Saturday for a *subbotnik*, an unpaid day of work for the sake of the party or the class struggle. Even Lenin did his *subbotnik* by helping to sweep the yard of the Kremlin. In reality, not much was achieved during a *subbotnik*. The symbolism exceeded the results, but the party, thus, demonstrated its control over the citizens' "free" time.

Official activity was run in a hierarchical, military way. Thus, it was subjected to linear time, which included a precise schedule—one that was hardly ever met. Meeting the plan was imperative, yet it was not enough. There was a constant push to overaccomplish, to fulfill the plan in advance, and thus to beat time, to transcend it. "Fulfill the five-year plan in four years," was one of Stalin's crucial slogans. "*Spi skorei, tovarishch*" ("sleep faster, comrade") is how writer Mikhail Zoshchenko satirized the compulsion of beating time. "Sleep faster, comrade, someone else is waiting for your pillow."[15] Indeed, the first five-year plan was declared fulfilled after four years and three months.

Beating time was a work collective's revolutionary vow of faith. Stephen Hanson called this transcended time "charismatic." As in a state of war, everything was to be done with urgency; indeed, urgency was needed to overcome the physical segregation. Beating the plan was primarily required of the industrial manufacturers, but agricultural production was also supposed to beat nature; the transport system or the snow removal in winter had to outperform their capacities as well. Even artists, tour operators, and the circus were to surpass their state-given goals.

Nevertheless, productivity was devastatingly low. "Charismatic" time was *oni*'s time, the time system of the others—the party, the superiors— and in reality, it was mostly ignored. Sickness, lateness, and absenteeism were common. During their day, many workers left to do their errands, see a doctor, or even go fishing. Others were present, but sat around or got drunk. In many Soviet offices, there was no scheduling and no compartmentalization of time (or space), except at the beginning and the end of the workday. People had lunch at their desks, which could go on for hours.

If time is not standardized, measured time does not matter. Thus, one could not trust a Soviet clock, except in the beautiful new world underground; the subway system was accurate to the second. One day in the Publichnaya, the main St. Petersburg library, I noticed that everyone of the five clocks displayed a different time, with differences of as much as three hours. Except for one, they were all running.

According to Hanson, the Communists' combined a concept of charismatic time with one of "rational" time: as a tool for modernization, time was rationalized; revolution, however, required transcendence, or charismatic time.[16] Any revolution, or carnival, for that matter, is a time outside time and a temporal threshold. It brings about the end of the previous time and starts a new era. For that purpose, it has to suspend the ordinary time system and declare a "state of emergency," or a carnival. Communism promised a bright future, an "endless summer vacation," as Hanson put it, or the end of history. The workers' paradise was just around the corner, with Lenin and the party its creators. A new time was dawning that banished the past (and the present) into prehistoric misery. And with the achievement of world Communism, there would be no need for any more development, except for technological progress. The superhuman depiction of the Communist leaders—the monuments—and Soviet historiography conveyed eternity; some, particularly the main Lenin statue on October Square, are set in environments stripped of history,[17] thus of temporality.

The Soviet regime groomed a distinct image of that "endless summer vacation." In a museum of the future, it displayed the achievements of socialism (to come). In fact, the VDNKh (Vystavka Dostizheny Narodnogo Khozyaistva, or the Exhibition of the People's Economy's Achievements), in the north of Moscow, showed off the accomplishments of Soviet technology. The theme park was structured around the different branches of science and engineering. Each field operated its own pavilion, with the ones for nuclear science and the space program being the most lavish. There were halls of radio technology, textiles, industrial poultry farming, and the production of ice cream. Also on display were the few innovations in consumer technology that the Soviets had accomplished. Exhibiting them proved necessary, since they hardly ever reached the ordinary consumer. By ideology, the future was technology, but this future was available only for the privileged, the *oni*.

In 1955, Disneyland opened in the United States. Walt Disney insisted that what he offered his visitors was "reassurance"; it should give them "peace of mind."[18] The VDNKh, the "Disneyland of Soviet technology," as Mikhail Ryklin called it,[19] served a similar purpose—to reassure the Soviet people not about the present, but about the brightness of their future, a future that was neither open nor unpredictable but seemingly stable, metered, and machine like. Both projects, Disney's and the Soviets', were deeply antiurban; they would not allow any disorganized melting pot to happen. And, indeed, they both catered to a pseudourbanized or suburbanized society.

Its architecture, however, betrayed the VDNKh as a folkloristic and backward-looking endeavor. Columns, cupolas, turrets, and fountains mocked a tradition of sorts, as if the celebrated future had to be rooted in a kitschy past. The Italian film director Federico Fellini called the some eighty buildings—the Parthenon of socialism—a "hallucination of a drunken pastry chef."[20] Opening in August 1939, the VDNKh was initially created to advocate collective agriculture. A pavilion was allocated to each republic. In a fairy-tale village, a model of *kolkhoz* life was enacted. It was not before the 1950s that the VDNKh was turned into an exposition of technology. In 1963, the national pavilions were abandoned; 1966 saw the conversion of the hall of farm machinery into one for space exploration, with the Sputnik as its main exhibit. One craze replaced the other. Stalin's one-hundred-foot statue gave way to a *Vostok* rocket of the same height.

Modernity has been characterized as the intertwined emergence of capitalism and industrialism.[21] In a modern society, money, interlocked with time and space, is the main source of social power. It coheres a society over space and time. Hence, its very existence transforms the meaning of space and time. A country without money—as an anonymous, abstract means of exchange—could not work as a modern society. However, the Soviet ruble lacked many characteristics of money; it was little more than a voucher system. One could not quickly transfer it over long distances or use it to safely store value over a period of time. Repeatedly in history some Soviet tenders, ruble notes, or state bond certificates were declared void. Lending rubles did not pay interest, certainly not in convertible currency or "real money." And no money, neither rubles nor "real money"— usually U.S. dollars—could buy time. Thus, there was little incentive to quantify time, or to linearize it, either in the private sphere or at work.[22]

"Charismatic-rational time," this alleged revolutionary fervor, favored appearance over reality. To lighten the burden of the plan, the bureaucrats initially understated the potential of their factories, only to later report higher results than they actually achieved. Beating time, therefore, was often turned into an exercise in beating truth. As with the language, Newspeak, most Soviets did not take monochronic time seriously. They had their strategies to deal with or avoid the demands of the state's phony Taylorism. If necessary, they made their time management *look* monochronic. From my Westerner's viewpoint, they wasted their own and other people's time in their bubbles of timelessness.

Only in the few moments of (public) self-organization was a quantitative value attributed to time. When waiting in a line for something, such as rare tickets, for which one had to queue for more than a few hours, people organized the line so that they did not have to stay there all day. One person was entrusted to take care of the "list" containing all the waiting people's names. Once a day, every one had to turn up to confirm their positions. By managing the list, its keeper assumed certain privileges, such as a speedier advancement of his or her own position and the possibility of receiving favors from other people in the queue. Of course, no fixed rules existed as to how far this "bookkeeper" could go. He or she had to test the others' willingness to "pay" for the service of saving them time.

The Soviet regime usurped historical time as well. By rewriting history, it deprived the people of their past. Central Asia was twice cut off from its (written) history. In the 1920s, Moscow ordered the Central Asian republics to switch from the Arabic to the Latin alphabet; a decade later they had to adopt the Cyrillic alphabet. Thus the Central Asian people were barred from reading their own written heritage. The destruction of banned books and the burning of letters added to the elimination of the past, including people's personal histories.

Popular Soviet historiography ignored the hardship of *byt*, or everyday life in general, and focused on the few (fake) legends of Communist achievements. The single most important was the victory in World War II. Human beings tend to forget the hardships they have had to endure and glorify their personal pasts. Again and again, I met people who earnestly tried to convince me how much better the food supply was under the Soviet regime. For the 1980s, as I had witnessed myself, this was not true: the stores were empty and people spent days "organizing" their provisions. One example was Ludmilla. For the better part of a decade, I met with this typical Russian *babushka*, sometimes almost daily. In 1990, she reported to me what food was available in the stores and what was not. Often, especially in 1991, almost nothing could be had—certainly not sausages, an indicator of some prosperity. To have access to something worthwhile to exchange, she worked in a dairy store. She vented about the tough times. That winter, her heating was turned off for weeks and the neighbors were rude. She had to stand in line, even waiting a half an hour for bread. A few years later, she still complained about her hard life, and rightly so. At least it was better than before, I argued. Surprisingly, she did not remember her own complaints. She accused me of making up the scarcity, or said I was exaggerating. Sausages had always been available, normally two or three kinds, and they were almost free. And the long lines? Yes, they happened, but they were exceptions, she said.

If the past is a foreign country, as Foucault[23] emphasized, then one should not be surprised that the Soviet people, barred from traveling abroad, were not allowed to visit that country, either. Glasnost was an attempt to reconquer the past. With Gorbachev's go-ahead, the media unearthed historical facts: for example, the truth about the murder of the czar and the imperial family, the collectivization that caused starvation, the gulag, the oppression of the church and the smaller nations, the purges, Trotsky, Bukharin, and the Motolov-Ribbentrop pact. Pictures of the czar and his family, street scenes of prerevolutionary Russia, and memoirs and political statements from the past were being published. History is a foreign country and the Russians had a very distant Russia to (re)discover.

What can be said about the past is even more true about the future: it is an unknown area, as foreign as any foreign country. There are two ways of approaching the future: actively and passively. The individual can step into the future, exploring it with a map and a route plan, shaping and thus creating it, or he or she can wait for the future to happen. Inevitably, the future comes to the passive individuals. Typically, this is, as Stephen Kern put it, a soldier's future.[24]

As a thoroughly militarized country, the Soviet Union discouraged individuals from going forward to explore their futures; personal initiative was unwelcome. And with the regime making arbitrary decisions, it was difficult for the individual to plan his or her future. Thus, not surprisingly, the Soviet attitude toward the future was passive; the future came to them—not the bright future the propaganda painted, but one of hardships and ugly surprises. No one expected life to improve; every one feared change. Those in charge enjoyed minor privileges that they were afraid to lose. They knew their rule was not supported, while the people had learned by experience that change was always for the worse.

The propaganda talk of a timeless, bright future further confirmed that. Most people believed that the opposite of what the party said was true. The Orthodox Church added to that. It assured the Russians that history—hence, time—was insignificant. The ultimate meaning of life was to be realized beyond this world, beyond time, in the face of God. The negation of time can thus also be seen as a characteristic feature of traditional Russian society.

With the denial of the past and future, the only remaining time was the present. But what kind of life did this present offer? People had to fight to make ends meet, while the propaganda blathered about the battle to build the bright future and timeless Communism.

By keeping Lenin's body visible, available for visitors to see, and thus seemingly alive; by naming cities after Stalin while he was still in power; by suppressing new fashions; and by maintaining price stability, the regime rendered the passing of time almost invisible. The group of old, ever-aging men on the balcony of the Lenin mausoleum only confirmed this impression. They seemed to have been around for an eternity. Their stony faces could not grow any older. New (elderly) faces were met as sensations; a ranking slightly different from the previous year was the most change one could expect on May Day and for the anniversary of the Revolution, year after year—as though there was only cyclical time. Indeed, the Brezhnev years were later to be called the period of stagnation. History had come to a standstill, time seemed to be halted, even on the fringes: the novelist Viktor Pelevin, in his book *Generation P,* ironically spoke of writers who worked for an eternal, bright future—and this future was already there. One had only to believe in it.[25]

Technology allows simultaneity; the telephone, radio, and television en-
hance the space over which a common present can be shared. The Soviet
Union boasted of mastering these technologies. However, for political reasons, such simultaneity was rarely allowed to happen. Long-distance calls
could not be dialed independently and television programs, radio shows,
and interviews were not transmitted live. On TV, recorded statements were
often paraphrased by a voice-over, so that one saw the interviewee's mouth
move, but heard only the voice of the reporter, except for the first and last
words of the interviewee, much as in interpreted interviews. Thus, the society at large was also denied a common present—even a present within
one country. The present was reduced to the present within one's own private spatial bubble. There, one projected one's wishes into a dreamworld
future that would never be reached; thus, one did not have to care much
about the present, or thus about time, as Sonja Margolina emphasized.[26]

Andrey Sakharov once said that the Soviet power would crumble if the
whole country went on a general strike, even if only for one hour: that is,
if the country, if only for a brief moment, would have a common present.
For one hour, the stagnation would have been suspended, finally, something memorable would have happened: the society would have been
united in space and time. Stagnating time would have been replaced by a
short period of charismatic time, independent of or actually against the Soviet system. Intuitively, Gorbachev seemed to understand that; in the
summer of 1989, to avert a general strike, his government conceded to all
the striking coal miners' demands (although it never made good on all its
concessions).

Time was not money in the Soviet Union, but speed meant prestige. In
sports, it qualified as a currency for international comparison. The Soviet
Union went to great lengths to prepare its athletes for competitions, such as
the (bourgeois) Olympic Games. It wasted resources to build airplanes, including a supersonic passenger jet, the Tu-144, that flew faster than its Western counterparts. Speed was the currency for prestige and a means of overtaking the West, but ordinary people could rarely take advantage of the
technological achievements. Fast travel was for the *nomenklatura;* even if flying was quick, securing a ticket for a flight often required a long struggle.

In moments of urgency, however, time became a commodity. To obtain
some immediately needed goods or (medical) services, one often had to
resort to bribery. If hospital workers refused to acknowledge an emergency as such, for example, one had to switch to a different time system,
one in which time could be bought. To this end, one had to resort to *blat,*
the informal network of favors and bribes.

For the better part of the 1980s, Soviet society remained paralyzed in its
state of timelessness or stagnation. Everything seemed permanent. In some
ways, this made a reporter's work easier. People's addresses did not

change; for decades, they lived in the same flats. They were almost always at home, with little to do in the evenings. Assessments of the political or social situation remained valid for months; whatever someone said in an interview this month was applicable for months to come. This may have convinced many people, including most (Western) observers, that the county would never change. Hence, the sudden acceleration of history took them by surprise. Communist propaganda had obviously succeeded in creating the fake impression of the USSR's strength, stability, and timelessness.

Despite slogans such as "forward," the Communist society petrified itself; there was little change. Why then did people perceive their lives as unstable? Why did so few of them invest time and work into their apartments; why did they hardly maintain them? In spite of the stagnation, people felt little permanence; anything could happen at any time. To most people, it did not make sense to build for duration or to acquire goods that would symbolize continuity. Cars and household appliances, such as washers, were chronically in need of repair. The only objects to reach beyond the temporal bubble, if any could, were small collector's items—objects of "personal temporal monumentality,", as one might call them after Lefebvre, such as flasks of foreign perfume, pins, stamps, some books, or tin soldiers.[27]

However, the desire for *private* permanence runs counter to the revolutionary fervor, or charismatic time. Thus, in addition to being deprived of time or change, people were also deprived of the security of permanence. Soviet stability was the stability of army barracks, where it can be quiet, but where one never knows what will happen next, since one's time is controlled by one's superiors. (Boris Yeltsin, at the time a party bureaucrat in Sverdlovsk, was praised as exceptionally courteous, since he did not call his subordinates at any hour of the night, as Gorbachev did.)[28]

Uskorenie (acceleration), Gorbachev's earliest slogan, coined even before "glasnost" and "perestroika," was an attempt to hypnotize the nation into reviving the country, especially its economy.[29] Gorbachev sought to have time propelled forward. As Hanson has read it, the last general secretary tried to relaunch the Communists' charismatic time as a disciplined revolutionary time. Gorbachev's attempts to accelerate time resulted in such fantastic projects as the "five-hundred-day plan."[30] Within that period, the centrally planned Communist economy was to be dismantled and transformed into a market-based democracy. The most fundamental restructuring of a country ever to be done was supposed to be completed within five hundred days; thus reform was approached with the fervor for beating time of a Soviet shock worker, the record-breaking hero workers celebrated by Soviet propaganda. The five-hundred-day plan was later abolished, but the quest for immediacy remained. Still, the conversion of the Soviet economy proceeded slowly, certainly compared to the most successful transitions from Soviet style Communism, such as Estonia's or Poland's. Yet, it has been labeled as a "shock therapy," a way to bring about a sudden transition to a market economy, thus stressing immediacy.

During perestroika, time finally caught up with Soviet politics. All of a sudden, coming first mattered. Many a race between the party conservatives and the reformers developed. Open battles were fought in the press. The Kremlin had difficulty keeping step with an ever more demanding population, particularly in certain Union republics: the Baltic countries, Ukraine, and the three Caucasus nations. The CPSU lost the only political race involving the population that domestic Soviet politics ever saw. When Gorbachev finally agreed to sign a "new union treaty" and thus to cede some power to the local elites of the independence-minded republics, the republics saw this as too little, too late. Meanwhile, Gorbachev's fellow party bosses conspired against him; to them, he seemed to be storming ahead. Had not Gorbachev said, while visiting East Berlin in October 1989, a time when hundreds of thousands of East Germans were crossing the Hungarian border, that "he who comes late will be punished by life"? He seemed to have been unaware of how time had finally begun to matter for his own country's politics.

In 1988, the changes in time became perceptible: the emerging people's fronts in the Baltic republics, then staunch supporters of Gorbachev's, demanded the introduction of a local Baltic time zone. Because Tallinn, the Estonian capital, was compelled to use Moscow time, it's winter dawn did not occur until shortly before noon. The Estonians claimed a right to a more natural day and night rhythm. Presumably, the symbolism of a time zone different from Moscow's, on the one hand, was at least as important for them as the inconvenience of a late dawn, which on the other hand gave them the advantage of a later dusk. If the hours of daylight had been the only concern, St. Petersburg might also have switched to Eastern European time; dawn occurs in St. Petersburg only twenty minutes earlier than in Tallinn.

Time zones constitute invisible borders and structured space. Belonging to a different time zone, the same as neighboring Finland, was supposed to make the Estonians feel closer to the West. With the change of the time zone, the clock they saw on Finnish TV, their main source of information, fell in step with the clock in their living rooms.

In March 1991, Moscow did not switch to daylight savings time, as it had done every spring since 1985. Estonia did. For the summer, that brought the two capitals back into the same time zone. Then, in September 1991, a few weeks after the putsch, no one seemed to be in charge of Russian time. Moscow, together with the European countries, "automatically" changed "back" to "winter time" (even though it had never gone to daylight time in the first place). Thence, Tallinn found itself still in Moscow's time zone, much to the Estonians' displeasure. Some of the newly independent states, such as Armenia and Kazakhstan, switched to a different time zone.

However, on January 19, 1992, Moscow changed the clocks back again (as did Armenia and Kazakhstan), putting them three hours ahead of Greenwich mean time in the winter and four during the summer. Time consensus, one of the most fundamental prerequisites for the functioning of society, seemed endangered. For a while, people did not know what time it was—or what time regime a railway or air traffic timetable observed.

In order to mark a new era, Russia had changed her time and calendar before. Between July 1917 and October 1921, there were no fewer than ten such changes.[31] Peter I moved Russia's New Year from September to January and provided a detailed prescription for how the holiday was to be celebrated, including the adoption of the Christmas tree. Two months after the Bolsheviks seized power, they switched the country from the Julian to the Gregorian calendar.

Russia spans eleven time zones. Until 1988, despite this expansion, air and railroad traffic ran on one time: Moscow time. Departure and arrival times on tickets were displayed in Moscow time, or "All-Union time" as it was called. Leaving Khabarovsk in the Far East at 3 A.M. was very convenient, since it was 10 A.M. local time. But since the locals did not use Moscow time in their everyday life, one was never completely sure of the exact time difference with Moscow. Symbolically, keeping transport on one time was an attempt to force the whole country into synchronization. All-Union time ignored nature's day-and-night cycle; it was linear, superior, and subjugating—the time of the center, the time of hailed technology. A decade after the end of Communism, in some smaller provincial railway stations such as Magnitogorsk, the clock still displays Moscow time.

When told that, in the West, departures were published in local time, Soviet people were incredulous. Was this not asking for chaos?, they wondered. Indeed, when the republics became independent, some administrations did not know how to replace Moscow time. Kazakhstan, for example, set the clocks at Almaty airport on Greenwich mean time as the superior time. The locals found it hard to believe when their airport finally switched to local time, although the tickets had already been issued in Almaty time for a while. For some months, one was never sure what time a train or plane ran, in what time the timetable was set.

As I showed in the chapters on the senses, to me traveling to Soviet Russia felt like traveling to the past. This was not specific to the Soviet era. Since the eighteenth century, European travelers conceived of their journeys to the East as traveling back in time to a "more primitive" state of Western civilization, as the postmodernist historian Larry Wolff showed.[32] But St. Petersburg was built as a window to Russia's future. Both Russian and the Soviet leaders spoke of catching up with and surpassing the West, jumping from the West's past into the (Western-like) future of humankind—basically skipping the present.

The collapse of Communism opened the door to time and to the past; the future is waiting to be shaped by the young generation. In the present, cyclical and linear time coexist as in any modern, complex society, as do polychronic or monochronic time—one is never sure what "time zone" one is in.

The bright Communist future has vanished. The attempts to beat time have failed; instead, the party has passed away. The VDNKh, the theme park for the achievements of Soviet technology, has been turned into a bazaar. Imported consumer electronics, computers, clothes, perfume, and washers are exhibited for sale, many for lower prices than in downtown. Ten years after the collapse of the Soviet Union, a Sputnik was still hanging from the ceiling of the pavilion for space exploration, while Western luxury cars were sold below. The Soviet museum of the future has turned into a shabby marketplace for the present. After 1991, a tidal wave of Western-style supermarkets and computer stores opened in the big cities, soon blurring the distinction between a "Western store" and a Soviet one. For a while, stores were either selling imported goods for "imported prices" or selling cheaper domestic merchandise. Now, many of the "imported" goods, such as Coca-Cola, Kellogg's cornflakes, or Swiss-brand bouillon cubes, are produced domestically. Young men spend hours in the computer stores, gawking and asking questions. These stores downtown have replaced the VDNKh as a museum of the future. Finally, a kind of a future has arrived, in full view, to touch, and for those who can afford it, to buy. But it is still an imported future, with a used Western car representing the "future" more than a new Russian one.

Even the past has become palpable. Since the late 1980s, the *fartsovchiki*, the small black marketeers catering to tourists around Red Square, in front of the museums, and near the international hotels, have taken advantage of the Westerners' wish to travel back in time. They have added icons of the past to their range of gadgets. To this day, they offer Soviet army watches, other army paraphernalia, KGB and Lenin insignia, old Soviet medals, wartime and prerevolutionary banknotes, old postcards, and books. The past is a foreign country and its souvenirs have been imported into the present.

Cultures around the world have been classified into a temporal hierarchy, with the defining power resting with the Europeans and Americans, who consider their own cultures to be more advanced than others. Westerners are the ones to decide who is "lagging behind."[33] The Soviets adopted that view and, with the help of Marx's temporal classification of the social systems, they wanted to jump ahead in time. Socialism was more advanced than capitalism; Communism was the final stage of social development. For that, the Soviet architects designed timeless buildings for a timeless future at the end of history. Their all-embracing style combined antiquity—namely, columns, sculptures, and quotations from the Greek—with nineteenth-century urbanism and crude modernism. They wrapped together the history of civilization from its beginnings to its (Soviet) peak.

To the young and adventurous, very few changes marked the passing of time. Soviet life seemed tedious to them, stagnant. They could spend time consuming, but there was little to be consumed—some nonofficial music, alcohol, drugs, movies, and sex—as Brodsky contended.[34] Thus, young people had much time to spend and one did not miss much when drunk: alcohol certainly helps to kill time. Gorbachev addressed alcoholism as a Soviet condition, inflicted by stagnation. Hence, in the Baltics many activists vowed not to touch alcohol as long as the fight for independence carried on. They did not want to miss an opportunity to act. Similarly, some New Russians tend to consume little alcohol; they do not have time to get drunk.[35]

An open future is the source of human freedom or, put differently, possessing freedom of action opens one future, Stephen Kern stresses.[36] No Soviet citizen was supposed to know the truth about the past since the past was fabricated to match Communist propaganda, and no one could plan for a particular future.

"If the time systems of two cultures are different, everything else will be different," said Edward Hall.[37] He, of course, had two separate cultures in mind—Japan and the United States. Yet, there is no reason not to apply his observation when looking diachronically at one changing culture.

When the Soviet leaders began to open up their country, when they finally allowed their people to get a hold of their pasts and to plan their individual futures, the very foundation of the Soviet society was shaken. The USSR's most hailed truths were no longer true. All of a sudden, people were allowed to shape their own futures, to reinvent themselves, and to have different individual futures, not soldiers' futures. Individual initiative suddenly became possible, if not mandatory.

The two-layered temporal order of the Soviet Union has broken down and is disappearing. The Soviet past has become a very distant, yet accessible, country. People's unpleasant memories are quickly fading. The general public's interest in history has vanished. Many people are cut off from their past again, but this time by their own will. The new Russian state does not indulge in transcendent or charismatic time. The Soviets' time doctrine has not been replaced. There is no standardized new time regime, at least not yet. No new language of temporal ideology has been imposed; there is no five-year plan. Ten years after the collapse of Communism, Russia is still desynchronized and temporally fragmented—pluralism at its worst reigns. The society harbors many different perceptions of time.

Uskorenie ("acceleration") for the economy obviously failed. Gorbachev did not succeed in reviving industrial production. However, in other fields, he triggered acceleration. People measure time in changes. By easing the repression, permitting cooperatives, and overseeing the filling in of the "blank spots" of Soviet history, Gorbachev tentatively opened up the country. The space of time interrogated by historiography and thus by popular knowledge increased dramatically. Any discovery of historical fact is perceived as new. Although its content involves the past, historiography happens in the present. The exploration of the past causes the sensation of time moving forward and, since so many historical facts were unearthed after the fall of the Soviet Union, time seemed to move in fast forward. The sheer number of events happening multiplied. This relative overabundance of events compared with the preceding period made people perceive time as accelerating. All of a sudden, things began to move and, soon, they were moving fast. Some events, especially the putsch in 1991, turned instantly into history. Soviet history was mined as though it were a quarry; banned books, suppressed thinking, and recountings of atrocities were excavated. Every week, some exciting new revelation was made public. Years of political and historical development were squeezed into weeks, days, or hours during the putsch. The Estonian novelist Jaan Kross once noted that he had always expected the Soviet Union to collapse, but he thought it would happen in fifty or one hundred years. Then he began to think that it would happen within one or two decades; later, he thought it would happen within years.[38] The regime finally crumbled within a week, only three years after Estonia's demand for independence could first be raised publicly.

The acceleration was mirrored by palpable changes: newspapers replaced books, writers switched to the shorter genres—essays, short stories, even poems—and news articles became more concise. The Russian language became livelier (and in some ways even more mutilated) than before; new words emerged, and others went out of fashion. Some words' life cycles were shortened and these words instantly faded away. The ubiquitous "worker" and the "proletariat" all but disappeared. Terms with positive connotations turned negative. As the St. Petersburg sociologist Leonid Kesselman recalled for me, in the 1960s being called an idealist was a positive characterization, to be a cynic was despicable. Today, a cynic is seen as reasonable, a pragmatist, while people unable to cope with post-Soviet realities are scorned as idealists or romantics. In the 1980s, the schools still taught collectivism as a higher value. Being publicly called an "individualist" was like being cursed. Privately, however, it was the other way around. "Perestroika," "glasnost," "democratization," and "market" initially stood for hope, but soon they were discredited.[39] In the last months before he stepped down, Gorbachev became devoted to the word "informal," thus, implicitly acknowledging the failure of his formal politics and literally asking for the violation of formal Soviet politics altogether. Post-Soviet politicians like to characterize themselves as "pragmatists." Other changes in language involved a whole set of new words that entered colloquial Russian: "skid" (sale), "businessmen," and many computer and fashion terms.

The Soviet society was not prepared for this acceleration of everyday life. Under these new stresses, people suddenly did not have enough time to complete everyday tasks—to eat, for example. The concept of fast food made it to Russia.[40] In the Soviet Union, one rarely saw anyone eating on the street.[41] Today, it is common for people to munch their burgers and pizzas while rushing around—a typical sign of modernity, according to the great Austrian novelist Robert Musil.[42]

Some of my Russian friends soon began to complain that they were under stress. An editor of a popular magazine, happy to finally be able to do what he considered useful and honest work, folded under the faster pace his new life suddenly reached. He continued to live in his polychronic time—a newly acquired *dacha* in Pskov, four hundred miles west of Moscow, had to be renovated; the carpenters had to be organized; the apartment in the city had to be rented out—while he stayed with his wife in his *dacha* in Peredelkino. The authors of newly discovered diaries and memoirs from the gulag that his magazine undertook to publish expected him to accommodate them with plenty of time and attention; for decades, they had been forced to keep silent, now they believed they had found a confidant. Eventually, he took refuge from the new fast-paced society he once longed for. He became an Orthodox priest.

Time not only accelerated, it expanded. The day underwent an extension. In the Soviet era, the grocery stores closed for the day somewhere between 6 P.M. and 8 P.M., the department stores no later than 9 P.M. Stores were closed on Sundays. Theaters, concert halls, and movie venues began their night performances between 6 P.M. and 8 P.M.; at 10 P.M., the last curtain fell. Hardly any restaurant would have served food later than 10 P.M. and bars did not exist. At night, people were supposed to relax. With the exception of the militaristically run enterprises, such as transportation, the Soviet Union slept at night. There was nothing else to do. The days were monotonous and the nights were long.

The opening up of society has turned the Soviet cities' fourteen-hour day into a place of nonstop activity. There is hardly anything one cannot buy at any time of day in Moscow and St. Petersburg. Many bars close only in the morning; some casinos operate around the clock. The Metelitsa in Moscow treats the gamblers still present at 7 A.M. with a free breakfast. Many a grocery store bills itself as "24 hours." Sleepy Moscow has turned into a sleepless city. To a lesser extent, this is true for St. Petersburg and the capitals of the former republics.

Oni and *my*, the separation of "them," the privileged, and "us," finds its equivalent in the citizens' relationship with time. *Oni*'s time was linear, but perceived as dull, slow, and imposed on the people. One coped best with it by being passive and evasive. It was a soldier's time, but there was little incentive to respect its imperatives. The people, *my* (we), observed a different time; this time was polychronic and required activity. One had to organize, to network, to socialize. People refused to plan this part of their time, because it was their "leisure" time. With the demise of the Soviet institutions, *oni* time lost ground. The temporal space in which one acted as a *homo sovieticus* gradually diminished and is still diminishing. The fact that many people have lost their jobs or are on permanent leave only contributes to this. However, with "our time" gradually expanding over the whole day, a leisurely, cavalier attitude has come to dominate everyday life and even business. Post-Soviet politicians and businesspeople tend to act as though their lives and the whole country were a single web of favor networks.

Many Russians perceive linear time as Soviet time and, since they want to avoid anything that is Soviet, they reject linear time. In addition, some of the more confident among the New Russians consider schedules to be a Western trait and associate it with the petit bourgeoisie; thus, they have little incentive to observe linear time. Also, people are time confused. The two systems coexist in parallel structures and, in some instances, they symbolically compete. For example, the two airlines, Aeroflot and Transaero, vie for business, with the latter aiming to stand for everything the Soviet Union was not: clean, friendly, and first and foremost, on time.

However, post-Soviet polychronic time is not the cozy peasant rhythm of Soviet life, in which people were open to different things happening simultaneously. It has taken on entirely new dimensions, comprising a high variety of time sets and paces. Many Russians these days, particularly of the younger generations, live in two different "time zones." They spend part of their time in a Westernized world, where they use mobile phones, the Internet, and electronic organizers. Their lives have a quick rhythm; many work hard, as they say, and they certainly play hard. They travel to London and New York, some on assignment. Yet, upon returning home, they reenter the old time system. Many working women in their thirties still live with their mothers, who raise their children. In the *babushkas'* territory, linear time does not matter. This is reflected by the economy of the lives of younger working women. On the one hand, these women live in the fast-paced New Russia; they live the lives of young, urban professionals in a world metropolis. On the other hand, they go home to a traditional Soviet *my*. They have privatized their humble apartments and their mothers shop thriftily. At home, everyday life is cheap, controlled, and traditional. Away from home, they waste money on a grand scale, in restaurants and discos, for example. For teenagers, living in different time systems simultaneously might not be uncommon. Their own society radically differs from that of their parents, as at school a completely different set of rules applies. In post-Soviet Russia, however, the society as a whole seems to indulge in a double life of living in separate times.

Russia's calendar confirms the parallel existence of the old and the new time systems. Most Communist holidays have been kept—the anniversary of the October Revolution in November, International Labor Day on May 1—although they have been downgraded to being merely days off work. At the same time, new holidays have been introduced, such as Russian National Day (June 12), Orthodox Christmas, and Easter.

Time is power; speed represents power. By traveling around town at high speed, politicians convey their importance. The fast lanes in the middle of the Moscow arteries are actually reserved for emergency vehicles, but top government officials and businesspeople (who buy the right to use emergency lights) are entitled to use them, too. They race dangerously along the middle lane with flashing blue lights, while the regular traffic moves on slowly. This has been justified by Moscow's permanent gridlock; important decision makers cannot waste their time in traffic. Their speed conveys status. If one recalls how the tycoon Boris Berezovsky allegedly wasted full days hanging out in the Kremlin, one must conclude that he also lives in two different time systems. When traveling about town, his time is sparse and linear, but it lapses into old Soviet timelessness after he arrives at his destination. Monochronic time is learned, as Edward Hall noted. It is arbitrary and imposed. In Western societies it has been so thoroughly learned and integrated that it is treated as though it were the only natural or "logical" way of organizing life.[43] Polychronic people, Hall believes, must stay "in sync" with their society. Does this explain why so many Russians, after a few weeks abroad, complain that they do not understand their own society anymore?

A carnival suspends ordinary time; it becomes a time outside time, as Bakhtin said.[44] And so does revolution. The society defies its fundamental truths. Bakhtin wrote: Carnival is "the true feast of time, the feast of becoming, change, and renewal, . . . hostile to all that was immortalized and completed."[45] Normally scheduled activities, such as dinnertime and bedtime, are put off. The participants switch into ceremony's time—sacred time. For the duration of the carnival, any temporal order beyond its own is placed on hold. However, a carnival is a ritual period of transition of limited duration, a time marker in cyclical time. Traditionally, it marks the end of winter, the passage to spring. A revolution, however, marks change in noncyclical time—history—

though, also as a rite of passage. Both carnival and revolution indicate a sudden change, though in both cases the transition process of adapting to this change actually occurs more gradually, flowingly. Hence a carnival is a temporal landmark and revolutionary events a "monumental period of time,"[46] to use Edward Hall's term.

In Russia, the state of emergency—thus the carnival—has not yet ended. Rapid transition continues; the society is still in turmoil. The year 1991 may be read as the climax of a carnival that started with Gorbachev's rise to power, although no end is in sight yet. This is expressed in the many conflicting values, tempi, styles, and customs; in spending habits and lavish feasts in new restaurants; in the orgies in nightclubs and *banias*. The Russians buy icons of affluence; exaggerating in any possible way, they dress up to be somebody else.

As mentioned earlier, some scholars have read Bakhtin's *Rabelais* as a coded attack on the cultural situation in Stalin's Russia.[47] Therefore, the entire Communist era would have to be seen as one extended period of transition from the authoritarian Russian empire to a more pluralistic rule, a state of emergency that lasted for almost a century, with the temporal order (and the rule of law) suspended since 1917. The Communist leaders would be the "lords of misrule and chaos,"[48] to borrow Milton's term, or *rois pour rire*, according to Bakhtin. The years 1905 and 1917 would be this *smuta*'s (time of troubles') call to arms and the collapse of the USSR its grand finale. What one sees now are a series of aftershocks, or the hangover.

Polychronic time still prevails as the main time system, even in Western-oriented institutions, such as a sociological research center. At lunchtime, scholars who use the most advanced sociological tools available to measure public opinion, people as Western-minded as they can possibly be, unwrap cold cuts, sausages, cheese, pickles, tomatoes, and bread. One woman takes the kettle to the ladies room to get water. Someone has baked a cake or brought strawberries from a *dacha*, or chocolate; maybe someone comes up with a reason to share a little drink, for a toast at least. The office is narrow; the two small tables are loaded with papers, books, staplers, pens, and floppy disks. The food is piled between the keyboards and documents and the computers are running; on top of one of the monitors is a box of cookies. Of course, the little feast lasts longer than the lunch break's scheduled hour.[49] However, work is not really interrupted. Whenever there is a call, someone answers it, and people discuss their work and make decisions during the lunch hour. From time to time, someone enters the office in search of work-related advice, to borrow a stapler, to borrow cash, to hunt for theater tickets or a used car. Most likely, he or she will be invited to stay, to have some food and a little drink. No one would see this person as an intruder, although the office is having its lunch break. Interestingly enough, the very same people behave much like Westerners when eating out for lunch. They choose small, frugal dishes, such as a salad or soup, and some *pelmeni*, Russian dumplings. They do not drink alcohol and within an hour or so they get back to work, observing an almost American time discipline.

As demonstrated before, the Soviet man's leisure activities were limited. Only a few people had hobbies, such as collecting stamps or pins. Men went fishing or to the *bania* or the *dacha*; they made repairs and organized supplies. For women, going to the hairstylist, the manicure studio, and the cosmetologist was one of the few ways to relax. To seriously engage in activities such as photography, mountain climbing, or music, one had to overcome many obstacles. There were few sports facilities for the population at large: maybe a swimming pool and in winter an ice rink. Sport existed mostly on TV, for the aggrandizement of the Soviet state. For young people, life is usually full of beginnings. Many Soviet youths, however, as Podnieks showed in his film *Legko li byto molodym?* (Is it easy to be young?), perceived their lives as monotonous and dull.

The end of Communism has fundamentally changed the Russians' attitudes toward their (free) time. All of a sudden, life is full of new starts, even for those generations who tend to look back. Many new things are there to be discovered—new activities, newly unearthed (historical) facts and objects. Tellingly, toward the end of the Soviet Union, Russian men began to wear digital watches, a symbol of time measured and commodified.

Time in Russia, previously a highly synchronized society, has become fragmented as never before; different temporal systems coexist. Russia has been desynchronized. This became obvious during the putsch in August 1991 and during the fight for the Russian White House two years later. The immediate neighborhood around which these events took place was plunged into revolutionary time, with the previous time order suspended—a few blocks away, however, everyday life continued as though nothing was happening. In Moscow, in front of the White House, history was in the making. On Lubyanka Square, on August 21, 1991, Feliks Dzerzhinsky's statue was toppled. Yet elsewhere in Russia the monuments honoring the founder of the KGB remain in place to this day.

Since the collapse of the regime, with a plurality of times and rhythms now coexisting, the passing of time has become visible as never before. Fashion for a mass market has reached Russia, not only in the form of mercurially shifting clothing styles, but also in the form of cars, furniture, services, tourism, and entertainment. Change—hence time—is accelerated. Russia's big cities, Moscow, St. Petersburg, and the capitals of the former Soviet republics, have become twenty-four-hour cities, especially for leisure activities. Many bars, restaurants, and stores are open around the clock. And people have adapted to and taken advantage of it, especially the young and those slightly older, but still young enough to try to compensate for what they think they missed in their previous Soviet lives.

The more affluent city dwellers have taken to playing tennis; some nouveau riche work out in the newly established gyms. Swimming has become more popular. People attend language courses. They have begun to schedule their free time, or that part of the free time they spend away from home. Much more entertainment, including high culture, is being offered than during the Soviet period. People tend to have more time at their disposal than before, though they have much less idle time. They do not waste time by standing in lines anymore; they spend it having fun, shopping, eating out, dancing, and studying. They also tend to work less; many do not have regular, full-time jobs anymore or they do business from home. Others, of course, find less time because their work has become their lives, which was inconceivable for the *homo sovieticus*.

In industrial societies, work is a "phenomenological marker of time"; in postindustrialist capitalism, according to Appadurai, it has been replaced by consumption, a necessity to keep the economy afloat.[50] The Russian society does not yet work in a Western way, but the consumption patterns of its newly affluent match those of the West. Free time, the previously barely structured evenings and weekends, has been transformed into consumption time. By actively consuming, one defines one's own status. Consumption, however, requires not only time, but also money. The ability to consume, therefore, is read as an indication of affluence. Moscow's emerging middle class shows off with cars, home computers, and trips abroad. The Russians have often been called patient, on the edge of stoic, but many new Russian consumers expect instant gratification.

As of late, many Russians themselves have embarked on a trip back in time, into their Soviet pasts, though only as tourists. River cruises have grown more popular, as people float from Moscow to St. Petersburg, to Astrakhan in the South, on the Lena in Siberia, or only for the weekend on the Volga Canal. Organized like a Soviet *putyovka*, as the package tours of the trade unions were called, these boat-trips include fixed eating hours, guided excursions, and entertainment programs for both children and adults. The revelers reminisce on the glossy side of the Soviet past.

Such boat tours, the kitschy urban design, the New Russians' estates, and the infamous *Okhotny Ryad* mall in Moscow, as different as they are, all express a nostalgia divorced from history—a "nostalgia without memory," as Appadurai called it.[51] This "interplay of fashion and patina" pretends a tradition that never was. It is supposed to provide those who can afford it with "roots," with history and thus with status, which might eventually—after the carnival is over—turn them into a new upper class. Or so they hope.

NOTES

1. The quote is generally attributed to Benjamin Franklin.
2. Stephen Kern, *The Culture of Time and Space, 1880–1918* (Cambridge, Mass.: Harvard University Press, 1983), and David Harvey, *The Urban Experience* (Baltimore: Johns Hopkins University Press, 1989).
3. Edward T. Hall, *The Dance of Life* (New York: Doubleday, 1983).
4. Hall, *Dance of Life*, 48. As Hall noted, Americans treat time almost the same way they treat money. They save it, they plan its use, they know exactly how much time they are willing to spend to be with somebody, and if they happen to waste time, they know exactly what this time was meant for. Most northern Europeans seem to divide their time the same way Americans do and have periods when they do not seem to care about time, as if setting aside a certain amount of time for nonlinear use.
5. Edward T. Hall, *Beyond Culture* (New York: Doubleday, 1976), 18–19.
6. "Loss of time through sociability, idle talk, luxury, even more sleep than is necessary . . . is worthy of absolute moral condemnation." Max Weber, *The Protestant Ethic and the Spirit of Capitalism*, trans. Talcott Parsons (London: Allen & Unwin, 1930), 158.
7. Arjun Appadurai, *Modernity at Large* (Minneapolis: University of Minnesota Press, 1996), 79.
8. Norbert Elias, *The Civilizing Process: The History of Manners and State Formation and Civilization*, trans. Edmund Jephcott (Cambridge, Mass.: Blackwell, 1994), 436–448, 457.
9. Hall, *Beyond Culture*, 150.
10. Hall, *Beyond Culture*, 150.
11. Hall, *Dance of Life*, 22.
12. Hall, *Beyond Culture*, 150.
13. Stephen Hanson, *Time and Revolution: Marxism and the Soviet Institutions* (Chapel Hill: University of North Carolina Press, 1997), 127.
14. Alexander Herzen, in his memoirs, complained about the noise of the many watchtower bells. Herzen, *My Past and Thoughts*, trans. Constance Garnett (London: Chatto and Windus, 1968).
15. Mikhail Zoshchenko, *Spi skorei* (Sleep faster) (Riga, Latvia: Logos, 1938). Interestingly, the book is printed in the pre-1917 Cyrillic alphabet, as if its publishers were longing for time gone by.
16. Hanson, *Time and Revolution*, 11. Hanson defines charismatic time as "ordinary time transcended for those accepting charismatic domination."
17. Mikhail Yampolsky, "In the Shadow of Monuments: Notes on Iconoclasm and Time," trans. John Kachur, in *Soviet Hieroglyphics: Visual Culture in Late Twentieth-Century Russia*, ed. Nancy Condee (Bloomington: Indiana University Press, 1995), 96.
18. Karal Ann Marling, ed., *Designing Disney's Theme Parks: The Architecture of Reassurance* (Montreal: Canadian Center for Architecture, 1997). Disney was inspired by the world's fairs, as Marling in her essay, "Imagineering the Disney Theme Park" (29–178) notes. The Soviets were most likely aware of what Disney was do-

ing. In the early 1940s, Eisenstein called Disney "the greatest contribution of the American people to art." And for Disney, just like for the Soviet art world, Richard Wagner with his idea of a work of total art, "Gesamtkunstwerk," had been an important influence.

19. Mikhail Ryklin, "Zeit der Diagnose," *Lettre International* 30 (Fall 1995): 112.

20. Quoted from Jamey Gambrell, "The Wonder of the Soviet World," *New York Review of Books*, December 22, 1994, 30.

21. Roger Friedland and Deirdre Boden, ed., *NowHere: Space, Time, and Modernity* (Berkeley: University of California Press, 1994), 1–60.

22. Harvey, *The Urban Experience*. Harvey wrote of the term "enlightenment projects" that it is "a unified common-sense of what space and time were about and why their rational ordering was important. This is based on 'common' availability of watches and clocks and the capacity to diffuse cartographic knowledge"(245).

23. Although the phrase "history is a foreign country" is generally attributed to Foucault and the quote "a foreign country is the past" is attributed to David Lowenthal, in 1953, L. P. Hartley published his book, *The Past Is a Foreign Country* (London: Hamish-Hamilton, 1953).

24. Kern, *Culture of Time and Space*. Kern cites Henri Bergson for distinguishing two types of future (89–91).

25. Viktor Pelevin, *Generation P* (Moscow: Vagrius, 1999).

26. Sonja Margolina, *Russland: Die nichtzivile Gesellschaft* (Reinbek, Germany: Rowohlt, 1994), 134. The projections into the dreamworld future, Margolina argued, further decreased people's interest in their own everyday lives and in reflecting on them.

27. For temporal monumentality, see Marc Augé, *Non-places: Introduction to an Anthropology of Supermodernity*, trans. John Howe (London: Verso, 1995), 60.

28. Leon R. Aron, *Yeltsin: A Revolutionary Life* (New York: Thomas Dunne/St. Martin's, 2000), 93.

29. *Uskorenie* included attempts to generate growth by allowing some degree of democracy on the shop floor, by easing the grip of Gosplan, the central planning agency. The workers were entitled to elect their management by introducing a certain level of self-management and increasing the investment in the construction of new manufacturing facilities, which resulted in hidden inflation and threw the Soviet economy off its delicate balance.

30. The five-hundred-day plan, originated by economists Stanislav Shatalin and Grigori Yavlinski and propagated by Yeltsin, was supposed to transform the Soviet centrally planned society into a market economy within five hundred days.

31. For instance on July 1 and December 28, 1917, and May 31 and September 17, 1918.

32. Larry Wolff, *Inventing Eastern Europe: The Map of Civilization on the Mind of the Enlightenment* (Stanford, Calif.: Stanford University Press, 1994), 17–49.

33. James Duncan, "Sites of Representation, Place, Time and the Discourse of the Other," in *Place/Culture/Representation*, ed. James Duncan and David Ley (New York: Routledge, 1993), 42.

34. Joseph Brodsky, *Less Than One* (New York: Farrar, Straus & Giroux, 1986), 22.

35. Alena V. Ledeneva, *Russia's Economy of Favour: Blat, Networking, and Informal Exchanges* (Cambridge: Cambridge University Press, 1998), 205.

36. Kern, *Culture of Time and Space,* 102–104.

37. Hall, *Dance of Life,* 92.

38. Jaan Kross, interview with author in Tallinn, June 1992.

39. Leonid Kesselman, a sociologist in St. Petersburg, interview with author, "Die Leben von Wörtern," *Weltwoche,* February 10, 1994, 11. Distinct layers of society—the youth, the prisoners, the soldiers—always spoke their distinct idioms in Russian, yet those were certainly more constant as long as the country was closed.

40. The *stolovayas,* or eateries, however, had existed before, as mentioned in chapter 5. They served regular meals, although the customers often ate standing.

41. The *piroshki* and the Georgian *khachapuria* were exceptions, though they were mostly available at the markets, not on the streets. The ubiquitous ice cream is not a meal, but a candy, entertainment for the palate.

42. In his *Man without Qualities,* Robert Musil repeatedly referred to eating while on the go as characteristic of modernity. Musil, *Man without Qualities,* trans. Eithne Wilkins and Ernst Kaiser (London: Secker & Warburg, 1953).

43. Hall, *Beyond Culture,* 20.

44. Mikhail M. Bakhtin, *Rabelais and His World,* trans. Helene Iswolsky (Bloomington: Indiana University Press, 1984), 7.

45. Bakhtin, *Rabelais,* 10.

46. Hall, *Beyond Culture,* 26.

47. Simon Dentith, *Bakhtinian Thought* (New York, Routledge, 1995), 71.

48. John Milton, *Paradise Lost* (1674).

49. The people in such offices may be slightly less extravagant than I assume, since I was welcomed and entertained in this instance as a guest; however, I have paid unexpected visits to such offices around lunch time and found as much food as when I was invited.

50. Appadurai, *Modernity,* 79.

51. Appadurai, *Modernity,* 82.

8

✢

To Buy Is to Be
Money Replaces the Fences

I buy, therefore I am. Until 1991, the Western consumers' maxim was alien to the Russians. If anything at all, they would have said, I obtain *po blatu*, therefore I survive.

The Soviet Union was a country virtually without money. The ruble did not buy much and no one respected it. People knew intuitively that it was not a real currency. It could neither be invested nor did it store value safely. The Soviet government repeatedly devalued people's savings. Owning foreign currencies was prohibited. Only taxi drivers in the big cities, waiters, and black marketeers accepted dollars; everyone else refused to take foreign money from strangers, from fear of being caught, for the lack of opportunities to use it, or out of habit. Therefore, money mattered little; people's lives did not depend on their finances—or not primarily. However, it was impossible to lead a decent life without a network of connections. They provided people with access to the goods generally unavailable in the stores.

For interactions for which a means of payment was needed, some widely appreciated goods were used. They had to be durable and easy to transport and conserve. In most crisis-afflicted societies, cigarettes meet these requirements. In Russia, vodka was used more widely as such a "hard" currency. Moonlighters and informal suppliers usually named their prices in numbers of bottles. Thus vodka kept circulating, much like money; it had the further advantage that a bottle could be disguised as a present.

Except for some canned food, Soviet grocery stores were usually empty, yet the country's refrigerators were full. Many Soviet jokes addressed this situation: in a store, a customer asks to buy the coatrack behind the counter, but he is informed that the store is a butcher shop.

Nothing shaped Soviet everyday life as much as the scarcity of almost all groceries, including soap and toilet paper. Durable goods such as shoes, coats, socks, apparel, tape recorders, TV sets, and washing machines were unattainable. Choices were always few and often the shops were empty. Officially or unofficially, all the goods sought after were rationed. As late as 1991, in some areas of the country, soap and basic foodstuffs could only be purchased with *talony* (ration coupons). In these places, no amount of money would have bought soap, at least not through the official channels. Thus, to meet the most basic needs, one had to find ways to obtain goods: to queue for hours, to ask friends for help, and to grasp and hoard what was available. An easier way to acquire searched-for items was to get them out of season—skis and winter clothing in summer, swimsuits in January.

One never left home without a canvas shopping bag because one had to grab something, such as soap or toilet paper, whenever one stumbled upon it. I have seen apartments stacked with more than a hundred toilet paper rolls. The Soviets' instinctive reaction to grab and save everything—and as much as possible—aggravated the shortages, for example, of toilet paper. This increased the demand, which by implication enhanced a commodity's value and subsequently its scarcity. That was particularly true for easy-to-store, nonperishable goods such as toilet paper, soap, or vodka. Sometimes, the Soviets' reflex to hoard might even have caused the deficit. If the authorities overnight provided the country with toilet paper in abundance, the shortage would still prevail for some time.

In obtaining goods and services, money was of little help. Only in niches would the Soviet regime tolerate islands of "capitalism," such as the *ptichi rynok* (bird market, actually a pet market) or the *rynok radio-lyubiteley* (literally, the radio amateurs' market), where radios, tape recorders, VCRs, and especially computer parts were sold. For everything else, people had to rely on friends and relations who would help them gain access to what was needed. That is, one had to resort to informal networks, called *blat*, which were essential for the Soviet Union's survival, since they corrected the command economy's deficiencies. However, by absorbing scarce commodities from the state's channels of distribution, *blat* additionally aggravated the shortages, hence rendering the informal channels, and *blat* itself, even more indispensable.

Soviet stores were run by the state; they merely mimicked normal retail outlets. However, what was on display was not necessarily for sale and not everything that was for sale was on display. Actually, whatever was sought after was not on display. The arbitrary prices were set by the government. They did not reflect the production costs, exchange value, or the utility of articles. The best stores, as I have shown in an earlier chapter, were beyond reach of the general public; not only the party leadership, but also many other groups had access to special outlets, to factory stores, or to privileged delivery. No attempts were made to hide the fact that some groups—collectives—enjoyed privileges, for example, military personnel at the Voyentorg department store. Single individuals, however, were not supposed to enjoy favored treatment.

Boris Yeltsin, shortly after becoming Moscow's party secretary, roamed the city's stores to inspect their storage facilities. Again and again, he unearthed goods that never made it to the counters. He called this crusade a fight against corruption and embezzlement, something for which he was lauded, both by ordinary Russians and by the Western press. The latter was outraged by the degree of fraud that seemed to exist. Yet Yeltsin in fact "exposed" what everyone knew about anyway. In one way or another, most people, presumably including Yeltsin, eventually profited from the possibility of obtaining scarce goods. Groceries withheld were redistributed through *blat* and thus reached those consumers who were willing to pay the highest price—not in money, but in *blat* credits; thus, those who obtained them probably needed them most urgently. Rather than uncovering a secret fraud, Yeltsin unmasked this generally accepted Soviet hypocrisy, a contradiction that society had learned to live with. Nevertheless, in Moscow this earned him his initial popularity.

Blat rules have never been recorded or told explicitly to others. People mastered them, but they would have had trouble articulating them to outsiders. Everyone observed the rules, which defined which acts were appropriate or inappropriate. They were written in practice but not yet read, to quote de Certeau.[1]

One of the best descriptions of how a *blat* system works can be found in Tom Wolfe's novel *The Bonfire of Vanities,* where he calls such a system a "favor bank." Everything in the New York criminal justice system operates on favors, Wolfe's lawyer Tommy Killian says. Everyone does favors for everyone else, since each favor is a deposit in a virtual bank, the favor bank. Favors are not supposed to be immediately reciprocated, just the opposite; it is mandatory for the reciprocity to be blurred. By making regular deposits, a participant gets into a position to receive big favors.[2]

Alena Ledeneva, in her excellent book, *Russia's Economy of Favours,* based on in-depth interviews, speaks of *blat* as a "counter-ideology of the Soviet system which nobody was supposed to follow, but could practice" by misrecognizing it. She calls the toleration of *blat* the Brezhnev regime's "Little Deal."[3] Thus *blat*, though violating the law, was seen as legitimate as long as the transactions remained limited, that is, within a closed, personal circle, conducted infrequently, modest in volume, and conducted mostly in situations of urgent need. People were not supposed to admit that they engaged in economic activities and, indeed, they thought of granting favors under this system as helping someone in need. Common excuses for using *blat* were the shortages, the fact that everyone practiced it, that Soviet institutions were unreliable, or that someone's situation was exceptional. However, as I will show, exceptional circumstances were often faked to obtain favors. Thus, "exceptionality" was as much merely part of the *blat* etiquette as it was the reason people relied on *blat*.

Contrary to the favor bank in the New York justice system, the Soviet *blat* networks were not all-embracing systems. They were complex, fluid, and grounded on cultural or personal relations. Ledeneva speaks of a "social alchemy." The networks were open to newcomers; one only had to be acquainted with an insider and pay a substantial initial deposit, a "big favor." I gained access to several networks by taking letters to the West, by bringing money and medication to Moscow, by introducing journalists and writers to Western editors or publishers, by editing application letters in German, and by helping people to obtain visas. These kinds of deposits meant that I could buy my way into an existing favor bank, or "make friends." In the beginning, I naively did this for people I considered my real friends, not because I thought I was eventually going to be repaid. It took me a while to grasp the crucial economic aspect of my friendships.

Every single client of a favor bank held a different status. One could easily participate in several *blat* networks. Moreover, one was well advised to do so. Since many favors, as I will show, consisted of providing access to other people, one's potential value increased with one's number of connections. Thus, two or more of the metaphorical bubbles people lived in could be linked.

In the Soviet Union, *blat* served as a "survival kit," as Ledeneva says. It was "reducing uncertainty in conditions of shortage, exigency and perpetual emergency, in which formal criteria and formal rights are insufficient to operate."[4] Friends helped each other to obtain what they needed by taking advantage of the special accesses each had. Ludmilla, who worked in a dairy store, set aside milk for her friends and also for the friends of her friends. Yet, not everyone needed milk. Ludmilla, for her part, required the services of a doctor who did not need milk, but had trouble getting gasoline. Someone else was looking for a flat. This person worked in a car park where gasoline could easily be obtained. Another person desperately wanted a phone line to her apartment and she could provide other people with boots. If a *blat* network was well connected and large enough, one could find anything through it. Direct exchanges were rare, no accounting was done, and cash payments exceeding the official retail price were all but excluded. Gifts, such as perfume or cognac, only symbolized the appreciation for a substantial favor, like a tip. They were not taken into account. Yet, the regular giving of gifts, such as cigarettes or flowers, preceding a substantial request could establish a *blat* connection. "Friends" presented each other with gifts for many occasions, such as the new year or a birthday. Well into the post-Soviet period, and perhaps even more so today, students gave gifts to their professors, journalists to their sources, and some sources to the journalists. While I conducted an interview in the editor in chief's office of a local daily in the Urals a few days before New Year, we were interrupted every few minutes. Well-wishers stopped by with plastic bags. *Ne pomazish, ne poluchaesh,* the Russians say: "If you do not grease, you do not get anything." Or, as another saying goes, small presents keep a friendship alive.

Although no accounting was done, the "friends," the participants of a *blat* network, were aware of each other's balance in the favor bank. If someone withdrew too much credit without debiting any favors to others, his or her creditworthiness was gradually reduced. However, lack of compliance rarely resulted in being ousted from a network; one's "credit" limit was merely lowered.

Usually, the groceries acquired *po blatu* were not stolen, unlike the materials that were siphoned off from factories or construction sites, but were bought at state prices. *Blat* only helped to circumvent queuing, to obtain fresh, boneless meat or fresh vegetables, as opposed to getting the rotten ones on display or no vegetables at all. The major favor of the "friend" at the grocery store was to set articles aside and make them available only to her friends and friends of friends. In short, the benefit consisted of privileged access and greater value for the same amount of money. Luxury goods would have been practically unavailable were it not for *blat*. These goods included whatever was hard to come by, such as decent meat, smoked fish, and fruit, as well as durable consumer goods, such as washing machines, tape recorders, TV sets, and VCRs.

Blat not only meant keeping in touch with one's "friends"—to be pleasant, to not forget to bring chocolate or cognac for New Year or flowers for International Women's Day—but also, and primarily, it meant being ready to "help," to grant favors at any time. The *blat* techniques included establishing "friendships" with people in the right places and personalizing one's relations, having contacts in as many institutions as possible. In cases of emergency—illness, a family death, a failed exam, something lost—people had to resort to *blat*. A favor had a better chance of being granted if requested with urgency. If the favor seemed to be at risk of not being granted, people threatened to deprive the "friend" of love or esteem, thus to depersonalize the contact, which might never have been personalized if not for *blat*. A friend who did not help a friend was no friend. On the other hand, some people who used *blat* often made every request look urgent, as if one had to dramatize to be taken seriously. For them, every case became a special case.

For many months, my friend S. stopped at the apartment allocation office daily, presenting the clerk with flowers. The clerk knew all along that S. would eventually need an apartment. After almost a year, she finally offered him two small flats, which he then exchanged for a bigger one. A "friendship" between the two was established; thus it became viable for her to procure privileged treatment for her new "friend." Neither considered the flowers a bribe; that would have been too little for such a valuable favor. Anyway, *blat* did not require reciprocity. My friend would not have had access to what the woman needed, but he may have had the necessary "friends." Even more important, direct reciprocity was dangerous, because the violation of law would have been too obvious and people's morals required the reciprocity to be blurred. If a deal could be camouflaged as a favor to a friend, it involved fewer scruples than taking a bribe. My friend's steady delivery of flowers only conveyed reliability, faithfulness, and permanence. Thus S. made a "friend" in the city's housing administration. (This happened in Communist Warsaw, not the Soviet Union, but the mechanisms were the same.)

I tried the trick with flowers and cigarettes. In 1990–1991, it was still hard to get tickets for domestic flights. Every time I needed a ticket or just an inquiry, I went to the same Aeroflot clerk, giving her a package of Marlboros. The first time, she refused to accept it, but then she told me her son was a smoker. Later, I made sure I stressed the cigarettes were for her son, a person I had never met and who might not even have existed. The son just helped her to see the cigarettes as a sign of friendship, to ignore the reciprocity we had established, which was unusual for *blat*.

Ledeneva quotes a former *apparatchik* who explained why people in key positions such as the housing office were willing to make new "friends," to make a deposit into a new favor bank: "The more you help, the more people are obliged to you. You may get nothing out of it at a particular moment, but the more people are obliged to you, the easier your problems will be solved in future."[5] And the more people connected to a particular *blat* network, the more useful the network becomes.

Most *blat* networks were formed around a master organizer, often a woman—a hairstylist, for example. This person served as a go-between and was called *blatmeister*. On rare occasions, she could act as an arbitrator and compel people to grant certain favors.

Corrupt behavior tends to blur the reciprocity. Most Westerners would not consider tipping to be a form of corruption, but a standard form of recognition or gratuity for good service or a small gift. The etymology of the English word "tip" proves them wrong: tip derives from the acronym "t.i.p.," for "to insure promptitude," written on tipping jars in London's sixteenth-century coffee houses.[6] Today, our tips conceal their original purpose, and thus the reciprocity, through institutionalization. They may not have effect anymore, anyway. In Soviet Russia, even substantial tipping or bribing would not have worked. With the need for secrecy and in the absence of a currency, a more sophisticated system of settlement was required: *blat*. This system served basically as an informal, nonmonetary banking and credit system. By offering favors to other members of such an open circle of "friends," one placed value in the favor bank, mostly by providing information and access. Contrary to its claims, the Soviet Union's power structures were weak and fuzzy; decision making was personalized. Therefore, getting to the right person with the best possible recommendation was essential. In a society as secretive as the Soviet one, information about who to contact was hard to come by.

For *blat* networks to succeed, they had to be well connected with the local power, which was the source of information, including most rumors. Ergo, *blat* served to disseminate both information and disinformation, thus adding to the mistrust that different groups felt for each other. The ability to distinguish relevant facts from mere rumors was an important benefit of such "friendships."

Blat primarily eased individuals' everyday hardships by softening some flaws in the state's distribution network. At the same time, it exacerbated these hardships, not only because it set aside goods, but also because the system was used in the state's economy, too. Soviet factories got their resources and raw materials by allocation from Gosplan, the planning agency in Moscow. Accounting of Gosplan was shady and secretive. The workers' salaries and the supplies available in their factory's stores depended on the (over)fulfillment of the plan. Therefore, it was important for the management to keep the plan's target low and to cheat on production numbers. It tried to obtain raw material from alternative sources, in case a delivery was late or of poor quality. To that purpose, many Soviet companies relied on a specialist engaging in *blat*, the *tolkach*. This person had the necessary connections and was used to dealing in gray areas. Unlike in the private *blat* networks, the *tolkach* kept a record and his deals sometimes involved cash, although Soviet companies were always short of cash, which they did not use except to pay salaries. Thus, the *tolkachi* had to find (state) customers willing to pay cash, because they so desperately needed what he could offer.

Mostly, however, a *tolkach* tried to find partner factories with which he could exchange surplus goods. These so-called barter deals gained in scale and importance during the Gorbachev years, since the enterprises obtained the right to freely trade on their own—first the surplus and later the whole production. *Tolkachi*, it was understood, were ready to bribe people. By smoothing deals that would never otherwise have been struck, *blat,* in addition to its effect on the citizens' provisions, might have improved the performance of the Soviet economy.

As mentioned earlier, phone directories were not published in the Soviet Union, which is why even knowing an influential person's phone number reflected potential access and, thus, power.[7] Since connections were the most valuable asset, giving someone a phone number was seen as an act of friendship, a favor, and an invitation to enter a *blat* network. Eventually, the favor would have to be returned. One could distinguish three levels of phone-related *blat:* if one received the phone number of someone who could help, that could be read as distant "friendship." People closer to the network were invited to call the person in question and tell him or her that they were calling on behalf of the friend who had given out the number. This was more obliging; a favor to a friend of a friend was a request to credit the favor bank. For "real friends," however, the friend with the phone number called the person himself or herself to announce the forthcoming call of the friend in need of the favor.

If many Russians are still reluctant to hand out phone numbers, it is for a different reason. In the Soviet period, they did not want to give away a privileged access (or to betray someone). Nowadays, security issues seem to be the main motive for secrecy.

To get interviews as journalists, one had to rely on the sort of "friendships" that were behind *blat.* My Swiss newspaper's name did not open many doors in Russia; therefore, if I needed to meet a politician or businessman, I looked for a "friend" who had an informal access to that person.

Blat only works in a stable situation. To rely on delayed and indirect compensation, one has to be sure that the network is still around when needed; stagnation thus was *blat*'s prerequisite. Contracts did not have to be enforced. One could wait because, eventually, "friends" who did not meet their obligations would need favors themselves. Favors were treated as acts of friendship and not, in the absence of any admitted reciprocity, as an economic activity. People simply "cared" for each other, so they helped each other. And they would continue to care. The fact that these networks, despite their economic purpose, were based on personal relations helped to contain the requests made. "Friends" tried to find the right friend for a particular need; they adapted their requests to that friend's possibilities and abilities. In order to not abuse a friend's generosity, they limited their requirements to spare both sides the embarrassment of a refusal. This helped to keep their own debts at bay.[8]

Blat may even have stabilized relationships by securing them for future use and by providing them with a clear purpose, as Ledeneva argued. It created a mutual dependence.[9] If Russians now complain that, in the Soviet era, the future seemed secure—as in jail, one might say—then they express a nostalgia for the stability of these camouflaged networks of distribution.

With the end of the command economy in January 1992, *blat* lost its importance. To find everyday necessities, one did not have to rely on friends anymore. The lines disappeared. The stores filled, and prices rose; soon, there were no more shortages. Overnight, the skills with which to navigate around the Soviet rules and obstacles, and to obtain the goods and services for survival, became obsolete. Gradually, the ruble became a currency. What one needed was cash, but that was scarce. There were no more bottlenecks in distribution, of which some bureaucrat was in control. These could be bypassed, since goods were shipped on many roads. New techniques and tricks to make money—especially cash—became vital, skills that almost no one had even considered important just a few years earlier.

On the streets, in subway entrances, in the markets—*kolkhoz* markets as they were called, since they had been established for the collective farms to sell the production that exceeded the plan targets—and around railway stations, flocks of small traders appeared, mostly younger people and *babushkas*. They displayed their merchandise on cardboard on the ground, on little camping tables, or by simply holding it in their hands.

Already in 1991, the first vendors of regular Soviet merchandise appeared on the streets, though this was still officially prohibited. During the late hours, after the stores had closed, they sold vodka, Soviet champagne, sausages, and flowers at higher prices. Most of them had obtained their merchandise through *blat*, from a factory outlet, or through the backdoor of a public store: this still illegal activity was the first step to "real" money, as it helped to smooth the inefficient distribution system.

The liberalization created new types of activities, such as shuttle trading. For some time already during the Soviet era, black marketeers had traveled around and *kolkhozniki* would fly to Moscow with baskets of fruits or vegetables from the Caucasus and Central Asia. The ticket prices were so low that they made a profit by selling their fruit at the *kolkhoz* markets. At the same time, people from Moscow's hinterland went to the capital to buy goods; the trains to the provinces around the capital were called "sausage express." But people made this journey to supply relatives and "friends." With the ban on private business revoked, shuttle trading became a full-time activity. Many people turned their traveling to Moscow to obtain imported items into a regular business. Soon, wholesale markets emerged and imports were sold in bulk out of trucks or freight containers. The more adventurous began shuttling abroad—to Eastern Europe or China. Some groups specialized and monopolized certain trading paths. As early as the summer of 1990, a friend—as a favor—introduced me to members of a Polish gang working the triangle of China, Russia, and India. They traveled in circles, from the Soviet Union to India, on to China, and back to Russia, smuggling gold from Russia to India, foreign currency from India into China, and pearls from China to Russia. To secure safe passage, they established permanent personal relations with border guards. All of a sudden, in the summer of 1990, the KGB cracked down on the pearl trade. Some Poles were arrested; others switched to a different commodity— leather jackets. However, while the pearls could be smuggled by hiding them, leather jackets could not. The group brought the jackets into the country officially, declaring them as being in transit from China to Poland. They then sold them in Russia, anyway, always to the same wholesale customer, a former Olympic athlete who had enough protection from above. With the exception of the cooperatives, private trade was still prohibited. On the black market, the Poles converted the rubles they obtained into dollars, which their girlfriends smuggled out of the country, concealed inside their bodies. The men themselves left the USSR empty-handed. They claimed to have lost their customs declaration forms, and since they were traveling with empty pockets nothing could be confiscated, anyway. After a while, they would embark on the next rotation. Similar trading paths existed between Poland, Hungary, Romania, the Soviet Union, and back to Poland; there, the major commodity was electronics.

In 1991, "friends" or friends of friends—scholars and scientists— repeatedly approached me to find potential customers for nonferrous metals in the West. The quality and purity were excellent, they assured me. They could massively undercut world market prices. The metals were "stolen" from defense industry plants, though in Soviet times, stealing modest amounts of material or gasoline from one's employer was generally condoned. It was called to *vynosit* (to siphon off or carry away). At the time, it was still difficult for Russians to obtain travel documents. My only contribution would have been to make the connection to potential Western buyers; I would not have been involved in the deal itself, I was told; nevertheless, I was offered a percentage for every deal made. Nothing was illegal or dangerous; the metals were not even smuggled out of the country. The group had found some legal loophole through Estonia. They could not understand my refusal. How could I be so foolish as to refuse free money?

One of these people, a former scientist, has become a successful post-Soviet *tolkach*, a barter broker, as he calls himself, a well-accepted Moscow businessman. He finds companies that need to trade energy for machinery, butter for gasoline, or textiles for a new factory and he mediates their complex deals. Most important, he finds meat for the supplier of spare parts to airlines or arranges trades of jeeps for cheese. Thus, for almost a decade, he has done what a *blat* network did for the private citizens; only, he has kept a record of the deals. Since direct barter trades are rare, he has acted as the favor banker for this nonmonetary exchange of equivalents. As such, he has taken his commission either in cash or in commodities, goods he can then sell for cash. Aside from the real bankers, these brokers or favor bankers have been the only players in the cash-stripped post-Soviet economy with substantial amounts of cash. Some of them have become very rich.

"When Russia started its transition, it had no category of people trained in dealing with accumulated wealth for their own interest and (indirectly) that of society (one could use the terms bourgeoisie and entrepreneurial class)," John Loewenhardt wrote in his book, *The Reincarnation of Russia*. "Its elite and population had been brainwashed into thinking that individual property was reprehensible."[10] Only the collapse of Soviet power brought about the chance to acquire economic skills. The borders opened and finally Russians could also engage in international shuttle trading. The number of business opportunities multiplied. In the wild capitalism that emerged, the rules of *blat* were crucial for the traders.

A twenty-two-year-old friend was one such businessman who learned his trade quickly. He had saved some money and, during his summer vacation in 1992, left for Vietnam. He returned with bags full of shoes and shirts. Together with his brother, he sold the merchandise in the Lushniki stadium. The profit, some 100 percent of the original savings, was reinvested in the next trip, which was to China. The two brothers went together, taking along borrowed money as well as their own. Over time, they traveled more often. Eventually, they organized trucks to ship the merchandise to Moscow. In 1993, the two brothers bought a kiosk that sold *kvas*, a Russian summer drink made of fermented bread. They turned their outlet into a tiny twenty-four-hour supermarket. A year later, with their profits, with loans raised from friends, and with credit from the group of racketeers who "protected" them, they opened a store and coffee shop. Within two years, they became successful entrepreneurs.

The sums of money involved in their business grew bigger and their store was abundantly stocked and had plenty of customers. In an article, I praised the brothers as model young Russians. Yet, eventually, these school teachers turned "businessmen" began to engage in increasingly shady deals. They had no idea about how to service their debts; instead of repaying their creditors, they accumulated higher debts, with little understanding for what was right or wrong. They began to cheat their creditors. Having been extorted of money themselves, they became extorters. They did not treat the business seriously, but as a masquerade, a game. The bigger their deals, the more they impersonated businessmen. Today, they are wanted by Interpol.

To find profitable paths for shuttle trading, to raise and accumulate capital, to run the gauntlet of obtaining the (six) permits necessary to open a *kiosk* or a store, to negotiate with racketeers, the police—if the latter are not racketeers themselves, the taxman, and the supervisors all require skills and a mindset unheard of during the Soviet period. Ten years earlier, many young Soviets, when first hired by Western companies in Moscow, needed guidance for the simplest tasks. As *homoni sovietici*, they were not supposed to take initiative, but to obey orders.

In dealing with administrative bodies in today's Russia, corruption is widely accepted as a method of smoothing things over. Many people, especially the young who came of age under the post-Soviet system, see it as informal taxation—unpleasant, yet unavoidable. As long as the required bribes remain within certain limits and are calculable, people are willing to pay them to insure a timely execution of their request, "to insure promptness" (t.i.p.). Everyone knows that it is impossible to live on a clerk's, a policeman's, or a taxman's salary; therefore, though grudgingly, people resign themselves to furnishing state employees with additional income. Only when the claims get too high do the Russians complain about corruption.

To obtain foodstuffs, Russian customers had to develop a whole new set of skills: they never had to compare prices before. The state fixed prices and they were the same everywhere; they did not matter, anyway, not for goods obtained through *blat*. At the same time that people began learning to develop price-comparing skills, the need to jump ahead in a line or to bully other customers vanished. Many connections lost their importance. People had to haggle over prices; they had to learn which prices were fixed and which were negotiable. Huge regional price differences emerged, both nationwide and on a local level. In 1992, I met a teenager who for a short time bought roses at one end of a subway station and sold them at the other end, at a profit of 20 percent.

The daily supply is an important part of people's lives, particularly when it does not work smoothly. A fundamental change in the way people obtain food affects their other interactions with their environment and the way they see the world. In today's Russia, providing for oneself does not differ much from the way it is done in other countries; there are huge supermarkets, grocery stores, street *kiosks*, and farmers' markets, the former *kolkhoz* markets. Food has become relatively expensive and there are enormous price differences, but anything is available at any time.

Even during times of scarcity, a privileged few enjoyed access to imported goods. With the gradual opening up of the society, such goods became attainable for more people, theoretically. Subsequently, the obstacles to trading them vanished. With the easing of the law against "speculation," the U.S. dollar gradually evolved into a second currency, or rather the first and only real currency in the country. The ailing Soviet Union and later the emerging Russian Federation, starved of cash, turned into a two-currency society. Rubles were used to obtain what the state's distribution system offered; dollars *(valuta)* were required for everything else. With more stores for imported groceries opening in Moscow and St. Petersburg, two distinct distribution networks established themselves.

For some time, through *blat*, one could still obtain goods for rubles that would otherwise have been available for *valuta*, but at a higher price. However, increasingly, cash was required. The de facto convertibility of the ruble opened the dollar economy up to everyone who could acquire enough rubles, yet for a few years the two distribution circuits remained separate. The enormous price differences prevailed in the official retail sector, as well as in the unregulated street vendor's market. They have since faded.

Before, when arriving at a major airport in Russia, domestic or international, the first thing one had to do with a prospective taxi driver was to convince him to accept payment in rubles. That meant that one wanted to be treated as a local. On the average, the ruble prices amounted to around one-third of the dollar price. The (unofficial) airport taxi drivers seemed unaware of the paradox; by simply changing money and speaking Russian, one got a steep discount from them. They maintained the two different prices, as if catering to two different classes of consumers. Only gradually did this practice disappear.

These days, many of the techniques needed in the first years after the collapse of the command economy are slowly vanishing. The one-on-one price haggling, for example, seems to be proving transitional. As a regular customer at one of Moscow's vegetable markets, I have noticed that the need for bargaining seems to be abating. The people who negotiate accept prices substantially closer to their asking price than they did a few years earlier.[11] Rather than haggling, people hunt for bargains by comparing the different merchants' prices. For most goods, a general price level has established itself and people accept it. Plurality and choice have become a part of daily life; people have to make comparisons and dozens of singular decisions. During the Soviet period, there was no choice. One was happy that anything was available.

Shopping as a leisure activity, common in Western societies, would have been inconceivable in the Soviet Union. To find the basic necessities was a struggle. Even if they were available, obtaining them was a time-consuming process. It took three steps to buy something. First, after queuing, one chose; then one had to queue at the cashier's counter to pay. With the receipt, one went back to the salesperson to receive the purchased goods. The department stores were not set up for people strolling around, looking and touching, as in their Western counterparts. The different GUMs and TsUMs[12] were cold and impersonal, as was the Detsky Mir, or Children's World (a toy store). Only in some *Beriozka* shops was the merchandise displayed in a Western way and available for touching. But the

Beriozka stores were reserved for foreigners with hard currency; until 1989 they were off limits to Soviet citizens. In Soviet bookstores, one had to ask for a book to browse through. With the emergence of Western-style stores, this began to change. Branches of foreign companies, Benetton and Lego, opened in the GUM building, with shop windows appealingly displaying their clothing and toys. In the beginning, long lines formed in front of these stores, but more opened and, eventually, there were whole malls—some very luxurious and expensive, such as the Petrovka Passage. People strolled around the renovated nineteenth-century arcades to the sounds of soft music, even those people who could not afford to buy anything; they watched, touched, and became acquainted with a category of goods they had never seen before.

The abacus, the icon of Soviet retail, has finally given way to pocket calculators and cash registers. For a long time, many vendors still preferred to use their abaci. With unbelievable speed, they calculated the prices, only to type the sum into the registers afterward. This simultaneity of old and new was a sign of transition. This transition is over; the abacus has disappeared.

Starved of luxury for so long, the Russians have become avid shoppers. Women search for clothes and shoes, while men browse the stores for consumer electronics and computers. Shopping is a new pastime. People spend hours exploring the top brands; they know the details and the prices and those who can afford them hunt for bargains. Some others seem to think, "I would buy, therefore I am." Or "I would be, if I could buy this or that." Even if they cannot afford anything, they experience choice and a fundamental plurality; they can dream about what they see. In the Soviet Union, there were no goods, but people had rubles; now there are goods, but many people do not have the money. Yet, as time goes by, more and more people will be able to afford to buy these goods.

In the beginning, affluence caused adversity. Some people, particularly pensioners, still feel insulted by their neighbors' wasting huge amounts of money. Did not they, until recently, live as humbly as the pensioners themselves? And would it not be the elderly's turn, according to the Soviet seniority principle, which they had respected all their lives?

As Igor Kliamkin emphasized, long before the advent of the market economy, the Russians were consumers, if consumers with little to consume; they were thus prepared for the change. The Brezhnev years made them withdraw into the private sphere and become "private citizens in a society without private property," urban petit bourgeois who focused on their private interests.[13] They "unlearned" how to think or act according to their "productive interests," but behaved exclusively in terms of "consumerist interests."[14]

To obtain everyday necessities, the networking connections, and thus the *blat* techniques, were not needed in the open market. However, to obtain permissions and to circumvent laws and bureaucratic obstacles, *blat* is still and will be needed, for dealing with both companies and the state. Having bought a newly built Moscow apartment, for months my friend T. haggled with the workers about paint, cracks, and faucets; she negotiated prices and tips. Furbishing the interior was up to the new proprietor of the apartment. When all was done, she wanted to get the keys from the construction company so she could move in. This, however, proved to be impossible, since a long line—in fact, a waiting list—had formed at the private company's office. After several weeks, when she finally made it to the clerk, this person found a flaw in T.'s registration. There was no way she would give her the keys; instead, she moved to throw her out of the office. T. asked for help *po chelovechesky* ("as a human being"). Attempting to bribe the clerk appeared impossible; too many witnesses were around. However, T. happened to have some smoked salmon in her bag (actually a present for someone else). Hoping this would pave the way for a slightly more favorable treatment, for the creation of a space and time in which a bribe could be negotiated, she offered the fish to the clerk, just as a little something from her home region, as she would have done *po blatu*, to initiate a "friendship." The clerk accepted happily and told T. to come back the next day *bez ochered* (without waiting in line). The next day, she handed her the keys, not even mentioning either the flaw in the documentation or a possible bribe. T. had expected to be asked for a few hundred dollars.

T.'s apartment lacked a phone line, as did all the others in the building. Yet a friend of hers had a friend who worked for the phone company. Through that friend, the installation of the phone line could be arranged; it "cost" U.S. $700 (for many Russians, this would have exceeded their yearly income). T. paid and got her phone. Then, a less fortunate neighbor asked how she managed to get it. She revealed her connection, only to be reprimanded by her friend. The $700 were a price for a friend, a *blat* discount, so to speak; for other people, the bribe was $1,000. T., like many other people, complains that she does not know the rules anymore. "If I ask a 'friend' in the local registration office for a favor that is difficult for her to grant, do I have to compensate her, does she expect me to pay for it, or would she be offended if I would try?"

Contrary to everyday life, in big business *blat* still works. Some of the old skills have become essential, not the least because there are much higher rewards at stake. In the absence of other ways to get credits, resources, land, and permissions, people resort to the old methods. Thus, raw material, energy, and finances are now distributed in the same way that sausages and TV sets were before. Cash starved and unable to rely on a law that does not provide any means to enforce a contract, businesses have to deal with partners whom they can trust: "friends." Many of the new barter brokers came of age as functionaries of the Komsomol, the party's youth league, as *tolkachi* of the state. They had acquired a "wealth of connections" and some of them managed to convert this nonmonetary working capital into cash—and power.

The same was true for the privatization process. The so-called clans are accused of having looted the country and distributing its wealth among themselves and their friends. Yet, for people raised in the Soviet Union it only felt natural to trust one's "friends." Some people who worked with Anatoly Chubais believed that their group was the only one in Russia that could reform and Westernize the country.[15] They did not trust anyone else. And since Russia failed to establish the rule of law, there was no other way to trust people than to rely on long-established circles of loyal friends—or to enforce contracts by violence—especially in the quickly changing environment of the transition economy.

The newspaper *Argumenty i Fakti* once defined a clan as a group "based on informal relations between its members." It has no registered structure and its members can be widely dispersed. They are united by a commonality of views and loyalty to an idea or a leader.[16] This echoes the description of a *blat* network, but it also justifies the term "Chubais clan." Thus what looked like capitalism was essentially a web of sophisticated *blat* networks taking advantage of the new openness and mimicking a free market. Its fundamental difference from a clan was that it actually included a number of competing clans, thus making it at least somewhat pluralistic.

Other *blat* techniques are used by post-Soviet business. *Blat* provides access to bureaucratic decision makers and inside information and it allows its members to influence and speed up the administrative process. Of course, this often includes bribes. Businesses resort to *blat* when, for some reason, money does not help or to pave the way for a bribe. The distinction between *blat* and bribery has been blurred. There is little need to obscure reciprocity these days; morals do not limit the bureaucrats' greed.

A barter economy's chains of interdependence have to be relatively short for that economy to function properly; therefore, such an economy tends to be local and relatively self-sufficient.[17] Usually, a barter economy does not depend on an extended network of communication or on longer chains of action. With the poor state of transportation in Russia, with the limited number of transportation arteries, with unreliable phone lines, and with no dependable system for making quick payments over distances, an economy based on relative autarky at the local level would have been appropriate for the Soviet Union. However, ideology made the regime create the exact opposite. The Soviet economy was interdependent to the extreme, governed by a central planning office. Managed like a single company, it stretched the division of labor all over the country and even beyond, into the satellite states, from Central Europe to the Pacific Coast and from the coal mines to the family refrigerator.

Theoretically, a centrally planned economy could work. In reality, the Soviet economy never did. However, its failure was not primarily because of the drainage of resources through ubiquitous theft. Any economy of scale is probably too complex and too fluid to be successfully administered by a central authority; its plan would have to be constantly adapted and readapted. Yet the Soviet regime did not possess the necessary prerequisites—including a grid of communication and transportation—that would allow a central planning office to constantly modify its plan to changing needs. With the crumbling of the Communist regime, the command economy became terminally ill. A highly interdependent economy lost its guidance and was about to collapse. In the absence of real money and a central management, barter became the method of choice for settlements. Often it was the only available method, but it was difficult for companies to find trading partners and to settle deals by themselves. This opened the niches for the self-promoted barter brokers to mediate trades and thus to gain influence. By acting as nonmonetary banks, they saved the Russian economy from stalling; thus, they played a crucial role, one that allowed them to amass personal wealth. Despite growing up in an environment alien to economic thinking, and despite never having been exposed to practices such as haggling or even choosing from a selection of offers, the Russians have adapted to sophisticated ways of doing business quickly.

Blat, as long as the Soviet Union existed, was the grid on which the "second economy" ran.[18] Since the collapse, *blat* has shaped the "first economy."[19] The informal set of rules and codes—not cheating one's friends and relations, not letting a partner down but beating the system and "violat[ing] the rules for the sake of efficiency, cleverness and creativity,"[20] and treating everyone except one's friends as adversaries or even as prey—became the standard under which the Russian economy was run, while it formally adopted the rules of a market economy. This should not surprise anyone: the young teams of economists who took to reforming the Russian economy started as the Soviet economy's critics; for them, the state economy were *oni*, the others. They entered politics collectively, as a network of friends. Thus, they brought along the basic prerequisite to run the economy *po blatu*. And, ironically, they tried to "beat the system" on behalf of the state—that is, the system.

Blat is widespread in post-Soviet business and politics. The everchanging legal and tax environment makes personal contact with a bureaucrat who can process things even more essential than before; often the bureaucrat does not mind becoming part of a network. Also, in enforcing contracts, personalization is crucial. There is little law enforcement and contracts are not always legal. People are forced to meet their obligations by the threat of violence and to meet them on time, since, unlike during the Soviet period, no one has time to wait for compensation. Today, *blat* and overt corruption, two almost contradicting codes, are intertwined. One is never sure to which set of rules one should adhere, as the following example shows.

When the state bank of one of Russia's autonomous republics applied for a license to deal in foreign currency, namely U.S. dollars, one of their middle managers working in the Moscow branch was dispatched to the Russian Central Bank. She filed forms and chatted with the clerks until, eventually, all the paperwork was completed. Nevertheless, every day this manager was sent to the Central Bank. Gradually, she got to know personally two clerks; they became "friends." This allowed her to find out how the clerks would want to be rewarded—that is, bribed. One day, her boss joined her to offer an envelope containing $5,000 to one clerk and jewelry to the other. Since a personal relationship had been established, the receivers could consider these obvious bribes as being gifts.

The transition from the Soviet to the post-Soviet economy has brought about a whole new system. Real money was introduced. The Russians had to do away with their tried and tested skills, their Soviet reflexes. For the individual, *blat* became obsolete. Instead, Russians had to learn to compare prices and, at times, wait for them to fall—they had to learn that prices matter. Today, they are bombarded with temptations, new goods, and values. An abundance of riches, unheard of only a few years earlier, has come to the Russian cities; it is in plain view, yet there only for a happy few to enjoy. Overnight, making money has become acceptable. The younger generations have adapted quickly, while others find this new life difficult. In the jungle of an emerging bazaar capitalism, they have trouble orienting themselves.

However, the transformations that the ex-Soviet economy are undergoing are not limited to the changing ways of provision. The well-stocked stores, as opposed to the empty ones, reshaped the cities, as tens of thousands of new sales outlets, from the kiosks to the huge American-style shopping malls, emerged. But these changes, as far-reaching as they may be, are less fundamental than a far less noted phenomenon beyond any genuine economic activity. Soviet society at large was never involved in the shaping of its own structures. One centrally controlled bureaucracy made all decisions regarding the way the country was fed, dressed, housed, and entertained. *My* ("we," "the people") did not have any say. On behalf of the party, some indifferent bureaucrats in Moscow determined what clothes were allowed to look like and what colors were to be used; they decided how and where goods were to be distributed and they set the prices, regardless of the production and transportation costs.

The same is true for the selection of sites for manufacturing, distribution channels, and allocations. In the Soviet era, these were determined from above, regardless of whether they made any economic sense; now they are set to maximize profits, often by any means. These decisions are made by countless individuals and companies with often conflicting interests and by the actors who compete for market share and profit. Thus, despite the ongoing manipulations from above, the Russian economy has become truly pluralistic.

The first post-Soviet Russian government gradually monetized the former command economy. It legalized private ownership in real estate and companies and introduced financial instruments: securities, (state) loans, and even derivatives. The government started to control the money supply and to cancel subsidies for companies, which became private after all. These steps turned the ruble into a currency. However weak, the ruble adapted a value that reflected the inner strength of the Russian economy. Eventually, it could be freely exchanged with foreign currencies.

Only money allows anonymous transactions over long distances, and only money includes the most diverse persons into a single system. Money accommodates individualism, otherness, and social fragmentation, as David Harvey emphasizes. The absence of money limits people's participation in an economy to their physical presence. A free-price system, Harvey stresses, is "the most decentralized socially coordinated decision-making mechanism."[21] Finally, Russia enjoys the benefits of money, that great "radical leveler and cynic."[22] Today, by simply making their choices, almost all Russian citizens are minutely involved in the shaping of their country's economy. In that sense, money by itself has a democratizing effect.

Money allows private citizens to buy power or, as the early German sociologist Georg Simmel said, permits political participation without personal involvement.[23] This is common in the West, where the rich and the corporations pay for access to political power, legally or illegally. Russia only saw this pattern emerge in 1996, when the so-called oligarchs struck a deal to pave Yeltsin's way to reelection by funneling some U.S. $100 million into his campaign. In the Soviet Union, power was political and secured by the threat of violence. Economic potential did not translate into political leverage. Now, with people making huge profits, and with the possibility of storing (private) value (inside or outside the country), a phenomenon that is new to Russia, almost all power can be bought. Money may have corrupted Russian politics, but it has opened up the circles of power by granting influence to anyone who can pay for it; this greatly increases the number of people who influence decision making.

Permitting agreements across previously unbridgeable borders, social or geographical, money allows the coordination of political actions between individuals of very diverse interests, that is, between competitors such as the oligarchs, as seen in 1996. Through its social power, money is a means of control. As such, it has replaced the Soviet-style controls—the fence and *propusk*. There is no need to check someone's documents if a high entrance fee is required. The opposite has become true: by being able to pay high fees, one qualifies for (almost any) access. Eventually, those with money will be those who control the people in office. Russia has not yet institutionalized this, unlike the established democracies. That's why some observers consider Russia's ways of "influence for sale" to be morally inferior. One might counter this by saying that Russia has not had time to shape her laws according to how influence is normally exerted. The sale of political leverage has not been institutionalized yet and thus it has not been legalized.

The collapse of the Soviet Union rendered its attributes of power obsolete, and new ones have not yet been found. Hence, money has become the only means of social distinction. It allows everyone who makes money to acquire a higher social standing, for example, by gaining access to schools and universities or by simply purchasing a diploma. In the absence of other accepted social markers, money has become the Russians' sole symbol of social power—an object of greed, lust, and desire—and the universal measure of success.[24] "I am ugly, but I can buy for myself the most beautiful women. Therefore I am not ugly," Karl Marx noted: he who has money "can buy talented people for himself, and is he who has power over the talented not more talented than the talented? . . . Does not my money, therefore, transform all my incapacities into their contrary?"[25]

In the Soviet Union, equality meant equality in the distribution of goods. In theory, the state made sure that everyone received the same allotments.[26] This, however, implied an inequality in treatment. There was no freedom to achieve wealth, neither by taking advantage of opportunities nor by honest work. Soviet people were supposed to be equally poor. They were severely restricted in managing their tiny assets and prohibited from openly selling what they had, so those with the capability to improve their lot were discriminated against. In favor of an alleged common welfare, the citizens' "agency freedom" was suffocated in favor of a common "well-being freedom," to use the Nobel-laureate Amartya Sen's distinction.[27] The consequence of this policy was the widespread sapping of the country's economic performance, hence there was not much well-being either.

Equal opportunity could not exist in the Soviet Union; this would have jeopardized the regime's solely materialistic perception of equality. Equal opportunity creates inequality. Therefore, even if someone had the necessary skills or means, he or she was not free to use them to pursue his or her well-being. The Soviet ideology hailed this as being morally superior and just. The higher a person's potential, both in terms of competence or buying power, the more he or she was disadvantaged by the compulsion to equality. Thus, there were no material incentives to excel.

The collapse of the command economy has transformed the *homo sovieticus* into a *homo economicus*. The Russian's life has become immensely demanding—full of choices, insecurities, traps, and temptations.

When, suddenly, the former Soviet cities were shelled with all sorts of advertisements, the people initially seemed to believe their claims, but soon they began to read them with a little skepticism, as well as irony. Subsequently, the advertisers started to reflect the public discourse. Some ad campaigns played on the word *vybor*, Russian for "choice" and "election," while another used the term "dictatorship of good taste," echoing President Putin's slogan "dictatorship of the law." The *otvetni udar*, or "retaliatory strike," is a campaign for a cigarette. Its images mock American icons, such as the space shuttle or Marilyn Monroe.

Russian society, deprived of the tiniest economic freedom for so long and never before subjected to marketing techniques, is learning to cope with all the tricks of advertising. The city dwellers, in general, do that surprisingly well. They have adapted to the completely new, chaotic conditions. They compare, choose, dismiss, and favor possibilities; they improvise and there is no reason to believe that those new skills are limited to their economic behavior. They may not abide by the law, but they certainly have mastered the fluid, unwritten rules that have established themselves.

NOTES

1. Michel de Certeau, *The Practice of Everyday Life*, trans. Steven F. Rendall (Berkeley: University of California Press, 1984).

2. Tom Wolfe, *The Bonfire of the Vanities* (New York: Farrar, Straus & Giroux, 1987), 400.

3. Alena V. Ledeneva, *Russia's Economy of Favours: Blat, Networking, and Informal Exchanges* (Cambridge: Cambridge University Press, 1998), 67.

4. Ledeneva, *Russia's Economy of Favours*, 76.

5. Ledeneva, *Russia's Economy of Favours*, 164.

6. Richard Pipes, *Russia under the Old Regime* (New York: Knopf, 1993).

7. See chapter 6, n. 17. Only at Mosgorspravka could one obtain private citizens' phone numbers.

8. Soviet property rights limited excesses. Bureaucrats could hardly amass wealth, because they would have had trouble explaining its origin; today, there is no limit.

9. Ledeneva, *Russia's Economy of Favours*, 141.

10. John Loewenhardt, *The Reincarnation of Russia: Struggling with the Legacy of Communism, 1990–1994* (Durham, N.C.: Duke University Press, 1995), 48.

11. Of course, there is a cultural dimension to it, too. Russian vendors are much less open to haggling than are Georgians and Azeris, fitting certain clichés.

12. GUM, or Gosudarstveno Universalni Magazin (State Universal Department Store), and TsUM, or Tsentralni Universalni Magazin (Central Universal Department Store).

13. Igor Kljamkin and Tatjana Kutkowez, "Der postsowjetische Privatmensch auf dem Weg zu liberalen Werten" (The post-Soviet private individual on his path to liberal values), in *Das neue Russland in Politik und Kultur* (The new Russia in politics and culture), ed. Forschungsstelle Osteuropa an der Universität Bremen, Hartmute Trepper (Bremen, Germany: Temmen, 1998), 97.

14. Igor Kljamkin, "Postkommunisticheskaja demokratiia i ee istoricheskie osobennosti v Rossii," *Polis* (1993): 9–10, quoted in Loewenhardt, *Reincarnation,* 49.

15. Janine R. Wedel, "Rigging the U.S.-Russian Relationship: Harvard, Chubais, and the Transidentity Game," *Demokratizatsiya* (Fall 1999): 469–500.

16. Olga Kryshtanovskaya, "The Real Masters of Russia," *Argumenty i Fakti* 21 (1997), quoted in Wedel "Rigging the U.S.-Russian Relationship."

17. Norbert Elias, *The Civilizing Process: The History of Manners and State Formation and Civilization,* trans. Edmund Jephcott (Cambridge, Mass.: Blackwell, 1994), 457.

18. There was never anything called "the first economy," as stressed in Ledeneva, *Russia's Economy of Favours.*

19. Wedel, "Rigging the U.S.-Russian Relationship," claims that economic reform itself, foreign aid, and U.S.-Russia relations had been privatized and run as a *blat* network, though she does not use the term.

20. Ledeneva, *Russia's Economy of Favours,* 162.

21. David Harvey, *The Urban Experience* (Baltimore: Johns Hopkins University Press, 1989), 176.

22. Karl Marx, *Das Kapital,* Vol 1., chapter 2, and Harvey, *Urban Experience,* 168.

23. Georg Simmel, *Philosophie des Geldes* (Leipzig: Drucker und Humboldt, 1900).

24. David Harvey, *The Condition of Postmodernity: An Inquiry into Cultural Change* (Cambridge, Mass.: Blackwell, 1990), 101.

25. Karl Marx, *Ökonomische und Politische Schriften* (1844), in *Werke, Frühe Schriften,* ed. Hans-Joachim Lieber, vol. 1 (Darmstadt, Germany: Wissenschaftliche Buchgesellschaft, 1971), 633.

26. In practice, the Soviet regime never tried to distribute goods equally, in spite of the propaganda claiming they did so.

27. See Amartya Sen, *Inequality Reexamined* (Cambridge, Mass.: Harvard University Press, 1992).

9

✛

Mafiosi and Prostitutes

The New Role Models

L ife is a story. Reality is what we construct—individually and collectively. In retrospect, many people in Russia downplay the hardships they had to endure and the restrictions to which they were subjected during the Soviet era. Human memory is selective; it gradually omits or replaces dreary and embarrassing details. One polishes the memories of one's life to make them consistent with the narrative.

However, not only do people recast their personal histories to shape them as the stories of their lives, but they also project these newly made personal histories onto their own futures. The plans they make have to fit into the trajectory of their life stories. And while people tend to brighten their pasts, the futures they foresee are blends of hopes, dreams, and expectations. They assess their potential or what they assume to be their possibilities and try to fit these into what they perceive as the future of their society. Role models, therefore, mirror the society as much as personal preferences.

A 1994 survey asked Russian high-school students who their role models were. To many people, the results, although disputed, were shocking: a majority of the responding boys named mafia activities, such as racketeering, as their preferred future occupation; the majority of the girls wanted to become prostitutes, to "earn hard currency, travel and meet people."[1] The appeal of prostitution contrasts drastically with an increasing occurrence and public awareness of sex slavery, the victims of which are often minors. It is doubtful this is what the teenage respondents had in mind and, in any case, the published survey results may have exaggerated the numbers. However, as everyone knows who has lived in post-Soviet Russia, as a trend, these findings cannot be disputed.

Paradoxically, the teenage girls who fancied becoming prostitutes named the female protagonists of imported TV serials, such as *Santa Barbara, Dallas,* or the Mexican serial, *The Rich Also Cry,* as their models. They mistook beautiful young women who meet rich, attractive men, have fun, fall in love, and enjoy luxury for prostitutes. These TV beauties are not bothered by regular work or by early morning work hours. They own beautiful clothes and expensive cars, but they do not engage in selling sex at all. Yet the responding high-school students gave little consideration to the actual job of a prostitute.

Generally, prostitution can be seen as being of two different types: modern slavery on one hand and that performed by the smart, often well-educated, young urban women who work freelance on the other. The latter often boost their incomes as part-time sex workers and many claim to enjoy their "work." When criminal gangs control the business, the former type is the reality, particularly in Russia. However, the image of the happy freelance working girls is the image young Russians have of prostitutes.

The Soviet Union praised itself for having done away with prostitution. Indeed, there was no streetwalking to speak of, there were no brothels or specialized bars, and prostitution was barely visible. Women would not solicit openly. Yet, also in the Soviet Union, sex was for sale. One could distinguish two classes of prostitutes: women whose clients were Soviet men (and who worked the railway stations) and women who sold sex for *valuta* in the hotels for foreigners, usually cooperating with the hotel's guards and the KGB. With the end of the strict controls, selling sex became an everyday feature of post-Soviet city life; working girls loiter on Moscow's most luxurious streets, such as the Tverskaya.

Only toward the end of the 1980s could one find specialized bars, such as the Night Flight on Tverskaya, that catered to the affluent sex customers, who initially were Westerners. The women working there identify themselves as students, academics, and clerks; they claim to be "looking for fun." Some of them prefer to accept "presents." However, many appear to be professional sex workers with fixed rates. The girls in the street, meanwhile, sell cheap, quick sex.

Women who are forced into prostitution are victims, completely deprived of their freedom. The freelancers, *per contra,* make their own fate, as free agents—at least, that's how they are perceived. A similar pattern seems to exist for the mafiosi. Being victimized is not what the young respondents had in mind when they expressed their wishes to become prostitutes or gang members. The future they envisaged, as unreal as it may be, ought to be read as a projected future beyond the state's control, even beyond the traditional Soviet-Russian society's reach and certainly beyond *byt,* the burden of Russian everyday life. Although this career goal seems to reflect a loosening of morals in the society at large, morality plays hardly any role in the pondering of these young people, and there is little reason for observers to be alarmed about the country or its youth falling into a moral abyss.

"For young people, to embark on an adult life based on conformism and lies, with a sense that it was not their achievements that counted but the 'weight' of their parents' connections—the hierarchy—this was a devastating start to a life," Russia-born essayist Sonja Margolina wrote.[2] To envisage a future as prostitutes or mafiosi thus meant to break away from "a culture pathologically committed to tradition,"[3] all the more so, since the trope of prostitution has proliferated in Russian literature and film. The scholar Helena Goscilo reads this as a reflection of the transition to the market, with "the myth of boundless Russian generosity" collapsing.[4]

A Soviet future was a soldier's future; choosing a profession meant selecting among a very limited number of possibilities offered by the state. For the most part, these options have disappeared or they have lost their attraction. Soviet propaganda created idols to teach socialist values to the young, but these role models are obsolete, though they have not been replaced by other idols. The post-Soviet society offers few models or career paths; young people are compelled to invent themselves. And not only the young have to find their own ways: so do the peddlers and street vendors—many of whom are elderly women—and the shuttle traders and the legendary *babushkas* who grow vegetables on their *dachas* to feed their families. There was no model for them to follow. Thus people not only have to come up with new models for their dreamed-of personal lives, but they also have to think up the ordinary activities necessary for survival.

In the Soviet Union, money did not define a person. Only the collapse of Communism has made affluence acceptable. The self-made millionaire is a post-Soviet hero; before 1989, his neighbors would have reported him to the authorities and he would have gone to jail as a "speculator." Even attempting to make money was against the law.

Soviet heroes were of a particular breed. Basically, one could distinguish two types, each lacking any individuality: the prototype of the New Man, a worker-athlete who mastered nature as a tractor driver or coalminer, and his healthy, strong girlfriend, an athlete-farmer herself. The double statue in front of the VDNKh grounds depicts these two archetypically; to this day, the film company Mosfilm uses the sculpture by Vera Muchina in its logo. The Soviets gradually transformed the image of the Russian woman from the prerevolutionary Mother Russia, a frail grandmother, into a slender, urban doll, a girl of the 1920s with muscles and firm skin. This female athlete later metamorphosed into a sturdy farmer, ready to go to war. The New Man and his Socialist Wife were superhumans, pure, innocent, and determined, with no individuality or sex. They echoed antique sculptures, faceless models of even features.

Still, the authorities allowed a limited number of individuals to attain fame, as "shock workers," that is, true Communists sacrificing themselves for the just cause. The best known is Aleksei Stakhanov, the record-breaking coal miner. His name has become synonymous with hard work beyond the Soviet Union.[5] Pavel Morozov became another type of hero, a Communist saint, the so-called Informer 001, the child who denounced his father to Stalin's secret police. Other state heroes include Yuri Gagarin, the first cosmonaut; some exceptional athletes who won Olympic gold medals; obviously, the party leaders; and, curiously enough, certain writers, even some of the writers of nineteenth-century Russian classics. In contradiction to the state ideology, and in contrast to anyone else, these heroes were granted individuality. However, they achieved it by sacrificing themselves. The stories of both Morozov and Stakhanov have been distorted, their details fabricated by the propaganda apparatus and then exploited.

In 1930, in the Siberian village of Gerasimovka, Pavel Morozov, twelve years old at the time, denounced his father Trofim, the chairman of the village council, to the secret police. To this day, it remains unclear of what crime the father was accused, as Yuri Druzhnikov wrote in his biography of the little boy.[6] The authorities changed the legend several times, molding it to meet their current needs. Trofim was deported to a prison camp, where he is presumed to have been executed, though documentation of this has never been found. It is believed that he was charged with obstructing collectivization; according to one version, he provided deported *kulaks* with documents that allowed them to return to European Russia.

Two years after the denunciation, Pavel was murdered—allegedly by *kulaks*, relatives of his father, though his biographer Druzhnikov considered the possibility that a Soviet agent killed him to provide the state with a martyr. Druzhnikov found few hard facts and many contradictions in the story as it was passed on. Original documents do not exist. After having betrayed his father, Pavel is said to have established a network of Bolshevik informers in his village to fight *kulak* activity, or so the Soviet myth went. Druzhnikov, however, suspects Pavel's mother Tatyana to have masterminded the denunciation. Trofim had left her for a mistress. By plotting against him, she hoped to compel her husband to return to the family home, Druzhnikov believes. In the end, Tatyana was the only member of the family to gain from the tragedy. Stalin gave her a pension and a home on the Crimea. After his assassination, Pavel was turned into a hero for Soviet schoolchildren. Nicknamed "Pavlik," he was made the patron saint of the Young Pioneers, the Communist children's organization. His example served to teach generations of Soviet children to become informers, even on their own families.

As the example shows, the agency permitted in the Soviet Union was that toward overcompliance with the system for the system's benefit, and even that required self-sacrifice. This genuinely Christian idea is another piece of evidence of how the Bolshevik ideology mimicked religion, taking advantage of a symbolism with which the Russians were familiar. Most likely, Pavlik's story, as it was taught to the Soviet schoolchildren, was not true. If the boy acted on behalf of his jealous, distressed mother, he was victimized repeatedly, first by being abused by the mother so he would report his own father, then by being killed, and finally, by having his memory abused by the state.

Fraud was also the foundation of the story of Aleksei Stakhanov, another Soviet individual turned into an icon during the 1930s. Pavlik stood for the totalitarian police state; Stakhanov became a model "shock worker" at the forefront of industrialization, the man who beat the machine. On August 31, 1935, in the pit Tsentralnaya Irimina, Stakhanov extracted 102 tons of coal in one single shift of five hours and forty-five minutes. This amounted to fourteen times the standard output. But the record was staged; a journalist was present in the pit, as was a representative of the Central Committee. Roughly a week later, Stakhanov more than doubled his record to 227 tons and, soon afterward, he broke it again with over 320 tons. Stakhanov was equipped with the best machinery of the time; he had the help of top miners, yet he was held up as an example for the coal miners who still worked with shovels and pickaxes. The accuracy of the numbers cannot be verified; perhaps they were made up. When I visited the Stakhanov Museum in the city of Stakhanov, the museum's director and his assistant could not agree on the exact figures. Either way, other miners considered him a cheater, considering the equipment and the helpers he had. His effort won him few friends among those who had to extract coal with outdated tools.

After a fourth record, Stakhanov was resettled to Moscow. Kadivka, his hometown, a sleepy mining settlement in the Donbass region in eastern Ukraine, was renamed Stakhanov. And there he still stands on a square at the end of a dusty boulevard. Some thirteen feet high, in bronze, boyish, wearing a heavy jacket, he carries a pneumatic drill on his shoulder. Some of his name's letters are missing from the pedestal, but nobody cares to replace them.

Within days after Stakhanov's records were publicized, other workers made names for themselves as "Stakhanovites": Alexander Busygin, Smetanin, Petr Krivonos, Maria Demchenko, Evdokiia, and Mariia Vinogradova—household names for many elder Russians. Stalin needed heroes to push industrialization ahead. By November 1935, more than six hundred production records had been registered.[7] Roughly ten weeks after Stakhanov first hit the news, Stalin called for an All-Union Conference of Stakhanovites. In such a short period, a grassroots movement had sprung up and a central conference had been organized—spontaneously, as the propaganda tried to make the world believe. In his speech to the conference, Stalin celebrated the Stakhanovites' victories over the technical standards and their ability "to squeeze out of technique the maximum that can be squeezed out of it"—to beat nature and, thus, time. He stressed their will to sacrifice themselves and to risk being dismissed by refusing to obey the "conservative" orders of their superiors. Praising their selflessness and modesty, Stalin said, "It even seems to me that they are somewhat embarrassed by the scope the movement has acquired, beyond all their expectations."[8]

If Pavlik Morozov was the "Informer 001," we can speak of Stakhanov as the "Shock Worker 001." They were both praised for their model behavior and both won fame by breaking the rules. Stakhanov overrode his immediate superiors for the sake of the state. The Stakhanovites helped to destroy the society by sowing insecurity. Their successful refusal to follow orders turned the hierarchy upside down; other people were persecuted and jailed for revolting against their superiors. This caused confusion. No rule could be taken for granted. By shaping a movement of Stakhanovites, Stalin created a vanguard, a troop of fools he could use to violate his own rules, to manipulate the seemingly revolutionary or carnivalesque situation. However, as their master puppeteer, he could reprimand them at any time. Obviously, it did not matter that the Stakhanovites achieved their goals by deception or unfair means. What was labeled a major contribution to the construction of a new society was in fact destructive, contributing to the carnivalization of the state. No one knew what rules applied at a given moment and what rules should be violated. No one could trust anyone else anymore, since anyone could be an informer or a Stakhanovite. Of course, this contributed to the atomization of the society.

Yuri Gagarin became the great post-Stalinist hero, the first human being to travel into space. He defied gravity, an endeavor symbolic of the Soviet Union's drive to defeat nature. Contrary to his prewar fellow heroes, his was no contribution to the uprooting of society. His flight reassured the nation, enhanced its reach (its space), and thus gave evidence of Soviet superiority. Gagarin may have been an early Soviet consumer, at least as he was depicted. He was granted individuality and even some personal gain. The press pictured him as a happy father of his daughter, a social dancer with his wife, and most surprisingly, the proud owner of a sports car. The son of a cabinetmaker and a milkmaid who made his way to fame and personal success, albeit in the name of the Soviet cause, Gagarin may have been one of the first Soviets privileged with a distinguished private life, visible to the public eye.

Particular heroes were the writers, celebrated personalities who enjoyed the rare privilege of being individuals (at the risk of overstressing the point). In her book, *The Soviet Novel*, the scholar Katerina Clark gives a simple, yet convincing explanation for the Soviet Union's will to produce its own literature: "All previous world systems had produced a great literature, and it was time to show the world what Soviet communism could do."[9] To the writer of novels, a certain degree of individuality had to be granted.

The ideal Soviet Man subordinated his personality to the identity of a shock worker; he was a tool of the party, ready to react on its behalf at any moment—in short, a soldier. In private, meanwhile, at least beginning with the Brezhnev years, he or she shaped himself as a bored consumer, waiting for something to happen, for a bit of entertainment to be delivered.

Brezhnev's Soviet Union did not take the tales of Pavlik Morozov or Stakhanov literally anymore, yet the two remained common knowledge and became Soviet folklore. Privately, some people may have worshiped other heroes, such as Western film stars, pop musicians, or Italian soccer players—people who stood for "decadent" values, such as affluence, which gradually became desirable. Publicly, in the realm of Newspeak, the cult of Pavlik and Stakhanov was kept alive.

Life in the Soviet Union was standardized. The regime forced people into a limited number of preformed careers. It tried to consolidate the system by preventing people from embracing identities that the regime defined as undesirable.[10] Of course the Soviet youth had their antiheroes, such as Jean-Paul Belmondo, the Beatles, or Soviet rock groups, but they could only be worshiped privately. Anyway, they were considered teenagers' idols and not to be taken seriously.

The Soviet society treated young adults as children, all the more so since they seemed to be living as parasites off their parents, dependent into their late twenties or longer. Young people did not have the chance to go to an out-of-town college or to earn their own living. Young couples could not find flats. They were treated like children long into their adult lives. Hence, their home-grown alternative idols—the singer Vladimir Vysotsky, rock bands such as DDT and Akvarium—were tolerated as marginal. To keep these groups under control, the authorities harassed and even jailed their heroes, but no one seemed to understand the social implications of this unspecified dissent. While the young dismissed the state's role models as folk figures, their own idols were treated as trivial. There were no role models that a majority of the society was able to share.

Soviet people had no convictions, the protagonist in Aleksandr Zinoviev's novel, *Homo Sovieticus*, says: "I've only got a more or less stable reaction to everything I bump against: a behavioral stereotype. Convictions are something Western man has, not Soviet man. Instead of having convictions the latter has a 'stereotype of behavior.' This does not presuppose any convictions, and so it's compatible with every sort of conviction."[11] And without conviction one cannot adopt a role model. Indeed, the idea of self-identification was absent from the Soviet discourse, just as the Western emphasis on individuality. That each person ought to realize his or her potential was a notion unheard of. Anthony Giddens called the search for self-identity "a modern problem."[12] In a society that took all responsibility away from its citizens, he wrote, there was little space for a self as a "reflexive project, for which the individual is responsible."

The Soviets hardly strove for individuality, which is a paradox, since historically, the increasing division of labor turned the society's focus toward the individual.[13] Yet the Soviet society, despite driving the division of labor to the extreme, oppressed almost any manifestation of individuality.

It was not until Gorbachev's perestroika that this began to change. More and more people despised the values for which Morozov and Stakhanov stood. In 1988, Gorbachev approved the revelation in *Yunost*[14] and *Komsomolskaya Pravda*, which depicted Pavlik as fabricated. Today, only Gennadi Zyuganov, the post-Soviet Communist leader, still reveres him.[15]

For Russians who grew up in the 1960s and 1970s, Pavlik Morozov is a remnant of a carefree childhood. Therefore, when the fabrications finally became known, that did not stop them from expressing affection for the little traitor, almost as if he were a fairy-tale figure. Nonetheless, the street named after him in Moscow's Krasnaya Presnya district near the White House changed its name and the flag-waving statue in the adjacent park was removed. The statue's granite pedestal, a round, five-foot column with the inscription "Pavliku Morozovu Geroyu" (to the hero Pavlik Morozov) lies abandoned next to the gardener's hut in the park. A newly erected wooden monument symbolizes the Orthodox Church; a playground and tennis courts have been added to the park. Next to its entrance, a large notice board remembers the Communist and nationalist casualties of the street battles of 1993, when the White House was stormed. But nobody stops for the somber faces of yesteryear, or their erring heroes.

Pavlik and Stakhanov could not survive the decline of the system, so they became obsolete. Yet there were no reputable alternatives ready. By design, celebrities were alien to the Soviet society. Its media ran hardly any personality stories; the politicians' private lives were unknown and their spouses not seen in public. With the advent of perestroika, all of this changed. Raisa Gorbacheva acquired a very public stature, yet many Soviets disapproved of her visibility. The perestroika-minded media began to feature individuals, artists, sport stars, and persons with critical views or unique fates. These changes were carefully orchestrated and sanctioned by the Kremlin. In real life, the New Man had died long ago. At last, the CPSU reluctantly buried him, just before its last work shift was dismissed itself.

The press's new heroes were people who crossed borders, who criticized and defied the old rules and rulers, who tried to violate the boundaries, though this time not for the price of self-sacrifice, but for their own (personal) benefit. Below are listed a few of them, as depicted by the magazine *Ogonyok* during the crucial year of 1988.

- *Elem Klimov.* The magazine started the year by profiling the filmmaker and screenwriter. His 1983 movie *Proshchanie s Materoi* (Farewell to Matyora), based on Valentin Rasputin's novel, features a Siberian village that is to be evacuated to give way to a reservoir that will power a hydroelectric power plant. The censors withheld the film for five years. In the interview, Klimov openly advocated a political cinema in which the filmmaker expresses his convictions.[16] Klimov thus acts as a shock worker or Stakhanovite on behalf of a higher cause, for the preservation of nature. He violates the limits drawn by the censors. His idealism echoes the drive of the *shestdesyatniki* (the generation that came of age in the 1960s) to renew the stagnating, rotten Soviet society. Gorbachev shared this view.
- *Oleg Blokhin.* A few months after its story on Klimov, *Ogonyok* introduced the first Soviet soccer player to play as a professional abroad. In Austria, Blokhin was to earn sixty thousand dollars, an inconceivable amount of money for a Soviet at the time. The magazine recounted his laborious struggle with the Soviet bureaucracy to obtain the travel documents: as if on behalf of the readers, Blokhin crossed the line to wealth and crossed the border of the country to conquer spaces yet inaccessible to almost all Soviet citizens.[17]
- *The Man in the Wheelchair.* Handicapped people were not acknowledged to exist in the Soviet Union. Neither were they visible nor was anything made accessible for them. An *Ogonyok* reporter accompanied a man in a wheelchair—allegedly the only wheelchair-bound person to use the subway—on his arduous travels through Moscow's underground.[18]
- *Beauty Queens.* March 1988 saw a story, about Russia's only cosmetic surgeon, that expressed sympathy for people's desire to feel physically valuable.[19] Miss Airspace was on the *Ogonyok* cover in April, Miss Moscow in August.

In 1989, the media featured more serious personalities. The first session of the Congress of People's Deputies in May 1989 revolutionized television coverage. The discussions were aired live; the deputies became people, heroes and villains, in short, individuals. In lengthy testimony, Yaroslav Karpovich and Oleg Kalugin, retired KGB colonels, confessed to foul play as agents of the secret service, but claimed remorse.[20] In August 1990, *Ogonyok* visited Anatoly Gorbunovs, the president who was going to lead Latvia to independence, in his summer home.[21]

Eventually, the scope of people who became celebrities was widened: a professional tennis player became a cover girl; the previously banned rock star Grebenchikov appeared in *Ogonyok*. Within a short period of time, the regimes' mouthpieces underwent a transition from rejecting individuality to offering a shallow endorsement of people who violated the traditional Soviet standards. They promoted personal success, beauty, and wealth. For a brief period, politicians, writers, and activists, for example, Yeltsin and Gavriil Papov, then mayor of Moscow, achieved stardom. Then, gradually, the party-sanctioned press lost its monopoly. Independent publications began to emerge, promoting different values and heroes. There would never be concert over a set of models again. This was the moment when the prostitute, the mafia hit man, and the stockbroker moved into focus. In a state of overt confusion, these free agents replaced the Soviet icons and perestroika's virtuous persons. They stood for the rejection of traditional Soviet values and the naive optimism of the perestroika period.

Post-Soviet Russia values individualism, determination, success, and efficiency; Lededeva called the New Russians "young wolves" and "children of a wild market."[22] Such was their self-perception: what seems more independent than a prostitute freelancing her services? Who could be more determined and successful than someone who makes money by having fun? Who could be more efficient than someone who extorts money from others? No doubt, the girls who see themselves as future prostitutes believe that the choice is theirs. And the boys who dream of becoming racketeers do not waste any thought over the immorality, the lawlessness, and the risks of this activity.

Soviet society did not encourage people to wonder about their own identities. Today, however, everyone is obliged to define himself or herself, to take sides (not least politically), to express opinions. Even in purely bureaucratic terms, the identity of many a Soviet citizen became unclear. Suddenly, clarification was required. People had to decide if they were Russian or Estonian, Russian or Jewish, a Russian-speaking Ukrainian or a Russian living in Ukraine. Should they identify with Moscow, or with their birthplace, which for many people all of a sudden was in a different country? In Soviet times, many people were hardly aware of, say, their national identity. In a Catholic church in Minsk, I met some elderly women who answered "Polish" when I asked them what religion they belonged to. They named Catholic as their nationality, unaware that their passports noted "Belarus." To this day, Russian authors' quest for identity points to a collective, national identity rather than an individual one.[23]

Many post-Soviet individuals' identities have been lost in transition; their old identities have become useless and no new ones have been established. The traditional Soviet careers are not available anymore; they have given way to a void or to some miraculously promising opportunities for those who seek them. The society is in fundamental turmoil. There is no longer a hierarchy, no widely accepted way to display status, making it very much like a carnival, particularly since the collective identity has also collapsed. What is Russia? Who is Russian? What does Russia want? Where should Russia go? Such are the questions debated in post-Soviet Russia.

The Communists' society was supposed to be a society of equals. But they could not (or did not want to) prevent stratification from emerging. People in any society search for means to situate themselves against each other: by what they do, by what they own, by what they wear, by what they know, or even by the hardships they have suffered. For some time, during the lean years of perestroika, people tried to outdo each other in their boasts about how long they had stood in line. Nancy Ries writes in her excellent book, *Russian Talk,* that her Soviet interlocutors "seemed more interested in impressing and astonishing each other with increasingly dire accounts of shortages and tales of how difficult it was becoming to buy anything" than in the actual problems of the food distribution.[24] With these lamentations, they bragged about their skills in finding what could not be found.

With the liberation of prices, this opportunity to distinguish oneself vanished, and with the need for special access and connections becoming obsolete, the hidden classes of Soviet society disappeared, too. Never was the allegedly classless Soviet society as classless as in the moment of its collapse, when it was a true carnival.

Deprived of the tested ways to display status, some intellectuals and engineers reshaped themselves into "former dissidents." The Soviet intelligentsia lost its sense of reality to the extent that people took inactivity as a form of resistance, Sonja Margolina commented.[25] For a brief period, this provided them with status; the self-promoted former dissidents were sought after. But with the interest in the past vanishing again, being a "former dissident" lost its appeal.

Russians who are able to do so rely on their newly acquired wealth to display status. A New Russian is not a Tatar or a physicist anymore, but a businessman—and incredibly rich. The New Russians brag about the amounts of money they have made.

Pavlik Morozov has been replaced by the prostitute, the shock worker Stakhanov by a racketeer. To many observers—Russians or Westerners—this is reason for grave concern. Yet one might read these post-Soviet counterparts of the Informer 001 and the "Shock Worker 001" as exaggerated icons of a drive to have fun and get rich. The prostitute and the bandit, like Pavlik and Stakhanov, are overachievers in their own right and reflect the nation's current state of mind. They reach for their share, by any means. Why should not these new idols be accepted for what they are—misguided exaggerations, caricatures, like the old Soviet ones? A mafioso cheats, just like Stakhanov; a prostitute's activity may seem amoral, but where are the morals of betraying one's own father? Neither the mafioso nor the prostitute would claim to be a paragon of moral virtue. They are honest about what they do. No party will place them on a pedestal. The most important transformation, however, is this: the prostitute, the stockbroker, the hit man, and the racketeer are free agents, or perceived as such; Pavlik and Stakhanov were slaves, even though by choice, as the propaganda would have people believe.

With the increasing availability of Western media, or Western news and entertainment in the Russian media, the diversity of idols has also increased. Today, the young Russians' range of stars reflects that of their European and American counterparts; it includes Madonna, Leonardo DiCaprio, Brad Pitt, rappers, skinheads, plus Russian actors and singers, such as Alla Pugacheva. Positive role models for young people interested in a professional career, though, are hard to find. Gagarin has not been replaced.

Post-Soviet Russia sizzles with irony. Little is taken seriously. It is therefore not surprising that irony does not even spare the space program, the pride of all Soviets, including the dissidents.[26] In his aforementioned novel *Omon Ra,* the writer Victor Pelevin pretended to reveal the true nature of the unmanned Soviet flight to the moon, which was celebrated as a major victory of Soviet automation. Omon Krivomazov is the book's protagonist. The boy's first name itself is satirical, as it mocks the Soviet habit of giving children names that refer to socialist institutions: the paramilitary special police forces are called OMON (Otriady Militsy Osobogo Naznachenya). Since the Soviet computers are far weaker than publicly admitted, the flight to the moon has to be piloted by human beings, teenage boys, one in each section of the spacecraft. Their lives end the moment their section of the carrier rocket is burned out and ejected from the craft. Omon is one of these boys; he tells the story of his short career and its surprising end. Pelevin dedicated the book to "The Heroes of the Soviet Cosmos," thus ridiculing the only heroes whose fame may have survived the collapse of the system.

A carnival cannot last; a continuing absence of any transparent order soon becomes intolerable to people. They crave order and hope for a hierarchy to redevelop. For Russia, returning to the old social system is not an option. A new hierarchy is not available, even within many families, where the fathers are absent and the mothers are working. Russia still lacks a commonly accepted value system; there are no class distinctions people can turn to and, except for that determined by money, there's no order of status. Communism denied people any dignity beyond the party's hierarchy; now even its phony honor system has collapsed.

Class is determined by the past; class is where people come from. With people cut off from their individual pasts, class is not an option for a restructuring of Russian society. Status, however, is forward-looking and fluid. Status can be achieved; it can change at any time.[27] Many intellectuals' efforts to refashion themselves as "former dissidents" were attempts to acquire higher status. Contrary to class, status needs permanent confirmation. The society at large acts as a mirror through which the individual looks for approval. However, it is all but impossible to have one's status confirmed by a society that cannot agree on values—except money. That's why the (New) Russians furnish themselves with as many signifiers for wealth—signs of social power—as they can.

Life is a story. In the Soviet Union, people tended to hide their particular stories. Being different or attempting to differ generally meant trouble. Excelling was only possible on officially sanctioned tracks—in school, at university, at work, in sports, in music. Since the collapse of Communism, most people have begun to actively shape their fates and thus their stories. They tell these stories with words as well as with the way they style themselves. Cosmetics were among the first Western goods to be imported on a large scale, followed by fashion, body care products, diet plans, and health food. The body, in the Soviet Union a passive object, has become a tool to express one's personality. It can be shaped, altered, trimmed, and displayed in the best possible light. Russian women have begun to take care of themselves or "to be true to themselves," an expression no one would have understood ten years ago.

A limited number of ready-made lifestyles have been replaced by an apparent lack of any pattern. People have to come up with their own life plans. Anything goes. It is thus not surprising that some youths dream of becoming prostitutes or mafiosi. Since there are no longer any manners, there is hardly any threshold of embarrassment.

The Shock Worker 001, a miner, has been replaced by a criminal, an extortionist; the Informer 001 has been replaced by a sex worker. And who will work? Conventional jobs have lost their appeal. Russia's ideal future, it seems, is a future without work. Yet the sex worker and the extortionist have as little in common with the average person's reality as had Pavlik and Stakhanov, who were the exaggerations depicting the rule. But if average people strive to become free agents, unlike their enslaved Soviet predecessors, then Russia is on her way to becoming a society in which more and more people are in charge of themselves and responsible for their own actions.

NOTES

1. Barbara Von der Heydtl, *Corruption in Russia: No Democracy without Morality*, Heritage Foundation, Committee Brief no. 13 (Washington, D.C.: Heritage Foundation, June 21, 1995).
2. Sonja Margolina, *Russland: Die nichtzivile Gesellschaft* (Reinbek, Germany: Rowohlt, 1994), 88.
3. Helena Goscilo, "The Gendered Trinity of Russian Cultural Rhetoric," in *Soviet Hieroglyphs: Visual Culture in Late Twentieth-Century Russia*, ed. Nancy Condee (Bloomington: Indiana University Press, 1995), 70.
4. Goscilo, "Gendered Trinity," 78.
5. In English as in German, "stakhanov" and "stakhanovite" are colloquial metaphors for hard work and people who work hard.
6. Yuri Druzhnikov, *Donoshnik 001, ili Voznesenie Pavlika Morozova* (Informer 001, or the ascension of Pavlik Morozov) (Moscow: Moskovsky rabochy, 1995).
7. Lewis H. Siegelbaum, *Stakhanovism and the Politics of Productivity in the USSR, 1935–1941* (New York: Cambridge University Press, 1988).
8. J. V. Stalin, Speech at the All-Union Conference of Stakhanovites, November 17, 1935, in J. V. Stalin, *Problems of Leninism* (Beijing: Foreign Language Press, 1976), 775–794.
9. Katerina Clark, *The Soviet Novel: History as Ritual* (Chicago: University of Chicago Press, 1981), 36.
10. George W. Breslauer, "Identities in Transition: Introduction," in *Identities in Transition: Eastern Europe and Russia after the Collapse of Communism*, ed. Victoria E. Bonell, International Area Studies, Research Series no. 93 (Berkeley: University of California, Center for Slavic and East European Studies, 1996), 6.
11. Aleksandr Zinoviev, *Homo Sovieticus*, trans. Charles Janson (Boston: Atlantic Monthly Press, 1985), 11.
12. Anthony Giddens, *Modernity and Self-Identity: Self and Society in the Late Modern Age* (Stanford, Calif.: Stanford University Press, 1991), 74.
13. Emile Durkheim, *The Division of Labour in Society*, trans. W. D. Halls (London: Macmillan, 1984).
14. *Yunost* (Youth) (Moscow), March 1988.
15. Gennadi A. Zyuganov, *Rossiya—Rodina Maya* (Moscow: Informpechat, 1996), 327. Zyuganov maintains that within the old CPSU there were two parties: a patriotic, Russian party, which was "the party of Sholokhov and Korolev, Zhukhov and Gagarin, Kurchatov and Stakhanov," and the antipatriotic "party of Trotsky and Kaganovich, Beria and Mekhlis, Gorbachev and Yeltsin, Yakovlev and Shevardnadze."

16. *Ogonyok,* no. 2 (1988).
17. *Ogonyok,* no. 21 (1988).
18. *Ogonyok,* no. 9 (1988).
19. *Ogonyok,* no. 52 (1987) had already celebrated female beauty on its cover with the words, "We want to be beautiful," along with numerous stories.
20. *Ogonyok,* no. 29 (1989).
21. *Ogonyok,* no. 32 (1990).
22. Alena Ledeneva, *Russia's Economy of Favours: Blat, Networking, and Informal Exchanges* (Cambridge: Cambridge University Press, 1998), 202.
23. Evgeny Barabanov, *Katalog zur Kieler Petersburg-Ausstellung,* quoted in Eckhart Gillen, "Das Fangen ist vorbei: Positionen der St. Petersburger Kunst," *Frankfurter Allgemeine Zeitung,* January 2, 1995, 25. Barabanov is quoted: "Scheuen wir immer und immer wieder voller Unruhe die Frage nach unserer Identität: Was bedeutet unser historisches Ich, und wo ist unser Platz in der Weltgeschichte?" (Again and again, restless, we fear the question of our identity. What does our historical "I" mean, what's our place in the history of mankind?).
24. Nancy Ries, *Russian Talk: Culture and Conversation during Perestroika* (Ithaca, N.Y.: Cornell University Press, 1997), 36.
25. Margolina, *Russland: Nichtzivile Gesellschaft,* 91.
26. Even people who openly criticized the Brezhnev regime were proud of the space program, as Leonid Gozman confirmed in an interview in November 1989.
27. The distinction between class and society is made by Andrew Sullivan in *New York Times Magazine,* November 15, 1998, 59.

10

Conclusion

Ikea, or the Furniture for
a Modern Russia

In March 2000, on Leningradsky Chaussee, just north of Moscow's city border, a long line formed—not of people, as was common during Soviet times, but of cars. Ikea, the Swedish furniture company, had finally opened its mall. Some people had been waiting in their cars for several hours.

At the height of the economic crisis, a line of cars—then a familiar sight, but now all but forgotten—indicated that a particular gas station had fuel. Nearly a decade later, Ikea caused a similar scene, as if Muscovites were starving for its inexpensive, easy-to-assemble beds, sofas, closets, and bookshelves and its kitchenware. They *were* starving. Soviet furniture was bulky and not meant to ever be disassembled again. (People did not move, anyway.) Ikea furniture, unlike the old Soviet furniture, is light, cheerful, sleek, and easy to put together or dismantle. In Western Europe, Ikea is the choice of the young and mobile, such as university students, for whom it initially implied their refusal to comply with the established society's ways to convey status. Today, it marks their indifference or expresses antistatus. In the West, if anything, Ikea is an antibrand. In Russia, Ikea, more than any other company, has been read as bringing the future into homes of the emerging middle class.

Western furniture—mostly expensive luxury brands for the showy New Russians—has been available since the beginning of perestroika, at least in Moscow and St. Petersburg. Ikea counters those brands; its customers hope to communicate their desire for a new and different *byt*, or being, of "visible decency," as the Moscow journalist Irina Sandomirskaya wrote in her essay in the Swedish monthly *Moderna Tider.* "Ikea is a guest from the future. It has landed at the fringe of Moscow's ideological land-scape like a spaceship from another world with a message of lightening public spaces, open personal relations, and a predictable healthy life."[1] Ikea goods stand for modesty; their practical style understates their true value.

However, Ikea is more than just another adaptation from the West; it is the latest in a long list of imports meant to improve Russian life, which started when the czars invited scholars, teachers, architects, and other specialists, including military men. Architectural style, court etiquette (in-cluding the use of the French language), dress codes (including blue jeans), and opera have been borrowed to turn the Russians into "Germans or Englishmen, instead of making them Russians," as Rousseau wrote[2]— in this case Russians would become Swedes, which was particularly ap-propriate since Ikea is not imposed from above.

Appearances matter in Russia and, as we have seen in chapters 3 and 4, they often matter more than content. Moreover, appearances have often been manipulated: by the state, both czarist and Communist, and by the elites as well. Again and again, the Russian society has wasted its energy to disguise the reality, in language as well as in signs.

Carnival is a moment of truth. Any disguise risks being torn off. To mock the rulers and symbolically turn society upside down, the partici-pants of the Swabian-Alemannic carnival, for example, mask themselves; during their parades, they distribute fake coins (sweets), night is turned into day and day into night.[3] Carnival and revolution cause, or are caused by, a crisis of signification: the festivities or upheaval cause people to lose the ability to distinguish the deviation from the standard, if they have not lost it already. However, by mocking, inverting, intensifying, and manip-ulating everyday life, carnival prepares for its restoration. Some kind of normality has to succeed the wild times; the same is true for revolution. People soon tire of the masquerade, of again and again being swept up in the disruptive and destructive immediacy of misrule, and their fatigue and disillusionment pave the way for a return to some stable order, the old one or—in the case of a revolution—a new one.

In Russia, the first "Lords of Misrule," the Bolsheviks, are long gone. They were repeatedly replaced by new leaders who promised to finally reform the country, to reinstall (a new) order. Each time, however, the new order turned out to be just another fools' society. Most Russians, as shown when the former KGB officer Vladimir Putin was elected president, crave order and stability.

With the collapse of the Soviet Union, millions of people lost their place in the world, some literally. They lost their country. In place of the Soviet Union, fifteen new states emerged. All of a sudden, members of some families were separated not only by distance, but also by state borders. Some are even required to apply for visas to visit one another. Time is not Soviet time anymore; space is experienced in ways it never was before. To many, life has become complicated, the familiarity of the Soviet "home" is all but gone.

The patterns of social interaction have changed, too. Unwritten norms and rules, many of them so minute that people are barely aware of them, govern the daily routine—where people learn and practice their social skills. It is this canon of codes that keeps a society together. However, the old Soviet rules are void and there are no new ones the post-Soviet societies have agreed upon. The Soviets' design for life has been abolished, people's expertise thus invalidated; their Soviet education is not applicable anymore and their tested skills, such as *blat*, have become useless. Many people feel that there is nothing left in their lives that can be taken for granted.

Soviet order was based on "suspended punishment," "collective guarantee," and "personalization," as Ledeneva wrote, hence the society was ruled by fear.[4] At the same time, the police state provided its citizens with the security of a jail. No one could escape, and no one would be abandoned; this afforded the citizens a sense of stability. Most people feared the state, but they knew it would take care of them. Constant control evoked a feeling of being protected.

Most Soviet people may have hated the party leaders, as my friends and acquaintances kept reassuring me. However, they still could love their rulers, as the Moscow psychologist Leonid Gozman maintained in his book published in Germany, *Von den Schrecken der Freiheit* (The scare of freedom).[5] People related emotionally to the regime; in one way or another, against all reason, they trusted it, relying on the firmness of the system and the permanence of its rules. Most of them displayed, as Sonja Margolina asserted, borrowing from Theodor Adorno, an *authoritarian personality*; they willingly accepted the regime's authority and readily obeyed and subordinated themselves to it.[6] Authoritarian personalities, according to Adorno, participate in the aggressive humiliation of weaker individuals or groups. This pecking order added to the society's inertia and thus made it seem even more stable.

In the wake of the collapse of the Soviet regime, the Soviet Union's social fabric crumbled and its institutions disintegrated, both the formal and the informal ones. People's skills became obsolete and, at the same time, the state institutions' expertise vanished (much of this expertise had been phony anyway, a Potemkin-style expertise). Yet, until the beginning of perestroika, the society had been in a precarious balance.

Nolens volens, people began to adapt themselves to the changing situations, even before the final collapse. The state, however, did not manage to replace its antiquated expertise; after 1991, many Russian institutions

failed to meet their most basic obligations. In general, post-Soviet offices,
like the Communist ones before them, have been make-believes, serving
some purpose other than their names allege. Most institutions do not
serve the citizens as they are supposed to—their bureaucrats do not
even know how. The new Russian state fails to enforce the law, to keep
its citizens safe, or to provide them with minimal welfare or education,
or with a health service; it botches the tax collection and seems to be unable or unwilling to safeguard the nation's assets, such as its natural resources. In some of the former republics, the situation is even worse than
in Russia.

Thus, even if the post-Communist governments had been more honest than any previous regime and cared more about the citizens' well-
being than their Soviet predecessors, they would have been defeated by
their own incompetence and the people's trust would still have fizzled
out. A majority of Russians never comprehended what Yeltsin and his
government were trying to achieve.

Overnight, the "authoritarian personalities" of Russia were deprived
of their sense of security. For many people, especially the elderly, this
was a shock. A nation as comfortable with a pecking order as the Soviets' had lost all its social markers; it was virtually orphaned. However,
many people adapted quickly and overcame their authoritarian personalities (some may have faked their pathological love for totalitarian
regime in the first place, as Gozman contended).[7] In the new social disorder, money has become the sole discriminating feature. Most people
cope with this change either by adopting the new status symbols, ridiculing them, or doing both simultaneously. Anyhow, who would want
to waste their money on expensive make-believes, particularly on designer furniture, status symbols that will be hidden away in a not-so-
fancy apartment? Thus most Russians will not want to spend thousands of dollars on a sofa or a bookshelf by some fancy Italian or
Danish designer brand; the majority could not even afford it. Yet people have grown tired of the bulky Soviet furniture—furniture that may
have served its purpose, but has not met any aesthetic requirements
and in most cases is worn out, often handed down from one tenant to
the next. For almost a decade, hardly any reasonable alternative had
been available. Many people resorted to building their own shelves and
beds.

This was the situation when Ikea started the construction of its mall.
Ikea promised to fill the gap between the pretentious, prohibitively expensive designer brand furniture and the musty Soviet stuff. Many Russians of the emerging middle class and expatriates rejoiced. The Moscow
city government, however, raised all sorts of obstacles to block Ikea's way,
which delayed its opening by several months.

With its reasonably priced furniture with simple lines and clear, cheerful colors, Ikea enables the consumers—many for the first time—to escape the rough feel and the stench of its Soviet counterpart and to simultaneously avoid the showiness of the New Russians and the high prices this entails. Ikea stands for value and utility and thus serves as a social leveler, reducing distinctions and allowing its customers to gain a foothold in the post-Soviet world.

Ikea appeals particularly to the emerging middle class, the mostly well-educated people who are making a relatively smooth transition from Soviet to post-Soviet life. Among them are some of my friends who were once proud of being mistaken as foreigners, though to them, as well as to many other customers, Ikea is still rather expensive. Not to speak of the Russians in the provinces, a substantial number of Muscovites, presumably still the majority, could not yet afford to shop at Ikea.

By buying furniture from Ikea, Moscow customers obtain a handy, decent piece of equipment that also helps them to display their new middle-class status. At the same time, they convey their refusal to compete with the New Russians, to boast about their status, or to comply with the old Soviet style. As a status marker, Ikea allows its customers to ignore the New Russians' pecking order and to simultaneously affirm their own identities. These people reject the old Soviet Union and despise the newly rich. Their model is a Western society in which, as my friends repeatedly said, "normal people" live with "normal furniture." Asked what they meant by "normal" (or *normalno*, in Russian, which is also used in the sense of "good" or "acceptable"), they stressed that they did not want to live as before any more, in a permanent state of emergency. "Normal" thus stood for "not the Soviet way."

Their buying furniture from Ikea can be read as evidence of how they imagine their future. They hope for the Russian society to Westernize—they often called that "to normalize"—and for themselves to be living in an unpretentious, nice-looking, and comfortable home. At the same time, by making major purchases, they are expressing confidence. They assume that for the foreseeable future, they will be able to maintain their new lifestyle.

In 1989, when McDonald's opened its first restaurant on Pushkin Square in Moscow, one friend justified his willingness to wait in line for up to an hour with the fact that at McDonald's, unlike any other restaurant at the time, he knew what was on the menu would be available. He therefore believed he would get fair value for his expenditure, both in waiting time and money. In other words, he trusted McDonald's.

In premodern societies, people trusted other people, rather than institutions. Often, there were no reliable institutions, anyway. The Soviet Union, however, placed the institution above the individual, at least theoretically.

Nominally, the institutions were at the citizens' disposal, although in reality people were reluctant to rely on them. The authorities did not serve their nominal purposes, but abused the citizenry, while hiding behind the facade of the institutions. As I have shown earlier, to get anything done, people were well advised to revert to personal connections.

With the unwritten laws obsolete and the written ones, including those passed by the post-Soviet government, unobserved, with the personal connections of limited use and hardly any institutions to turn to, many Russians feel lost and unable to trust anyone.

Modernity has been called "the intertwined emergence of capitalism, the bureaucratic nation-state, and industrialism"; it "changed the representation of space and time and hence the way we experience and treat them," as Friedland and Boden wrote.[8] Modernization implies a shift of trust, from individuals to institutions. However, industrialization does not equal modernization. The German scholar Dieter Hoffmann-Axthelm called it a basic mistake to read technical innovations as indicators of social developments.[9] Yet the Soviets cultivated this mistake in their aspiration to create the appearance of modernity.

On an individual level, modernization is an educational process. The individual aspires to "civilize" himself or herself, as Sonja Margolina put it. In post-Soviet Russia, diverse lifestyles differentiate people of different status.[10] In Soviet times, the Russian language barely knew the term "lifestyle";[11] the concept of having a choice of lifestyles did not exist. Nowadays, people have a plurality of options. However, for the transition to this multitude of lifestyles to succeed, a civil society should already be in place, as Margolina emphasized. The (former) *homini sovietici,* therefore—lacking any experience of a civil society—must create the building blocks of that society from scratch.

Stalin's Taylorism may have been compatible with the Soviet apartheid, since industrialization requires a certain atomization of the society, the separation of work and living, for example. Modernization, however, would have caused a dialectical tension between individualism and the individual's compliance with the needs of the system, something the Soviets suppressed by all means. "Modern concerns with identity stem also from ways in which modernity has made identity distinctively problematic," Lash and Urry wrote in *Economies of Signs and Space.*[12] "The discourse of self is distinctively modern, and modernity distinctively linked to the discourses of self, not just because of the cognitive and moral weight attached to selves and self-identity."

With Soviet Taylorism little more than a facade, and individualism, the quest for self-identity, and even the discourse of selves violently oppressed, neither thrust to modernize the society had any chance to materialize.

In early modern Western Europe, complete strangers shared hostel beds—beds, not bedrooms. It was not before the eighteenth century that sleeping was "privatized" and the child's right to have his or her own bed became a sociopolitical demand.[13] In provincial Russia, hotel guests are still made to share a room—to Westerners, common sleeping rooms are only acceptable for children, backpackers, and soldiers, although not so long ago, affluent European travelers happily shared their bedrooms with strangers.[14]

As with the sharing of rooms, in the eighteenth century Western European families ceased to eat from a common bowl. At the same time, Western European restaurants began to set individual tables for separate parties. The desire for privacy had reached the dinner table.[15] In Russia, especially in the provinces, such developments have only just begun.

The Czech émigré novelist Milan Kundera believes that freedom is impossible in a society that refuses to respect the fact that "we act different in private than in public." By forcing them to live in a glass house, totalitarian regimes "deny their citizens the status of individuals," Kundera maintains. The transformation of man from subject to object evokes the experience of shame; thus a certain degree of privacy is necessary for the development of human individuality.[16] In modern societies, people wear various masks, each appropriate to a specific situation. One takes on different roles according to the particular social setting. If such a mask were to be violently torn away, Jeffrey Rosen wrote in the *New York Times*, what would be exposed is not the true self but the spectacle of a wounded and defenseless person. For individuals to freely relate to the society, the mask is essential. It allows them to influence the way they are perceived.

The fragmentation of the society, even of the single life—the unity of disunity,[17] the "maelstrom of perpetual disintegration and renewal"[18]—and the "disembedding" of social institutions are essential to modernization.[19] In their quest to modernize Russia, the Bolsheviks engaged in what they considered "creative destruction."[20] But they failed to start any forward-looking reconstruction, to build a future, to furnish their cities with an architectonic equivalent of Ikea's convenient and pleasing ensembles. Instead, by the 1930s they had silenced their avantgarde and begun to commission edifices that represented eternity and immutability.

With modernization, personal relations are increasingly replaced by dealings with anonymous institutions. Urbanization has a similar effect; modernization and urbanization usually go hand in hand. As I have shown, the Soviet Union cultivated a Potemkin-style urbanism, when in fact it was a peasant society where people lived semirural lives in citylike landscapes. If industrialization and urbanization are inseparable, as Lefebvre stresses, then a Potemkin-style urbanism matches a Potemkin-style industrialization.

It's not the size that makes a city, but its soul, as the early sociologist Os-wald Spengler wrote.[21] A city speaks its own language—or languages, in-cluding the nonverbal ones; it harbors a specific alertness. A city is aware of itself; a big agglomeration is not. The city condenses exchanges—or "semiotic activity," to use Umberto Eco's term[22]; an agglomeration com-presses people. A city is a place of centralized wealth, in a situation in which wealth is mobile, according to Lefebvre.[23] In the USSR, wealth was immobilized, if it existed at all. Thus urbanity, the way I use the term here, could not exist in the Soviet Union—and neither could modernity, since there was neither condensed exchange nor centralized wealth.

"All that is solid melts into air." To title his book exploring modernity, Marshall Berman quoted Marx's *Communist Manifesto*, which says, "All fixed, fast-frozen relations, with their train of ancient and venerable preju-dices and opinions, are swept away, all new-formed ones become anti-quated before they can ossify."[24] The *Übervater* of the Soviet leaders un-derstood the mercurial nature of a modern society, while they, more than a century later, still tried to petrify the nation. "All that is holy is profaned," the *Manifesto* continues. Marx' executors, however, turned the profane in-signia of their dirty power into their Holy Grail, heavily borrowing signs from the church. Thus, with their actions, the Bolsheviks clearly set against Marx's own ideas of modernity. "To be modern is to find ourselves in an environment that promises adventure, power, joy, growth, transformation of ourselves and the world—and, at the same time, that threatens to de-stroy everything we have, everything we know, everything we are," Berman wrote.[25] In other words, people gain freedom at the price of secu-rity. This, however, requires some self-confidence—at least enough that the individual does not perceive the relative lack of security as a threat.

Trust begins at home. The house and the neighborhood provide a space in which (young) people practice their social literacy. The family home is where morals and rules are taught.[26] This is the place to learn to read and convey nonverbal messages, and to eventually acquire the judgment needed to survive. In the Soviet living environment, such learning oppor-tunities hardly existed. Many fathers were absent; their children were raised—spoiled and disciplined—by the grandmothers. Despite the stag-nation, the homes did not feel stable, even if nothing ever changed. Ap-pliances, such as refrigerators and laundry machines, were unreliable; the furniture with which people lived was hard to come by and unappealing. The heating could break down and getting things repaired was difficult, time consuming, and costly.

With the easing of the totalitarian system, punishment lost its deter-rence; fear no longer restrains people from violating the law. In an envi-ronment a majority of the inhabitants perceive as dysfunctional, ugly, and repellent, there is very little incentive to behave properly.

With its furniture, Ikea brings tiny counter-homes into being. With simple lines and functionality, its furniture represents the lightness and freedom of modernity, particularly since it is easy to dismantle and reassemble. Ikea expects its customers to be mobile. Its colors and material, however, its warm bright shades, its raw wood, metal, and glass convey stability—or "honesty and reliability," as one woman friend in Moscow said. There are no rusty springs hidden in an Ikea sofa bed that would make her back ache and her nights sleepless. For most people, when choosing a piece of furniture, its looks are as important as its comfort, and Ikea does look like a promise for a decent, healthy, and predictable life; it seems to put its owners in control of their own fates. Ikea furniture has to be assembled by the customer, which might be a setback in other countries, but most Russians have become very handy during the years of shortages. By assembling their own furniture, they feel that they are not wasting money. And add the fact that Ikea is from Sweden, the country many socialists and social democrats from all over the world admired as a model for their own, a state that takes care of its citizens but does not deprive them of their liberties.

On top of that, the Ikea mall on the highway north of Moscow, as Sandomirskaya insists, is a "spaceship" from the future. There are no lines inside the clean, air-conditioned store; the atmosphere is relaxed, almost like in a home furnished by Ikea. People are served well: there are no guards who bully people and keep them away, no metal detectors at the entrance, very few sport utility vehicles—bandit cars, as many Russians call them—in the parking lot, no bribes, and no hidden charges.

Ikea is a small island. Its furthest extension, the company's shuttle bus downtown, brings the customers back into Russia's harsh present, into a dirty, crime-ridden city of lost hopes and missed opportunities, run by clans and gangs looting the remains of the Soviet state. The formally democratic government includes thieves and, when fighting its critics, it resorts to crude pressure and violence. Returning from Ikea, one feels as if one is waking up from a sweet dream to the harsh, repulsive Russian reality, going from an orderly world to a moral vacuum, to the never-ending carnival. But how can it have been only a dream if one carries along an Ikea bag with plates and dishes or boxes containing the parts of a bookshelf? Ikea may be a dream, but the goods one buys there are real, and they remain real in the daily life of the emerging middle class. Furniture and appliances perhaps alter the way Russians view the world even more than do the changing eating and dressing habits. Ikea allows Russians to create a new world in their own home. They thus lose one of their reasons to disapprove of their environment. In apartments in which the furniture conveys some lightness of being, some people might find it easier to live with each other, possibly even to solve private conflicts. Ikea creates homes in a country where people never had a home.

True, prior to *Ikea* many other things had been imported to improve Russian *byt* (being), including socialism, democracy, and capitalism. However, Russians have russified anything they have adapted and too often they have criminalized it, as Edward Keenan once said.[27] There is no guarantee that they will not do the same to Ikea. Or, as Sandomirskaya put it: Neither Ikea nor other benign intruders "can be sure to be immune against the aggressive local bacteria." But different from most other such imports, Ikea has not been imposed upon the population from above; neither has it been brought to Moscow for reasons of ideology. Its purpose is not to Westernize the Russians from above, as has repeatedly been attempted ever since Peter the Great. Ikea is a commercial endeavor, brought to Russia to make a profit and embraced by the middle class— paying customers—and not by any anonymous authority with a hidden agenda. By buying furniture from Ikea, people distance themselves from the masquerade of the bragging New Russians, from the governing elite, and not least from the Soviet past. By doing so, they might well Westernize themselves.

Thus, shopping at Ikea could be called the Russian middle class's most ardent step toward the modernization of the society from below. Ikea drastically narrows the gap between the message an item conveys—good taste, affluence, openness, and maybe power—and its content or usability, or between signifier and the signified. Ikea furniture is not suited to boast.

Ikea, of course, is a multinational company that mass-produces its goods, taking advantage of low-wage countries—Russia and Latvia, for example—and the low fringe expenditures it has to pay in these countries, such as a trifle in social security. There is nothing cozy about Ikea's way of doing business: the company produces a reasonably priced—and thus highly profitable—line of products. Its promotions department has carefully designed Ikea's benevolent air.

According to Kotkin, other characteristics of modernity are mass politics and mass production, the latter usually implying mass consumption, and mass culture.[28] There can be no doubt that Soviet politics was mass politics—not politics by the masses but, in the regime's own words, politics for the masses—politics that treated the citizens as an anonymous mass. Soviet culture was mass culture, if only because of the sheer lack of diversity. Everyone read the same books and watched the same few films and television programs. Was the Soviet Union a country of mass consumption? There was very little consumption in the first place. For food and agricultural products, the techniques of mass production were used. Aeroflot was proud to run the world's biggest chicken factory; milk was converted into milk powder only to be rehydrated to become "milk" again. Obsessed with the success the United States achieved with the Fordist model of production, the Stalinists copied its industrial mass production. They tried to convert agriculture to a system based on Fordist principles. Time clocks and conveyor belts were installed; production was seemingly automated. Stephen Kotkin reads this as evidence of an early modernization. However, as Kotkin admits, such "modernized" Soviet factories needed hundreds of auxiliary workers to prepare the machines and to step in where automation failed. It has been argued that this faking of a Fordist production even decreased productivity. The main goals of mass production—to increase production with a reduced work-force, to streamline the manufacturing process and maximize efficiency—were therefore never met. Why would the Soviets have bothered—if not for the sake of appearances? They had human resources at their disposal for all but free. Soviet mass production was thus a phony mass production. If it indicated the degree of the society's modernization, the Soviet Union appeared to be a modern state, while in reality its modernization was a masquerade—with a mask of modernity glazing over a premodern society, in short, a Potemkin-style modernity.

In a modernized society, all that was solid has melted into thin air. There is no permanence except that of change; mobility, both social and geographical, is highly valued, even encouraged. At the same time, the civilizing process continues to compartmentalize people's lives, as Norbert Elias so convincingly showed. Bodily functions have become increasingly intimate, thus adding to the division between private and social. In some Western societies, any bodily odor or noise is considered rude. People's lives are split between an intimate sphere and a public sphere, with respective behaviors. The bourgeois Western societies have assigned particular enclaves for bodily activities, such as eating, sleeping, even napping, and of course sex and "using the bathroom." Thus modernization implies an increasing fragmentation of people's lives, which have become subject to permanent change. However, this is a different fragmentation from the Soviet apartheid. It requires steady mobility between the spaces. The Communist regime, by contrast, prevented any social or geographical transgression. It suppressed change; hierarchy and stability were its highest precepts—everything alive was frozen in a political ice age.

Theoretically, the Soviet state provided its citizens with all sorts of services, from preschool education to health care for the elderly. For each necessity, an institution was set up. The state assumed responsibility for its citizens, made most decisions for them, and arranged employment for everyone and paid their pensions. It pampered people, although with very modest perks. For a few decades after World War II, this welfare system worked, if on a poor level. It worked better for the privileged living in the big cities, for the intelligentsia, particularly in Moscow, and for those working for the party or the military-industrial complex. The Soviet

232 Chapter 10

Union appeared to have a mass welfare system. In hindsight, many Russians gloss over its flaws, particularly the beneficiaries, such as the former elite. Nevertheless, one had to rely on personal connections, even for basic needs. This paradox fits well into the general picture: the Soviet state appeared much more advanced than it really was.

Another paradox: the thrust toward modernization beginning with perestroika made the Soviet institutions, or what remained of them, increasingly irrelevant. At the same time, people's tested connections vanished. Therefore, since the collapse of the Communist regime, one could rely neither on the institutions nor on stable connections. A "tip" or a bribe was often the only means that helped achieve an end. Now that people have lost their confidence, their lives have become very complicated.

When rallying for the abolition of the state monopoly, Soviet citizens were hardly aware that they would be trading their social security for freedom. No one expected the extent to which the situation would deteriorate. For many people, life has indeed become more difficult, with the growing gap between rich and poor raising people's awareness of their material hardship. However, some Russians tend to complain for the sake of complaining. A friend who has succeeded in making the transition, who now has a nice apartment, an imported car, and a decent salary that allows him to regularly travel abroad, laments the increased difficulty of life. Joking about his paradoxical stand, this fifty-something expresses nostalgia for the "simple socialist life," as he calls it.

In addition, one has to ask, who are those who complain the loudest? The formerly privileged, rather than the *babushkas* who suffered hardships all their lives. Sonja Margolina, born and educated in the Soviet Union, considered the humanities' departments of the top Soviet universities as places of "unequaled laziness and corruption." In these "salons" of Soviet academia, an extension of the kitchen tables, everyone grumbled but no one felt obliged to act.

Human beings will never feel completely secure—that is, as safe as they feel at home—in a second language. An idiom one has acquired by studying remains slightly unfamiliar. The later in life one starts to learn it, the clumsier one feels. I assume the same is true for other codes, particularly a nonverbal language, a mode of communication that is not learned from textbooks.[29]

Despite its propaganda, the Soviet state ignored the needs of its citizens, but hammered the Communist ideology into their heads. Some governments of the post-Soviet states may still disregard their citizens' rights and dignity, but most refrain from preaching a belief-system—at least they have so far. From my Westerner's point of view, this seems to be a huge step forward. The *homini sovietici*, however, may feel abandoned. How can they respect or "love" a state that demonstrates its indifference toward them so. A little more than a decade ago, the Soviet state attempted to control every idea expressed on its territory; now the Russian government does not care at all. Repression—under which one is at least taken care of—may evoke a perverse assertiveness. Indifference, however, causes feelings of abandonment.

The permanent carnival thus has dramatically undermined people's sense of security. They lack any incentive to trust people outside their own circles or to trust the institutions. The state even refuses them the comfort of a greater purpose: there is no world war, no fight against imperialism, no supreme cause to sacrifice oneself for. Therefore, the people are starved for signs of righteousness and trustworthiness, for things that convey clarity and honesty, things that are easy to handle, reasonably priced, and useful. For "normality," as so many Russians say.

Ikea is an island of "normality"—or of simple Westernness. There are other "islands of civilization": some employers have adjusted their principles, while some factories have changed their modes of production, as well as their appearances. Private kindergartens, schools, and universities are emerging, as are private clinics. Certain restaurants and bars owe their success to their alleged Westernness; Transaero, the first private airline, stood for everything that was not Soviet. At the very beginning of the transition, the Western hotels, McDonald's, and Stockman (the first Western supermarket in Russia) were perceived as islands. But these—with the exception of McDonald's—were islands for a happy few, for foreigners and the privileged. The computer stores are now emerging as islands, but they sell awe-inspiring gadgets from a different world—and only to a computer-literate elite. Ikea, however, offers basic equipment for anyone's everyday life—for a new environment inside the home—thus Ikea allows people to change their own world.

Social-democratic furniture for a social-democratic society: Ikea, as shown above, represents simplicity, mobility, and reversibility, the lightness of being in a modern Western welfare state, or at least the Russian customers' idea of such a life. Ikea appeals to the people who wish to be the masters of their own domains. "Liberty and the pursuit of happiness," as mentioned in the U.S. Declaration of Independence, have never been on the Russian agenda. Either the quest for liberty was considered subversive, a kind of escapism, or its absence was not even sensed. Happiness was for the poets, or something one hoped to provide for one's children. To this day, it is hard to imagine a Russian *muzhik* (man) who would declare himself free or happy—or unhappy, for that matter—except when drunk.

While happiness may still be missing from the agenda, gratification, most often instant gratification, is on the minds of many Russians—all too often at the expense of others. Most Russians bemoan the selfish greed their fellow citizens evince, even more so since it often goes together with a blatant disrespect for human beings and the rule of law. However, the people who complain do not necessarily abide by the rules themselves. Many Russians call for law enforcement—and vote accordingly—but themselves steal, cheat, and embezzle. No one is afraid of sanctions. A society where the majority disrespects the rules, written or informal, remains in a state of social disorganization. Or, as once written in the *Economist*, "Post-Communist dry cleaning does for your suit what post-Communist social life does to your manners."[30]

Occasionally, people still depend on personal connections, but these connections have become dubious and unreliable. The bureaucrats come and go, and they can no longer be sure of their own connections. But since they no longer have to rely on the (hidden, indirect) reciprocity of the favor bank, they can ask for exorbitant bribes. In general, people and businesses can adapt to almost any environment, even if it is oppressive or criminal, as long as it is stable. In post-Soviet Russia, however, neither the clean and honest relations nor the corrupt ones are stable.

Thus the former Soviet citizens' attempts to trade security for liberty has stalled halfway. Security is lost, the price paid for freedom, but the freedom they have won is uncertain and many people lack the means to enjoy their newfound liberties.

The Russian society has not achieved the openness people have hoped it would. It is not democratic as the West defines it, or certainly not yet. Rather it has created what the Moscow philosopher Mikhail Ryklin calls "negative democracy": a "condition that prevents a single individual or a small group from imposing their will on all the others."[31] This is, as Ryklin believes, typical for formerly separated social strata that are forced to share a common space—a postapartheid phenomenon.

Nevertheless, the *homo sovieticus* is all but dead. Most Russian city dwellers cope surprisingly well with the instability of their new lives. They are becoming informed, they voice opinions, they take action, and despite all the odds, they display initiative; they are engaging in business, legal and illegal. In short, they are becoming citizens. Many people are modernizing much more quickly and radically than their state. They have gotten used to transient contacts and vanishing interactions, to the increasing pace of circulation, to a "structural differentiation and functional integration"[32] of their lives. They are constantly reinventing themselves by doing several jobs, as craftsmen, peddlers, drivers. Their lives are fragmented, but they travel easily from one realm to the next. Somehow, despite ever-changing preconditions, the majority in the big cities succeeds in making ends meet. Money has replaced the connections; the ruble is, though slowly, depersonalizing—modernizing—the society.

Yet, the post-Communist elite has little interest in supporting the completion of this transition. The new capitalists and the first shift of "democrats" can only lose their newly acquired privileges, and the former Communists have even more to lose. Time goes against them. Thus, the new Russian state shows a steady tendency of reossification. No wonder, then, that the new elite is cultivating architectural styles that hark back, that the Duma favors a return to the Soviet hymn and armory, the insignia of the past, the stability of stagnation. The VDNKh, the theme park for the achievements of Soviet industry, was meant to be a technological utopia. The post-Soviet mayor of Moscow, by contrast, attempts to turn the city center into a Russian Arcadia, a world mirroring the late nineteenth century.

"Creative destruction," to borrow a term from Nietzsche, has been crucial to modernization. How could a new world be created without destroying the old one? Thus the fieriest self-styled innovators justified themselves, including the early Bolsheviks, ardent readers of Nietzsche. In the name of progress, they denounced "all ornaments as crime, all individualism as sentimentality, all romanticism as kitsch."[33] Their declared goal was to detraditionalize the society.

Post-Soviet architecture has revived an inclination for ornaments and medieval-looking elements. The post-Soviet elite is reluctant to further shatter an already collapsing state. Instead, it is privatizing and looting its parts, only to then cultivate them as the fundament of a backward-looking imagery.

Despite the often retrograde architecture, the development of the post-Soviet cities should be read as a process of urbanization and modernization. Space is being differentiated, compressed, and commodified; its compartments, though, are highly permeable, although this quality often comes at a (financial) price. Also, the various urban spaces have been expanding; people have begun to convert basements and attics into living rooms and apartments, as if to recover the density of the prerevolutionary Russian cities. In Moscow, the state's construction committee has called a competition for exemplary reconstructions of attics.[34] Industrial buildings are being converted into residential or commercial space, shops and restaurants, for instance. In St. Petersburg, a former nuclear shelter has been turned into a night club, the Bunker.

The streets have changed, too. As early as the perestroika era, Moscow's Arbat was turned into a pedestrian street, the first of its kind in the Soviet Union. At the same time, the number of cars in the big cities has multiplied. Increasingly, bicycles can be seen. After decades of remaining unused, the St. Petersburg channels have again become waterways for leisure and moving goods. A city culture is reemerging. Or is it the *enactment* of a city culture, with artisans posing as old-fashioned shoemakers and silversmiths, just as in any other tourist city in the West?

The Soviet Union knew three types of cities, according to Margolina. First were the centers of government and administration, such as the union republics' capitals, which included facilities for state-run culture and science. Second were the factory towns, Magnitogorsk, for example, once populated by former *kulaks*, prisoners, and survivors of the famines. Third were the garrison towns. The Communists saw this separation of functions, as well as the destruction of the historical substance of the cities and the pseudourbanization of the countryside, as acts of modernization. However, since the 1920s, all three city types have been subjected to a process of deurbanization.[35] The destruction they suffered during the civil war and World War II only added to this process. The grown nature of most Russian towns—part of what makes up a city's soul—was lost and cities were prevented from developing any distinctiveness. They were shaped by some invisible party authority.

The collapse of the central power has allowed the cities to dodge Moscow's rule. More and more, the new social and economic realities are reshaping them, as well as the smaller towns. Cities and towns make their identities, construct some historicity, and market themselves, thus attempting to return to some historic roots, though not for the sake of tradition, but pressured by the market. The market's forces help to bundle certain functions, for example, shopping and nightlife; they make the new owners repaint the facades. Thus the market is creating neat inner cities that offer themselves to the consumers of nostalgia, inviting them to visit a Russia that never was.

Under Communism, a city's space was reduced to serving the four basic functions: work, housing, relaxation, and transportation. The gigantic central places made the people feel small and powerless. Now, the Russians find space to escape from the state's—or the society's—grip. Niches for privacy emerge, inscribed onto the urban space by individuals: little cafes, bars, parks.

On these islands of civility, people collect themselves, like actors going backstage. The availability of such spaces allows them to develop individuality. Resurfacing from the (often ad hoc) private places, they deliberately distinguish themselves from others. Thus they turn the city into a stage for the presentation of their selves. There can be no modernity without individuality and there can be no individuality without these private places of withdrawal.

The discourse of self is distinctively modern and modernity is distinctively linked to that discourse, as Anthony Giddens showed. In premodern times, the emphasis on individuality was absent. "The idea that each person has a unique character and special potentialities that may or may not be fulfilled is alien to premodern culture"[36]—as it was to the Communists. They refused to value individuality.

Modern societies see the self as a "reflexive project." "We are, not what we are, but what we make of ourselves."[37] A constantly reflected self-identity implies self-interrogation, self-presentation, and increasingly, body awareness, as Giddens stressed. Self-presentation is often used to justify consumption. Indeed, in modern societies, when acquiring something, many people deliberately buy brands—that is, objects intended to be signifiers. This kind of permanent self-actualization could hardly have existed in the Soviet Union, not least because people lacked space and the control of their own time. Plus, there were no brands and, mostly, there was no choice.

Citizens are distinct selves, responsible individuals, as opposed to *the masses*. Islands of civility, although it may be a mimicked or imported civility, allow people to behave like citizens. Ikea is one of those islands, and so far the only one that facilitates the creation of the people's own little islands at home.

But is a refined civic appearance evidence enough for a growing self-reflexivity? Is the post-Soviet society really modernizing? The ill-behaved, newly rich do not suggest this is so. Yet by playing a virtuous citizen, by dressing like one and mimicking bourgeois habits, the New Russians might gradually transform their underlying attitudes. They are eager to conform with the self-image they try to project, not least to exclude others. That's how, according to Norbert Elias's *Civilizing Process*, manners have become a marker of social distinction.[38] Therefore, even if they do not act responsibly, their imitating Western life may fuel the development of a civic society.

After all, despite the fact that the new civility is partly a masquerade, the Russian society is changing rapidly, even if, instead of getting rid of the Communist and post-Communist masks, people are putting on additional ones, enacting their idea of a "normal" life.

Nobody knows if the Russians will refrain from russifying Ikea, distorting it like they have other imports. However, Ikea furniture—simple, understated, and functional—is ill-suited for carnivalization. Many of the customers in the mall seem to see that as a relief; they are tired of the masks.

As a Western correspondent since 1988, I enjoyed an incomparable freedom of movement, physically and mentally, even before the Soviet regime collapsed. I was privileged to stroll through Russia's transition in the making, while my friends and neighbors had to "crawl through history."[39] I enjoyed (material) security, the backing of a foreign employer, and the safety of bearing a Swiss passport and a journalist card issued by the Soviet/Russian Foreign Ministry; thus I myself represented a lightness of being most Russians could (and did) only dream of. Now, at least, most can buy furniture that symbolizes this dreamed of way of being.

Some may question this optimistic picture I paint of Russia's future. Many citizens, particularly the elderly, have lost their savings and their apartments; they suffer daily harassment and have no security whatsoever. It is no wonder they are nostalgic for what they consider "the good old days," all the more since they compare their post-Soviet daily *byt* with a glossed-over memory; they have forgotten the ordeal of Soviet everyday life.

Outsiders tend to observe selectively: many Western colleagues, both scholars and journalists, draw a gloomy picture of Russia's future. Ridden by crime, looting, corruption, and incompetence, by alcoholism and slackness, the country, they believe, will never change. And history seems to endorse their point. The present work takes the liberty to counter this one-sided view. I am not oblivious to the burden of life in the former Soviet Union. On the contrary, I admire the Russian people's ability to adapt to ever-changing situations, I admire their endurance, and I admire their will to start anew for the umpteenth time. However, I have tried to put the present into a historical context, to think in broader terms, and to stress how fundamental a transition the Russians' attitudes and modes of communication are undergoing and how different today's Russia is from the country I explored only a little more than a decade ago. As implied in this book, some of the former republics' cities, particularly in the Baltic States, are well ahead of the Russian centers.

Russia is not the country of the *homini sovietici*, but a nation emerging from a long-lasting carnival, slowly getting ready for a new life. People try hard to trust their unstable country, and their children will never know what it meant to be a Soviet Man.

Happiness is still lacking from the Russian agenda. The carnival, with its multifaceted signs, is dragging on. It is not Ash Wednesday, yet. However, more and more people are breaking away from the carnivalesque bustle, getting ready for the postcarnival existence of responsible citizens in a modernized society—in a "normal" country, as they have been saying ever since the beginning of Russia's carnival of modernization.

NOTES

1. Irina Sandomirskaja, "IKEA's perestrojka" *Moderna Tider*, November 2000, 54–57.

2. Jean-Jacques Rousseau, *The Social Contract*, quoted in Larry Wolff, *Inventing Eastern Europe: The Map of Civilization on the Mind of the Enlightenment* (Stanford, Calif.: Stanford University Press, 1994), 199.

3. In my hometown, Basel, Switzerland, carnival begins at 4 A.M. and runs through the next seventy-two hours. It is believed to be most festive during the very early hours of the morning.

4. Alena Ledeneva, *Russia's Economy of Favours: Blat, Networking and Informal Exchanges* (New York: Cambridge University Press, 1998), 77.

5. Leonid Gosman (Gozman), *Von den Schrecken der Freiheit: Die Russen— Ein Psychogramm* (The scare of freedom: The Russians—a psychogram) (Berlin: Rowohlt, 1993), 17.

6. Sonja Margolina, *Russland: Die nichtzivile Gesellschaft* (Reinbek: Rowohlt, 1994), 166.

7. Gosman, *Schrecken*, 27.

8. Roger Friedland and Deirdre Boden, eds., *NowHere: Space, Time and Modernity* (Berkeley: University of California Press, 1994), 2.

9. Dieter Hoffmann-Axthelm, *Die dritte Stadt* (The third city) (Frankfurt: Suhrkamp, 1993), 179.

10. Margolina, *Russland: Nichtzivile Gesellschaft*, 178.

11. *Stil zhizn* (lifestyle) has become a very common term.

12. Scott Lash and John Urry, *Economies of Signs and Space* (London: Sage, 1994).

13. Hoffmann-Axthelm, *Dritte Stadt*, 110.

14. Norbert Elias, *The Civilizing Process: The History of Manners and State Formation and Civilization*, trans. Edmund Jephcott (Cambridge, Mass.: Blackwell, 1994), 135.

15. Hoffmann-Axthelm, *Dritte Stadt*, 110.

16. Jeffrey Rosen, "The Eroded Self," *New York Times Magazine*, April 30, 2000, 67.

17. Marshall Berman, *All That Is Solid Melts into Air: The Experience of Modernity* (New York: Simon & Schuster, 1982), 15–23.

18. Berman, *All That Is Solid*, 15.

19. Anthony Giddens, *Modernity and Self-Identity: Self and Society in the Late Modern Age* (Stanford, Calif.: Stanford University Press, 1991), 16.

20. The term "creative destruction" is from Friedrich Nietzsche, *Also sprach Zarathustra* (1883–1885). It's probably no accident that many of the early Communists venerated Nietzsche.

21. Oswald Spengler, *The Decline of the West* (New York: Knopf, 1928).

22. If we consider the exchange of commodities as a semiotic phenomenon where *use value* of the goods is transformed into their *exchange value*, a process of signification or *symbolization* takes place. Then the cities are points of condensed semiotic activity. This is perfected by the appearance of money, which *stands for something else*, according to Umberto Eco, *A Theory of Semiotics* (Bloomington: Indiana University Press, 1976).

23. Henri Lefebvre, *Writings on Cities*, trans. Eleonore Kofman and Elizabeth Lebas (Cambridge, Mass.: Blackwell, 1995), 109.

24. Karl Marx and Friedrich Engels, *The Manifesto of the Communist Party*, introd. and notes by A. J. P Taylor (London: Penguin Classics, 1967), 83.

25. Berman, *All That Is Solid*, 15.

26. Elias, *Civilizing Process*, 155.

27. Edward Keenan, during the conference for the fiftieth anniversary of the Davis Center for Russian Studies, Harvard University, Cambridge, Massachusetts, May 1998.

28. The criteria are Stephen Kotkin's, from "The Soviet Union: An Interpretation" (paper presented at the Davis Center for Russian Studies, Harvard University, Cambridge, Massachusetts, February 2000).

29. Inherently, semiotic systems are in a state of constant flux, therefore, any semiosphere is subject to change both in its inner structure and as a whole. See Yuri M. Lotman, *Universe of the Mind,* trans. Ann Shukman (Bloomington: Indiana University Press, 1990), 151.

30. "Ukraine's Merchant Adventurer," *The Economist,* May 13, 2000.

31. Mikhail Ryklin, "Warten aufs Christkind," *Lettre International* 44 (Spring 1999): 95.

32. Lash and Urry, *Economies of Signs,* 13.

33. David Harvey, *The Condition of Postmodernity* (Cambridge, Mass.: Blackwell, 1990), 40.

34. International concourse of the Gosudorstveno komitet RF. po stroitelstvu i zhilishchno-komunalnomy kompleksu (State Committee of the Russian Federation for Housing and Public Construction).

35. Margolina, *Russland: Nichtzivile Gesellschaft.*

36. Giddens, *Modernity,* 74

37. Giddens, *Modernity,* 75.

38. Elias, *Civilizing Process,* 424–436.

39. Kazimierz Brandys, *A Warsaw Diary 1978–1981,* trans. Richard Lowry (New York: Random House, 1983), 165.

Selected Bibliography

Appadurai, Arjun. *Modernity at Large*. Minneapolis: University of Minnesota Press, 1996.

Aron, Leon R. *Yeltsin: A Revolutionary Life*. New York: Thomas Dunne/St. Martin's, 2000.

Argumenty i Fakti, 1990-1997.

Augé, Marc. *Non-places: Introduction to an Anthropology of Supermodernity*. Translated by John Howe. London: Verso, 1995.

Azhgikhina, Nadezhda and Helena Goscilo. "Getting under the Skin." In *Russia, Women, Culture*. Edited by Helena Goscilo and Beth Holmgren, 94–121. Bloomington: Indiana University Press, 1996.

Bakhtin, Mikhail M. *Problems of Dostoevsky's Poetics*. Translated by Caryl Emerson. Minneapolis: University of Minnesota Press, 1994.

———. *Rabelais and His World*. Translated by Helene Iswolsky. Bloomington: Indiana University Press, 1984.

Bater, James H. *St. Petersburg: Industrialization and Change*. London: E. Arnold, 1976.

Berman, Marshall. *All That Is Solid Melts Into Air: The Experience of Modernity*. New York: Simon & Schuster, 1982.

Billington, James H. *The Icon and the Axe: An Interpretive History of Russian Culture*. New York: Knopf, 1966.

Bonnell, Victoria, and Gregory Freidin. "Televorot: The Role of Television Coverage in Russia's August 1991 Coup." In *Soviet Hieroglyphics: Visual Culture in Late Twentieth-Century Russia*. Edited by Nancy Condee, 22–51. Bloomington: Indiana University Press, 1995.

Boym, Svetlana. *Common Places: Mythologies of Everyday Life in Russia*. Cambridge, Mass.: Harvard University Press, 1994.

Breslauer, George W. "Identities in Transition: Introduction." In *Identities in Transition: Eastern Europe and Russia after the Collapse of Communism*. Edited by Victoria E. Bonnell, 1–12. International Area Studies, Research Series, no. 93. Berkeley: University of California, Center for Slavic and East European Studies, 1996.

Brodsky, Joseph. *Less Than One*. New York: Farrar, Straus & Giroux, 1986.

Certeau, Michel de. *The Practice of Everyday Life*. Translated by S. F. Rendall. Berkeley: University of California Press, 1984.

Certeau, Michel de, Luce Giard, and Pierre Mayol, eds. *The Practice of Everyday Life. Vol. 2: Living and Cooking*. Translated by Timothy J. Tomasik. Minneapolis: University of Minnesota Press, 1998.

Clark, Katerina, and Michael Holquist. *Mikhail Bakhtin*. Cambridge, Mass.: Belknap, 1984.

Clark, Katerina. *The Soviet Novel: History as Ritual*. Chicago: University of Chicago Press, 1981.

Colton, Timothy J. *Moscow*. Cambridge, Mass.: Belknap, 1995.

Condee, Nancy. "The Second Fantasy Mother, Or All Baths Are Women's Baths." In *Russia, Women, Culture*. Edited by Helena Goscilo and Beth Holmgren, 1–30. Bloomington: University of Indiana Press, 1996.

Cracraft, James. *The Petrine Revolution in Russian Imagery*. Chicago: University of Chicago Press, 1997.

Custine, Astolphe de. *Empire of the Czar: A Journey through Eternal Russia*. New York: Doubleday, 1989.

Demokratizatsiya (1998–1999).

Dentith, Simon. *Bakhtinian Thought*. New York: Routledge, 1995.

Douglas, Mary. "The Genuine Article." In *The Socialness of Things: Essays on the Socio-Semiotics of Objects*. Edited by Stephen Harald Riggins, 9–22. New York: de Gruyter, 1994.

Druzhnikov, Yuri. *Donoshnik 001, ili Voznesenie Pavlika Morozova* (Informer 001, or the ascension of Pavlik Morozov). Moscow: Moskovsky rabochy, 1995.

Duncan, James. "Sites of Representation: Place, Time and the Discourse of the Other." In *Place/Culture/Representation*. Edited by James Duncan and David Ley, 39–56. New York: Routledge, 1993.

Eco, Umberto, "The Frames of Comic Freedom." In Umberto Eco, V. V. Ivanov, and Monica Rector, *Carnival! Approaches to Semiotics 64*. Edited by Thomas A. Seboek, 1–9. New York: de Gruyter, 1984.

Elias, Norbert. *The Civilizing Process: The History of Manners and State Formation and Civilization*. Translated by Edmund Jephcott. Cambridge, Mass.: Blackwell, 1994.

Ellis, Frank. "The Media as Social Engineer." In *Russian Cultural Studies*. Edited by Catriona Kelly and David Shepherd, 192–222. Oxford: Oxford University Press, 1998.

Etkind, Alexander. "Psychological Culture." In *Russian Culture at the Crossroads: Paradoxes of Postcommunist Consciousness*. Edited by Dmitri Shalin, 99–126. Boulder, Colo.: Westview, 1996.

Ewen, Stuart. *All Consuming Images: The Politics of Style in Contemporary Culture*. New York: Basic Books, 1988.

Foucault, Michel. *Power/Knowledge: Selected Interviews and Other Writings, 1972–77.* New York: Pantheon, 1980.

Foreign Affairs.

Friedland, Roger, and Deirdre Boden, eds. *NowHere: Space, Time and Modernity.* Berkeley: University of California Press, 1994.

Geertz, Clifford. *Local Knowledge: Further Essays in Interpretive Anthropology.* New York: Basic, 1984.

Giddens, Anthony. *Modernity and Self-Identity: Self and Society in the Late Modern Age.* Stanford: Stanford University Press, 1991.

Goldhoorn, B. "State and Market: A Polemic View." In *Rotterdam Moscow, Architectural Training at the Academy of Architecture and Urban Design.* Edited by M. Provoost and J. Duursma. Rotterdam: 010 Publishers, Rotterdam and Moscow Architectural Institute, 1995.

Golub, Spencer. *Evreinov: The Theatre of Paradox and Transformation.* Ann Arbor, Mich.: UMI Research Press, 1984.

Gorbachev, Mikhail S. *Perestroika and the New World Order.* Moscow: Novosti, 1991.

Goscilo, Helena. *Dehexing Sex: Russian Womanhood during and after Glasnost.* Ann Arbor: University of Michigan Press, 1996.

Goscilo, Helena. "The Gendered Trinity of Russian Cultural Rhetoric." In *Soviet Hieroglyphs.* Edited by Nancy Condee, 68–92. Bloomington: Indiana University Press, 1995.

Gosman, Leonid (Gozman). *Von den Schrecken der Freiheit: Die Russen—Ein Psychogramm* (The scare of freedom: The Russians—a psychogram). Berlin: Rowohlt, 1993.

Gregory, Andrusz, Michael Harloe, and Ivan Szelenyi, eds. *Cities after Socialism: Urban and Regional Change and Conflict in Post-Socialist Societies.* Cambridge, Mass.: Blackwell, 1996.

Hall, Edward T. *Beyond Culture.* New York: Doubleday, 1976.

———. *The Dance of Life.* New York: Doubleday, 1983.

———. *The Hidden Dimension.* New York: Doubleday, 1966.

———. *The Silent Language.* New York: Doubleday, 1959.

Hanson, Stephen. *Time and Revolution: Marxism and the Soviet Institutions.* Chapel Hill: University of North Carolina Press, 1997.

Harvey, David. *The Condition of Postmodernity.* Cambridge, Mass.: Blackwell, 1990.

———. *The Urban Experience.* Baltimore: Johns Hopkins University Press, 1989.

Hoffmann-Axthelm, Dieter. *Die dritte Stadt* (The third city). Frankfurt: Suhrkamp, 1993.

Hollander, Anne. *Sex and Suits.* New York: Viking, 1976.

Kelly, Catriona, and David Shepherd, eds. *Russian Cultural Studies.* Oxford: Oxford University Press, 1998.

Kern, Stephen. *The Culture of Time and Space, 1880-1918.* Cambridge, Mass.: Harvard University Press, 1983.

Kljamkin, Igor, and Tatjana Kutkowez. "Der postsowjetische Privatmensch auf dem Weg zu liberalen Werten." (The post-Soviet private individual on his path to liberal values). In *Das neue Russland in Politik und Kultur* (The new Russia in politics and culture). Edited by Forschungsstelle Osteuropa. Bremen, Germany: Temmen, 1998.

Kon, Igor. *Sex and Russian Society.* Bloomington: Indiana University Press, 1993.

Kotkin, Stephen. *Magnetic Mountain: Stalinism as a Civilization.* Berkeley: University of California Press, 1995.

Klyuchevsky, Vasili. *Peter the Great.* Translated by Liliana Archibald. London: St. Martin's, 1958.

Lash, Scott, and John Urry. *Economies of Signs and Space.* London: Sage, 1994.

Ledeneva, Alena. *Russia's Economy of Favours: Blat, Networking and Informal Exchanges.* New York: Cambridge University Press, 1998.

Lefebvre, Henri. *The Production of Space.* Translated by Donald Nicholson-Smith. Cambridge, Mass.: Blackwell, 1991.

———. *Writings on Cities.* Translated by Eleonore Kofman and Elizabeth Lebas. Cambridge, Mass.: Blackwell, 1995.

Lettre International 30–44.

Levada, Yuri A. *Die Sowjetmenschen, 1989-1991: Soziogramm eines Zerfalls* (The Soviet people, 1989–1991: Sociogram of a disintegration). Munich: Deutscher Taschenbuch, 1993. Originally published as *Sovetskii prostoi chelovek.*

Literaturnaya Gazeta.

Loewenhardt, John. *The Reincarnation of Russia: Struggling with the Legacy of Communism, 1990–1994.* Durham, N.C.: Duke University Press, 1995.

Lotman, Yuri M. *Besedy o Russkoi kulture: Byt i Traditsy russkogo dvoryanstva (xviii–nachalo xix veka)* (Talks on Russian culture: Life and tradition of the Russian aristocracy [eighteenth–beginning of the nineteenth century]). St. Petersburg: Isskustvo, 1994.

———. *Universe of the Mind.* Translated by Ann Shukman. Bloomington: Indiana University Press, 1990.

Margolina, Sonja. *Russland: Die nichtzivile Gesellschaft* (Russia: The noncivil society). Reinbek: Rowohlt, 1994.

Matheus, Michael, ed. *Fastnacht/Karneval im europäischen Vergleich* (Fasnacht/ Carnival in Europe: A Comparative Study). Institut für Geschichtliche Landeskunde an der Universität Mainz e.V. Mainzer Vorträge 3. Stuttgart: Franz Steiner, 1999.

Moderna Tider (Stockholm).

Moscow Times.

The New York Review of Books.

Ogonyok, 1987–1993.

Pearl, Elizabeth Linn. "Semiotics and Politics: An Encounter on the Pages of Pravda." Ph.D. dissertation, Harvard University, 1990.

Pelevin, Viktor. *Omon Ra.* Translated by Andrew Bromfield. New York: Farrar, Straus & Giroux, 1996. Originally published in Russian under the same title (Moscow: Tekst, 1992).

———. *Generation P.* Moscow: Vagrius, 1999.

Pesmen, Dale. *Russia and Soul: An Exploration.* Ithaca, N.Y.: Cornell University Press, 2000.

Peterson, Nadya L. "Dirty Women." In *Russia, Women, Culture.* Edited by Helena Goscilo and Beth Holmgren, 177–205. Bloomington: Indiana University Press, 1996.

Pipes, Richard. *Russia under the Old Regime.* New York: Knopf, 1993.

Project Russia, nos. 1–12.

Rancour-Laferriere, Daniel. *The Slave Soul of Russia: Moral Masochism and the Cult of Suffering*. New York: New York University Press, 1995.

RFE/RL Daily Report, 1987–1997.

Ries, Nancy. *Russian Talk: Culture and Conversation during Perestroika*. Ithaca, N.Y.: Cornell University Press, 1997.

Rothstein, Halina, and Robert A. Rothstein. "The Beginnings of Soviet Culinary Art." In *Food in Russian History and Culture*. Edited by Musya Glants and Joyce Toomre, 177–194. Bloomington: Indiana University Press, 1997.

Ruble, Blair. *Money Sings*. Washington, D.C.: Woodrow Wilson Center Press, 1995.

Sen, Amartya. *Inequality Reexamined*. Cambridge, Mass.: Harvard University Press, 1992.

Sennett, Richard. *The Fall of Public Man*. New York: Knopf, 1977.

Siegelbaum, Lewis H. *Stakhanovism and the Politics of Productivity in the USSR, 1935–1941*. New York: Cambridge University Press, 1988.

Simmel, Georg. *Philosophie des Geldes*. Leipzig: Drucker und Humboldt, 1900.

Sinyavsky, Andrei. *Soviet Civilization: A Cultural History*. Translated by Joanne Turnbull. New York: Arcade, 1990.

Slavic Review (1998).

Smith, Hedrick. *The Russians*. New York: Ballantine Books, 1984.

Sombart, Werner. *Liebe, Luxus und Kapitalismus: Über die Entstehung der modernen Welt aus dem Geist der Verschwendung* (Love, luxury, and capitalism: On the emergence of modernity from the spirit of extravagance). Reprint of *Luxus und Kapitalismus*. 2d ed. Munich: Duncker and Humbolt, 1922. Berlin: Wagenbach, 1983.

Spengler, Oswald. *The Decline of the West*. New York: Knopf, 1928.

Starr, S. Frederick. *Red and Hot: The Fate of Jazz in the Soviet Union, 1917-1991, with a New Chapter on the Final Years*. New York: Limelight, 1994.

Troitsky, Artemy. *Back in the USSR: The True Story of Rock in Russia*. Boston: Faber and Faber, 1987.

Tuan, Yi-Fu. *Topophilia: A Study of Environmental Perceptions, Attitudes, and Values*. Englewood Cliffs, N.J.: Prentice-Hall, 1974.

Tumarkin, Nina. *Lenin Lives: The Lenin Cult in Soviet Russia*. Cambridge, Mass.: Harvard University Press, 1997.

Turner, Victor W. *The Ritual Process: Structure and Anti-Structure*. New York: de Gruyter, 1969.

Vainshtein, Olga. "Female Fashion, Soviet Style: Bodies of Ideology." Translated by Helena Goscilo. In *Russia, Women, Culture*. Edited by Helena Goscilo and Beth Holmgren. Bloomington: Indiana University Press, 1996, 64–93.

VTsIOM, Informationi byulleten monitoringa.

Waters, Elizabeth. "Soviet Beauty Contests." In *Sex and the Russian Society*. Edited by Igor Kon and James Riordan, 116–134. Bloomington: Indiana University Press / London: Pluto Press, 1993).

Weber, Max. *The Protestant Ethic and the Spirit of Capitalism*. Translated by Talcott Parsons. London: Allen & Unwin, 1930.

Weltwoche.

Wittfogel, Karl A. *Oriental Despotism: A Comparative Study of Total Power*. New Haven, Conn.: Yale University Press, 1957.

Wolff, Larry. *Inventing Eastern Europe: The Map of Civilization on the Mind of the Enlightenment*. Stanford, Calif.: Stanford University Press, 1994.

Yampolsky, Mikhail. "In the Shadow of Monuments: Notes on Iconoclasm and Time." Translated by John Kachur. In *Soviet Hieroglyphics: Visual Culture in Late Twentieth-Century Russia*. Edited by Nancy Condee, 93–112. Bloomington: Indiana University Press, 1995.

Yeltsin, Boris N. *The Struggle for Russia*. Translated by Catherine A. Fitzpatrick. New York: Times Books, 1994.

Zinoviev, Aleksandr. *Homo Sovieticus*. Translated by Charles Janson. Boston: Atlantic Monthly Press, 1985.

Zoshchenko, Mikhail. *Spi skorei* (Sleep faster). Riga, Latvia: Logos, 1938.

Index

Ikea, 104–105, 221, 224–225, 229–230, 233, 237
individualism, 44, 173, 201, 214, 226
individuality, 44, 208–213, 236
institutions, 26, 66, 69, 177, 231–233
intelligentsia, 3, 74, 89, 90, 94, 133, 136

jeans, 72, 103. *See also* dress code
Jewish, 71, 83

Kalugin, Oleg, 214
Karpovich, Yaroslav, 214
KGB, 9, 45, 70, 86, 89, 136, 138, 146, 151, 171, 178, 192, 206, 214, 222
Khrushchev, Nikita, 49, 66, 69, 126, 129, 148, 161
kiosks, 82, 83, 135, 142, 193–194, 200
kitchen table, 6, 25, 71, 131–132, 136, 232
Klimov, Elem, 213
kommunalka. See apartment, communal
Komsomol, 11, 26, 49, 84, 85, 109, 198

language, 7–9, 41, 81; non-verbal, 7–8, 48–49, 53, 87, 88, 99; Russian, 9, 81. *See also* Newspeak
Lenin, 24, 33, 64, 103, 148, 162–163, 166, 171; mausoleum, 87, 139, 148, 150, 166
Lords of Misrule, 4, 17, 22–23, 177, 222
luxury, 71–72, 93, 95, 124, 171, 187, 196
Luzhkov, Yuri, 75, 106, 150, 235

mafiosi, 205–207, 214
Magnitogorsk, 66–67, 75, 90, 127, 147, 151, 170, 236
make-believes, 1–2, 63, 65, 66, 73–74, 224. *See also* Potemkin
Manezhnaya Square, 20, 27, 68, 75–76, 101, 106, 150
maps, 118, 124–125; cognitive, 12, 120–124, 135–136, 143, 145, 151; falsified, 124
market, 67–68, 74–75, 87, 88, 91, 92, 99, 104, 143; farmers' *(kolkhoz)*, 191, 194; and haggling, 194, 197
Marx, Karl, 33–34, 228
masquerade. *See* carnivalization, and carnivalesque elements

McDonald's. *See* food, McDonald's
media, 35, 39–47, 80–82, 151, 165, 167, 212–213
metro. *See* subway
modernity, 12, 67, 100, 164, 174, 227–236; and self, 211–212, 217–218
modernization, 67, 119, 157, 161, 172, 226–238
money, 71, 140, 157, 164, 179, 183, 191, 200–202, 207, 234; investment, 140, 142; as means of social distinction, (*see* status marker); as means of social power, 71, 164, 201–202; monetization of society, 143; and U.S. dollar, 194–195, 206; *valuta*, 195
monument, 147–150, 163, 178
morality, 74, 130, 203, 207
Morozov, Pavlik, 208–212, 216, 217–218
music, 82–88; background, 88; classical, 87–88; jazz, 82–84; pop, 87; rock and roll, 82–87
my (we). *See my* and *oni*
my and *oni*, 132–133, 136, 145, 148, 162–163, 175, 199–200

names, 96, 144; of restaurants, 96–98
national (ethnic) identity, 66, 214–215
neighborhoods, 134–135
New Russians, 71–73, 75, 88, 101, 109, 133, 144, 175, 179, 214–215, 225, 230, 237
New Man. *See homo sovieticus*
Newspeak, 9, 164
New Union Treaty, 15, 169. *See also* August putsch
nomenklatura. See CPSU
nouveau riche. *See* New Russians
"normality." *See* normal life
"normal life," 43, 133, 233, 237, 225
nostalgia, 179, 232, 236, 238

Ogonyok, 41–45, 212–213
Okhotny Ryad, 75, 101, 150, 179
oni (them). *See my* and *oni*
Orthodox Church, 101, 103, 166, 212

party leaders. *See* CPSU
peasant society, 12, 94, 159–161, 227

About the Author

Christoph Neidhart is a senior columnist for *Die Weltwoche*, Switzerland's leading newsmagazine. As its correspondent, he lived in Russia for almost ten years. He wrote *Russia's Carnival* as a visiting scholar at Harvard University's Davis Center, and is also the author of the book *Nach dem Kollaps* [After the Collapse], describing the transition of the former Soviet republics into emerging states.